GROWING UP FEMALE IN AMERICA

GROWING UP FEMALE IN AMERICA

Ten Lives

Edited and Introduced by

EVE MERRIAM

BEACON PRESS   BOSTON

Beacon Press
25 Beacon Street
Boston, Massachusetts 02108

Beacon Press books are published under the auspices
of the Unitarian Universalist Association
of Congregations in North America.

First published in 1971 by Doubleday & Company, Inc.
Copyright © by Eve Merriam 1971
First published by Beacon Press in 1987 by arrangement with the author

97 96 95   8 7 6 5

Library of Congress Cataloging-in-Publication Data

Growing up female in America.

    Reprint. Originally published: Garden City, N.Y.:
Doubleday, 1971.
    1. Women social reformers — United States — Biography.
2. Women — United States — Biography. 3. Women — United
States — Social conditions. I. Merriam, Eve, 1916–
HQ 1412.G76   1986   920.72'0973   86–26473
ISBN 0–8070–7009–2

Grateful acknowledgment is made for the use of the following copyrighted
material:

THE STORY OF A PIONEER by Anna Howard Shaw.
Copyright 1915 by Harper & Brothers; renewed 1943 by Lucy E. Anthony.
Reprinted by permission of Harper & Row, Publishers, Inc.

MOUNTAIN WOLF WOMAN: THE AUTOBIOGRAPHY OF A WINNEBAGO INDIAN
    edited by Nancy Oestreich Lurie.
Copyright © 1961 by the University of Michigan.
Reprinted by permission of the University of Michigan Press.

CONTENTS

INTRODUCTION

No ten women, however diversified their life styles, could possibly represent what it was like growing up female in America. These specimen lives, portrayed first hand through autobiographies, diaries, journals, and letters, are intended as a beginning attempt only; let me note here at the outset that I hope successive efforts will broaden and deepen this initial venture.

One scarcely need be a vocalizing feminist to observe that women —along with blacks, Indians, and to a lesser extent other minorities —have not been given their due sufficiently in American history. More than these other groups, perhaps, women have been not so much misrepresented as missing: their presence cavalierly, boldly omitted. Men wrote the history books, men assigned themselves not merely center stage and the central roles, but all the roles; the colonists who left the Old World for the New in the early 1600s carried along with them a heavy cargo of prejudice and superstition. English law had discriminated severely against women; the colonies carried on that tradition.

Women, like children in the adage, were not to be heard. They were considered minors in every respect. Not only were they lumped with "children and idiots" as being unsuited to vote, they were held to be inferior beings physically (though fit for the most strenuous labor), and inferior mentally (generally attending only "dame schools"): the law prohibited their owning property, owning the wages they earned, even owning custody of the children they bore. Among other technical niceties, a husband was allowed to punish his wife for disobedience "provided he did not use a stick thicker than the judge's thumb."

Authoritarianism of the Great White Father state ruled supreme.

Despite all the restrictions, however, women wrote and spoke out from the very beginning, even though the quotations have not as yet made their way into our general American history textbooks.

There was Anne Bradstreet, emigrating from England to the Massachusetts Bay Colony with her father and husband in 1630, raising a brood of children and pricking the male order with her sharp pen:

> I am obnoxious to each carping tongue
> Who says my hand a needle better fits . . .
> For such despite they cast on Female wits;
> If what I do prove well, it won't advance—
> They'll say it's stoln, or else it was by chance. . . .

There was the Negro woman who signed herself simply Matilda in her letter to the first Negro newspaper *Freedom's Journal,* writing "I deplore the ignorance that blinds men's eyes. We women have minds that are capable and deserving of culture. While it is necessary to possess a knowledge of cookery, I do believe that something more is requisite."

Abigail Adams, *prima inter pares,* exhorted the Founding Fathers. In a letter to the playwright, Mercy Otis Warren, in 1776, she confided:

"Mr. Adams is very sausy to me, in return for a list of Female Grievances which I transmitted to him. I think I will get you to join me in a petition to Congress.

"I thought it was very probable our Wise Statesmen would erect a New Government & form a New Code of Laws, I ventured to speak a Word in behalf of our Sex who are rather hardly Dealt with by the Laws of England which gives such unlimited power to the Husband to use his wife Ill.

"I requested that our Legislators would consider our case and as all Men of Delicacy & Sentiment are averse to exercising the power they possess, yet as there is a Natural propensity in Human Nature to domination I thought the Most Generous plan was to put it out of the power of the Arbitrary & tyranick to injure us with impunity by establishing some Laws in our Favour upon just & Liberal principles.

"I believe I even threatened fomenting a Rebellion in case we were not considered and assured him we would not hold ourselves bound by any Laws in which we had neither a voice nor representation. . . ."

And how did John Adams respond to this threat? By treating his wife like the child that, in law and custom, she was. Abigail's letter continues:

"In return he tells me he cannot but Laugh at my Extradonary Code of Laws, that he had heard their struggle had loosned the bonds of Government, that children & apprentices were disobedient, that Schools and Colledges were grown turbulent, that Indians slighted their Guardians and Negroes grew insolent to their Masters. But my letter was the first intimation that another Tribe more numerous & powerfull than all the rest were grown discontented. This is rather too coarse a compliment, he adds, but that I am so sausy he wont blot it out.

"So I have helped the Sex abundantly, but I will tell him I have only been making trial of the disinterestedness of his Virtue & when weighd in the balance have found it wanting.

"It would be bad policy to grant us greater power say they since under all the disadvantages we labour we have the ascendancy over their hearts

"'And charm by accepting, by submitting sway.'"

To escape from accepting and submitting, education was necessary, for how ignorant even upper-class women had been kept.

In Massachusetts, in the mid-seventeenth century, half the women signing deeds or other legal documents could not write their names and had to sign by a cross. In New York the percentage of illiterate signers was sixty per cent, in Virginia seventy-five per cent. These were women of property; imagine what the degree of illiteracy must have been among the unpropertied.

The educational advancement of women was meager throughout the eighteenth century; Abigail Adams was keenly conscious of the fact. Writing to her husband when he was concerned that sons were not the scholars their fathers and grandfathers were, she wrote: "If you complain of education in sons what shall I say of daughters who every day experience the want of it? With regard to the education of my own children I feel myself soon out of my depth, destitute in every part of education. I most sincerely wish that some more liberal plan might be laid and executed for the benefit of the rising generation and that our new Constitution may be distinguished for encouraging learning and virtue. If we mean to have heroes, statesmen, and philosophers, we should have learned women. The world perhaps would laugh at me, but you, I know, have a mind too enlarged and liberal to disregard sentiment. If as much depends as is allowed upon the early education of youth and the first principles which are instilled take the deepest root great benefit must arise from the literary accomplishments in women."

Slowly, slowly, educational opportunities widened. From 1789 to 1822 girls in Boston might attend the primary grades of public school from April to October only, and then only if vacant places occurred through the absence of boy students out harvesting the fields. (Girls, too, were harvesting and working.) In other places, girls were sometimes accepted for two hours' schooling in the afternoon, once the boys had been dismissed.

By 1837 Mary Lyon had scraped together enough funds to establish Mount Holyoke Female Seminary in Massachusetts as "a permanent institution consecrated to the training of young women for usefulness . . . designed to furnish every advantage which the state of education in this country will allow." It was Mary Lyon's radical notion that a college for women should be run on the same basis as one for men: with fixed standards of work, and with the same subjects taught; that is, instead of the usual three graces of Embroidery, Music, and Deportment while Dancing, there would be the sterner but no less graceful disciplines of science, Latin, and geometry.

At almost the exact same time, Oberlin College in Ohio admitted three female students and permitted them to study for the same bachelor of arts degree that men students were granted. These pioneering steps in women's education were deplored not only by yahoos of the period but by leading scholars, and not only by men but by a preponderance of women. For the prevailing opinion, as expressed in most newspaper editorials and delivered from most speakers' platforms and pulpits, was that "all the higher mathematics any girl had to know was how many places to set at table. And no mother needed trigonometry to count twelve or fourteen children. . . . Chemistry enough to keep the pot boiling, and geography enough to know the location of the different rooms in her house—these were learning sufficient for any woman."

Widespread jokes of the time suggested that female graduates be awarded degrees of MPM—Mistress of Pudding Making—and RW —Respectable Wife.

In 1841, when the first arts degree was awarded to a woman, there were seven major occupations open to her sex: teaching, needle trades, keeping boarders, cotton mill work, bookbinding, typesetting, and domestic service. That same year, woman's sphere was enlarged by the opening of three public places in New York City: a Ladies' Oyster Shop, a Ladies' Reading Room, and a Ladies' Bowling Alley where girls set up the pins.

By the mid-1840s Elizabeth Blackwell was admitted to Hobart Medical College in upstate New York, and when she graduated ahead of all the one hundred and fifty males in her class, a certain Dr. Brockett of Hartford, Connecticut, allowed that "the medical treatment of women and children might someday be in the hands of highly educated female physicians," but on the whole Dr. Brockett recommended "the keeping of bees, rearing of silkworms, and care of some of the fanciful varieties of domestic fowls and

pigeons, guinea hens, ducks, geese, turkeys, and rabbits as employments better suited to women."

In 1847 Lucy Stone graduated from Oberlin and was informed
that one of the professors would read her graduating essay, for it
would be indelicate for Lucy to read it herself "before a promiscuous
audience." Deprived of the right to read it herself, she refused to
have it read at all.

In 1848 the movement for women's rights was launched officially
with a convention on July 19 and 20 in the Methodist church at
Seneca Falls, New York. Lucretia Mott, Elizabeth Cady Stanton,
and their "coadjutors," as Elizabeth called them, modeled their Declaration of Sentiments deliberately upon the Declaration of Independence. The Revolutionary Fathers had drawn up eighteen chief
complaints against the tyrannous reign of King George; so the
gathering of one hundred (mostly women, but with some male
supporters, including the great Negro orator and editor, Frederick
Douglass) listed what they considered eighteen of women's most
glaring grievances. In peroration their statement declared:

"In view of this entire disfranchisement of one-half the people
of this country, their social and religious degradation—in view of
the unjust laws above mentioned, and because women do feel
themselves aggrieved, oppressed, and fraudulently deprived of their
most sacred rights, we insist that they have immediate admission to
all the rights and privileges which belong to them as citizens of the
United States."

The newly invented telegraph spread the word of the first
women's rights convention in the world: "Insurrection Among
Women! The Petticoats Revolt!" The Philadelphia *Ledger* edito-
rialized: "A woman is nobody. A wife is everything. A pretty girl is
equal to ten thousand men, and a mother is, next to God, all-
powerful. . . . We trust that the ladies of Philadelphia will resolve
to maintain their rights as wives, Belles, Virgins, and Mothers, and
not as Women." From pulpit and podium Lucretia Mott was denounced as "a devil hiding in Quaker gray," Elizabeth Cady Stanton
was "a horrid monster" and "a professional lunatic." Others who

attended the convention were "modern Lucretia Borgias, planning war and murder." The men like Wendell Phillips and William Ellery Channing who supported equal rights for women were "weak-minded, Aunt Nancys, soft-spoken with upturned eyes," and were simultaneously reviled as "wild-eyed revolutionaries." The editor of the *State Register* insinuated that "People are beginning to inquire how far public sentiment should sanction or tolerate these unsexed women, who make a scoff at religion, who repudiate the Bible, and blaspheme God; who would take upon themselves the duties and the business of men; stalk into the public gaze, and by engaging in the politics, the rough controversies, and trafficking of the world, upheave existing institutions, and overturn all the social relations of life!"

It was bold indeed for the women to demand *"immediate admission to all the rights and privileges which belong to them as citizens of the United States."*

Those rights and privileges have not yet been granted.

The Women's Revolution, launched so frontally, went forward, went backward, forward again, into byways, foundered, and only today is being relaunched on an extensive scale as the young enthusiasts of the Women's Liberation movement spread out from campus to community. Now, as then, there is the danger that, without enlisting the massive support of working-class women and black women, the movement may be contained as a white middle-class enclave.

There is by this time a substantial body of writing in the field. Yet for all the outpouring of material it has been mostly propagandistic; necessarily so, perhaps, in order to effect changes in the legal, economic, social, and psychological systems that still continue to discriminate against women.

What has remained lacking, it appeared to me, was, despite the voluminous suffrage literature and the mounting case histories of the current scene, any kind of record of the dailiness of women's lives in our country's past.

We need such a record if we are to redress the falsities of our textbooks.

What was it like, really, to grow up in America marked *sex, female?* How did girls react to parents' strictures and ambitions for them, how did they react to school, to church, to the severely limited choices of work outside the home? What were their personal, private lives concerned with? How did they face their coming of age, what were their responses to the primal experiences of menses, maidenhead, motherhood?

One cannot rely on biographies to find out. Too often a life is filtered through the biographer's own predilections, prohibitions. So I decided to go direct to the sources themselves; the women would speak in their own tongues.

It has been a large undertaking these past four years, and if the result seems at all scant, I must remind the reader that I am in the position of the proverbial fisherman: you should see what got away. The winnowing was essential as I began to define what shape the book would take.

There were four principal factors governing my choices. I was seeking a chronological range, a geographical distribution, an economic cross section, and a cultural (or ethnic, if you will) diversity.

Now that it is completed, I see that it exists more in space and less in time than I first imagined it would. The geographical scope of the country is here: from New England to the Southern states to the Midwest and out to the West coast. But there are no figures earlier than the last part of the eighteenth century, and none later than the early part of the present century, for reasons that I will explain shortly.

At the risk of sounding tautological, I was limited first of all by who wrote in the forms that I was seeking. Many representative women I should have liked to include did not put down any first-person accounts of their lives. Then, too, not all journals, diaries, letters, autobiographies made their way into print or available archives.

One unpublished windfall came my way: Professor Keith Rinehart, of Central Washington State College, generously lent me a family document: his great-grandmother's account of a journey across the plains from Missouri to Oregon, written down some fifty years after the event as a memento for her descendants. Not only was it a lively, true story of the drama of a wagon-train trip through Indian territory to the Far West, it was also, in its style of narration, an illumination on growing up female in America: straightforward frankness and corseted repression vying for uppermost place. All the events of the journey are told by Mrs. Cooper in the first person until about two thirds of the way along, when she gives birth to a baby and states, "From now on, as my narrative will necessarily be so personal as to seem egotistical, I will write in the third person."

Although Mrs. Cooper's is the only unpublished manuscript, a number of the selections have long been out of print and not readily accessible: the letters dating from Eliza Southgate's schoolgirl days in 1797, Mary Ann Loughborough's journal of her life in a cave during the siege of Vicksburg, the diary entries of Maria Mitchell, the astronomer.

Throughout the compiling of the book I was concerned with trying to avoid weighting it with white, middle-class material: such women were the most vocal and also had the most leisure time in which to keep a journal or diary. At the other end of the economic scale, slaves were forbidden to learn to read and write; Sojourner Truth's "autobiography" is told in the third person, by a white woman, and so reluctantly I felt I could not include it. Instead, there is Susie King Taylor's reminiscence: her account of attending a clandestine school in 1858 in Savannah, Georgia, is, I think, outstanding in its understated, almost casual tone—not in accepting monstrous injustice, but in acknowledging its daily existence.

"Mother" Mary Jones's salty telling of her experiences as a union organizer in the coal fields of Pennsylvania is also far removed from the traditional middle-class experience, as is the autobiography of Elizabeth Stern, growing up in the Jewish ghetto of a Midwestern city at the turn of this century. Probably most removed from the middle-class milieu is the tape-recorded life story of Mountain Wolf Woman, raised in the tribal ways of the Winnebago Indians in Wisconsin.

The only professional writers in the group are Elizabeth Cady Stanton, the Reverend Anna Shaw, and Elizabeth Stern after her earlier career as a social worker. (The reader may or may not agree with my estimate that often these professionals describe scenes and express feelings with less directness than the amateurs.)

In addition to the objective limitation of what first-person material was available, and trying to maintain the chronological span, geographical spread, economic range, and cultural cross section that I had planned, there were, of course, subjective factors governing my choices.

Since I knew from the outset that I would be working on this book over a long period of time, my first demand was that each personality had to hold my own interest—all the way through. This eliminated a number of earlier lives I might have included, because so many of the journals and diary excerpts that I read struck me as lugubrious, tantalizingly evasive, and monotonous in their emphasis upon a spiritual afterlife to the exclusion of almost every activity in the secular world.

Beyond capturing and holding my attention as first reader, I felt that each life presented had to offer sufficient wordage by way of autobiography or journal or letters to give the sense of a whole personality, not just a fragment. This restriction, also, eliminated much early material.

Then, arbitrarily, I decided not to include the contemporary. The lives of modern women, narrated by modern women themselves, are readily available. What I sought was to restore our sense of the past, to listen to those who were long gone, and to learn how they echo down the years; in short, to give our lives today a continuity that has been lacking.

Listen to the voices: how varied, yet how unfailingly feminine, whether teen-age Eliza with her underlinings, girlish gushes, accents of enthusiasm ("Now, mama, what do you think I am going to ask for?—a wig. I must either cut my hair or have one, I cannot dress it at all *stylish*. How much time it will save—in one year we could save it in pins and paper, besides the *trouble*") or young Susie, already married to a soldier in the Union Army and working in the regiment herself ("I assisted in cleaning the guns and used to fire them off, to see if the cartridges were dry, before cleaning and reloading each day. I thought this great fun") or proud twelve-year-old Anna in the Michigan wilderness. ("At first we had our tree-cutting done for us, but we soon became expert in this gentle art, and I developed such skill that in later years, after father came, I used to stand with him and 'heart' a log.")

Listen to the voices: how overlapping, whether Elizabeth fasting by the banks of the Ohio River on the Jewish high holy day of Yom Kippur, or Mountain Wolf Woman fasting in the woods in appeal to Indian spirits.

Listen to the voices: how guarded, how euphemistic the language, attempting to gain privacy through the distancing of words when no physical privacy was obtainable: Arvazine, jouncing on a cramped wagon train across the plains, giving birth to "the little stranger"; Mountain Wolf Woman dressing for a marriage that her brothers had arranged, referring to her groom only as "that man" and to her prospective mother-in-law as "that man's mother."

Despite the sometimes flowery sentimentalizing (often from the professional writers), with what poetic female exactitude many of the daily moments are perceived: Elizabeth Stern's achieving an office, for instance ("a real desk, a typewriter, a telephone, and a tray—for what? For letters. It looked like the wire tray in which I drained dishes"). And Maria Mitchell's drudging detail work—and feminine vanity—along with the exaltation of realizing her scientific goal. ("As I did not know how to manage a spider's web, I took the hairs from my own head, taking care to pick out the white ones because I have no black ones to spare. I put in the two, after first stretching them over pasteboard, by sticking them with sealing-wax dissolved in alcohol into the little grooved lines. . . . I thought it nice ladylike work to manage such slight threads and turn such delicate screws; but fine as are the hairs of one's head, I shall seek something finer, for I can see how clumsy they will appear when I get on with the eyepiece and magnify their imperfections. They look parallel now to the eye, but with a magnifying power a very little crook will seem a billowy wave, and a faint star will hide itself in one of the abysses.")

With what spare majesty some of the traumas of growing up female in America are recorded. Mountain Wolf Woman's onset of menses, with its haunting (is it unconscious?) symbolism: "Because mother had told me to do so, I ran quite far into the woods where there were some bushes. The snow was still on the ground and the trees were just beginning to bud. In the woods there was a broken tree and I sat down under this fallen tree. I bowed my head with my blanket wrapped over me, and there I was, crying and crying. Since they had forbidden me to look around, I sat there with my blanket over my head. I cried." And Susie King Taylor's dry-as-dried-tears statement of widowhood, leaving her teaching career to go to work as a domestic: "I put my baby with my mother and entered in the employ of a family, where I lived quite a while, but had to leave, as the work was too hard."

The striking contemporaneity: how like a modern suburban housewife's lament is Elizabeth Cady Stanton's describing her daily life of 1847: "Our residence was on the outskirts of the town, roads very often muddy and no sidewalks most of the way, Mr. Stanton was frequently away from home, I had poor servants, and an increasing number of children. To keep a house and grounds in order, purchase every article for daily use, keep the wardrobes of half a dozen human beings in proper trim, take the children to dentists, shoemakers, and different schools, or find teachers at home, altogether made sufficient work to keep one brain busy. . . . I suffered with mental hunger, which, like an empty stomach, is very depressing. . . ." And how close to our current Women's Liberation advocates of twenty-four-hour-a-day child care centers and communes is her epiphany: "I now fully understand the practical difficulties most women had to contend with in the isolated household, and the impossibility of woman's best development if in contact, the chief part of her life, with servants and children. Fourier's community life and cooperative households had a new significance for me."

Sometimes, in these first-person lives, time works in reverse. There are strong echoes of Nora in *A Doll's House* as Elizabeth Stern, several generations after Ibsen's play became a landmark in the women's movement, dissembles with her husband: "He did not feel that I was as hungry for the full measure of human responsibility as he was. 'I like to work,' I said then, quietly. 'I enjoy—being important,' I said with a half laugh. He laughed then, relieved. He was delighted that I spoke like a child about my work. He kissed me and held me close."

Time becomes extremely fluid, and there are passages in Mary Ann Loughborough's journal of her cave life in Vicksburg that almost seem as if they could be lifted out of today's nightmare headlines, when home fronts become battle fronts, and one comes to take the most abnormal situations for normal. ("'Ah!' said I to a friend, 'how is it possible you live here?' 'After one is accustomed to the change,' she answered, 'we do not mind it; but becoming accustomed, that is the trial.' . . . And so I went regularly to work, keeping house under ground. Our new habitation was an excavation made in the earth, and branching six feet from the entrance, forming a cave in the shape of a T. In one of the wings my bed fitted; the other I used as a kind of dressing room; in this the earth had been cut down a foot or two below the floor of the main cave; I could stand erect here; and when tired of sitting in other portions of my residence, I bowed myself into it, and stood impassively resting at full height. . . .")

And painfully relevant are Susie King Taylor's "Thoughts on Present Conditions," set down as the nineteenth century turned into the twentieth: "The war of 1861 came and was ended, and we thought our race was forever freed from bondage, and that the two races could live in unity with each other, but when we read almost every day of what is being done to my race by some whites in the South, I sometimes ask, 'Was the war in vain? Has it brought freedom, in the full sense of the word, or has it not made our conditions more hopeless?' . . . There is no redress for us from a government which promised to protect all under its flag. It seems a mystery to me. They say 'One flag, one nation, one country indivisible.' Is this true? . . . No, we cannot sing, 'My country, 'tis of thee, Sweet land of Liberty!' It is hollow mockery. . . . Justice we ask—to be citizens of these United States, where so many of our people have shed their blood with their white comrades, that the stars and stripes should never be polluted."

Listen to all of these voices growing up female in America: how much there is to hear and hearken to in what is said—and what goes unsaid—as the women speak for themselves.

A brief note about the technical aspects of editing this material. I have made minimum alterations in original style. Punctuation and spelling have sometimes been clarified and modernized, such as capitalizing the word Negro. On fewer occasions, when old-fashioned phrases seemed to me to lead to unintelligibility, I changed them. As an example, so you need not worry that I have updated "glorious," for instance, to "groovy," there is a sentence in Susie King Taylor's memoir that read: "I did this; when he wanted to know if I could sew." In the text here, I have made the sentence read: "I did this; then he wanted to know if I could sew." Another example, "He spied a boat in the distance and thought they might be spies." To avoid ambiguity, I substituted for the verb *spied, observed.*

Sometimes when phrases seemed overly cumbersome I simplified the sentence structure. (Not often.) Both personal and place names have also been omitted when they were distracting and not germane to the narrative. Repetitive phrases have also at times been eliminated. Repetition is to be expected more often in journals and letters, since by their nature they are given to a more conversational and careless tone than formal essays or intentional historical writing.

Ellipses have been used only where obviously connective material has been excised. Otherwise I have not made use of this suspensive device; it always makes me feel hesitant . . . that I am waiting for somebody to drop the other shoe. . . .

Finally, I have added subheads and supplied continuity where it seemed to me helpful in keeping the narrative going.

The full titles and original sources are these:

A GIRL'S LIFE EIGHTY YEARS AGO. Selections from the Letters of Eliza Southgate Bowne. New York: Charles Scribner's Sons, 1888.

MARIA MITCHELL: *Life, Letters and Journals.* Compiled by Phebe Mitchell Kendall. Boston: Lee and Shepard Publishers, 1896.

EIGHTY YEARS AND MORE. Reminiscences of Elizabeth Cady Stanton. New York: European Publishing Co., 1898.

THE STORY OF A PIONEER by Anna Howard Shaw with Elizabeth Jordan. New York: Harper and Bros., 1915.

MY CAVE LIFE IN VICKSBURG *With Letters of Trial and Travel.* By A Lady (Mrs. Mary Ann Webster Loughborough). New York: D. Appleton and Co., 1864.

JOURNEY ACROSS THE PLAINS. Unpublished ms. by Arvazine Angeline Cooper.

REMINISCENCES OF MY LIFE IN CAMP by Susie King Taylor. Boston: Published by the author, 1902.

AUTOBIOGRAPHY OF MOTHER JONES. Edited by Mary Field Parton. With an introduction by Clarence Darrow. Chicago: Charles H. Kerr and Co., 1925.

I AM A WOMAN—AND A JEW by Elizabeth G. Stern (pseud., Leah Morton). New York: J. H. Sears and Co., 1926.

MOUNTAIN WOLF WOMAN. Edited by Nancy Oestreich Lurie. Ann Arbor: The University of Michigan Press, 1961.

Yaddo, October 1970

Eliza Southgate

LETTERS

ELIZA SOUTHGATE
1783–1809

Eliza Southgate was born in Scarborough, Maine, the third of twelve children. Her father's family had been long settled in Leicester, Massachusetts; he grew up there and studied medicine.

However, by the time he finished his course there was not room for another doctor in the town, so he went north to the newer community of Scarborough, in the District of Maine. There he met and married Mary King, the daughter of a large landholder.

Dr. Southgate's practice flourished. After a while he added legal knowledge to medicine, and in time he was appointed a judge in the Court of Common Pleas.

The Southgate children, as befitting the family station, were given what was considered to be the best education of the times.

After attending school in Scarborough, all the Southgate children were then sent to be "finished" at boarding schools near Boston. When she was fourteen, Eliza was sent to Mrs. Wyman's in Medford.

Medford, May 12, 1797

Honored Parents:

I am not doing anything but writing, reading, and cyphering. There is a French Master coming next Monday, and he will teach French and Dancing. Mr. Wyman advises me to learn French, he says it will not take up but a very little of my time, for it is but two days in the week, and the lessons only 2 hours long. Mr. Wyman says I must learn Geometry before Geography, and that I better not begin it till I have got through my Cyphering.

We get up early in the morning and make our beds and sweep the chamber, it is a chamber about as large as our kitchen chamber, and a little better finished. There's 4 beds in the chamber, and two persons in each bed, we have chocolate for breakfast and supper.

Your affectionate Daughter,
Eliza Southgate.

Dr. Southgate decided that the cramped quarters of Mrs. Wyman's school were not suitable for his daughter, and so he transferred her to Mrs. Rowson's school, also in Medford.

Medford, August 25, 1797

Dear Mother:

I received your packet of things the 20th inst. and was very glad of them.

Never did I know the worth of good parents half so much as now I am from them; I never missed our closet so much, and above all things our cheese and Butter which we have but very little of, but I am very contented. I wish you would send me up my patterns all of them for I want them very much indeed, for I expect to work me a gown.

I am with due respect
Your dutiful daughter.

Medford, Sept. 30, 1797

Dear Mother:

You mentioned in yours, of the 16th inst. that it was a long time since you had received a letter from me; but it was owing to my studies which took up the greater part of my time; for I have been busy in my Arithmetic, but I finished it yesterday, and expect now to begin my large manuscript Arithmetic.

You mentioned in your letter about my Winter clothes of which I will make out a Memorandum. I shall want a coat and you may send it up for me to make, or you may make it your self, but I want it made loose with a belt. I wish you to send me enough of all my slips to make long sleeves that you can, and I wish you would pattern my dark slip to make long sleeves. I want a flannel waist, and a petticoat, for my white one dirts so quick that I had rather have a colored one. I have nothing more to write, only give my love to all who ask after me.

Your ever affectionate daughter.

Boston, February 13, 1798

Hon. Father:

I learn Embroidery and Geography at present and wish your permission to learn Musick. You may justly say, my best of Fathers, that every letter of mine is one which is asking for something more; never contented—I only ask, if you refuse me, I know you do what you think best, and I am sure I ought not to complain, for you have never yet refused me anything that I have asked, my best of Parents, how shall I repay you? You answer, by your good behavior. Heaven grant that it may be such as may repay you. A year will have rolled over my head before I shall see my Parents. I have ventured from them at an early age to be so long a time absent, but I hope I have learnt a good lesson by it—a lesson of experience, which is the best lesson I could learn.

I have described one of the blessings of creation in Mrs. Rowson, and now I will describe Mrs. Wyman as the reverse; she is the worst woman I ever knew of all that I ever saw; nobody knows what I suffered from the treatment of that woman—I had the misfortune to be a favorite with Miss Haskell and Mr. Wyman, she said, and she treated me as her own malicious heart dictated; but whatever is, is right, and I have learnt a good lesson by it. I wish you, my Father, to write an answer soon and let me know if I may

learn music.—Give my best respects to my good Mother, tho' what
I say to my Father applies to my Mother as much as to my Father.

*After finishing school, Eliza returned home to Scarborough but
made frequent visits to Boston and wrote to her next younger sister
Octavia about her experiences.*

Boston, Feb. 7th, 1800

After the toil, the bustle and fatigue of the week I turn towards
home to relate the manner in which I have spent my time. I have
been continually engaged in parties, plays, balls, &c. &c. Since the
first week I came to town, I have attended all the balls and assemblies, one one week and one the next. They have regular balls
once a fortnight, so that I have been to one or the other every
Thursday. They are very brilliant and I have formed a number of
pleasing acquaintances there; last night, which was ball night, I
drew No. 5, & 2nd sett drew a Mr. Snow, bad partner; danced
voluntarily with Mr. Oliver, Mr. Andrews, Mr. McPherson; danced
until 1 o'clock; they have charming suppers, laid entirely with china.
I had charming partners always. Today I intended going to Mrs.
Codman's, engaged to a week ago, but wrote a billett I was in-
disposed, but the truth of the matter was that I wanted to go to the
play to see Bunker hill.

I have bought me a very handsome skirt, white satin. Richard
Cutts went shopping with me yesterday morn, engaged to go to
the play next week with him.

For mourning for Washington the ladies dress as much as if for a
relation, some entirely in black, but now many wear only a ribbon
with a line painted on it. I have not yet been out to see Mrs. Rowson
and Miss Haskell, but intend to next week. Uncle William King
has been very attentive to me—carried me to the play 3 or 4 times
and to all the balls and assemblies excepting the last which I went
with Mr. Andrews. Give my best respects to Pappa and Mamma,
and tell them I shall soon be tired of this dissipated life and almost want to go home already.

Approximately mid-Feb. 1800

Now, Mama, what do you think I am going to ask for?—a wig. Eleanor Coffin [*a neighbor from Scarborough*] has got a new one just like my hair and only 5 dollars, Mrs. Mayo one just like it. I must either cut my hair or have one, I cannot dress it at all *stylish.* Eleanor's mother bought hers and says that she will write to Mrs. Sumner to get me one just like it; how much time it will save— in one year we could save it in pins and paper, besides the *trouble.* At the assembly I was quite ashamed of my head, for nobody has long hair. If you will consent to my having one do send me a 5 dollar bill by the post immediately after you receive this, for I am in hopes to have it for the next Assembly—do send me word immediately if you can let me have one.

[*To Octavia, who by this time was at Mrs. Rowson's school in Medford.*]

12th of June, 1800
Hanover Street, Boston

I have heard that Eleanor Coffin received attentions from Sam Davis when in Boston, did you hear of it? Martha writes me too that Mr. Andrews is paying attention to a young lady in Boston, but does not mention her name, *Miss Pickman,* I guess; he was said to be her swain last winter.

Mr. Little, the bearer of this, another beau I send you, and here is poor *I* not a bit on a one, *Doc. Bacon* excepted, and even *him, Cousin Mary,* selfish creature, has lugged off his *heart* and left the remainder here, so we might as well have a stump—poor soul, his face looks like a *peony,* one continued blush—I suppose for fear of hearing her name mentioned, and she, unreasonable creature! thinks he is not all perfection. Unaccountable taste—he is very *delightsome* surely,—how long shall I rant at this rate. I long to go to Portland and then I shall see some being that looks like a beau—or a monkey, or anything you please;—To supply the loss I often look out the window, till my imagination forms one out of a tree or anything that I see, we can imagine anything you know. Bless my soul, Mr. L. is waiting!

July 3, 1800

My dear Mother, I don't know what I shall do about writing Octavia, as Mrs. Rowson told her I wrote on an improper subject when I asked her in my letter if Mr. Davis was paying attention to Eleanor Coffin, and she would not let her answer the question. This is *refining* too much, and if I can't write as I feel, I can't write at all. Now I ask you, Mamma, if it is not quite a natural question when we hear that any of our friends are paid attention to by any gentleman, to ask a confirmation of the report from those we think most likely to know the particulars. Never did I write a line to Octavia but I should have been perfectly willing for you or my Father to have seen. You have always treated me more like a companion than a daughter, and therefore would make allowance for the volatile expressions I often make use of. I never felt the least restraint in company with my Parents which would induce me to stifle my gaiety, and you have kindly permitted me to rant over all with my nonsense uncorrected, and I positively believe it has never injured. I must bid you good-night.

     Eliza

Pray don't forget to send some more shirts.

[*To Octavia*]

Scarborough, Sept. 14, 1800

We hear you were in Boston last Sunday. Momma thinks, Octavia, you are there too much, we do not know how often, but we hear of you there very often indeed. I think, my dear sister, you ought to improve every moment of your time, which is short, very short to complete your education. In November terminates the period of your instruction. The last you will receive perhaps ever, only what you may gain by observation.

I think, Octavia, I would not leave my school again until you finally leave it. You may—you will think this is harsh; you will not always think so; remember those that wish it must know better what is proper than you possibly can. Horatio [*their older brother*] will come on for you as soon as your quarter is out. We anticipate the time with pleasure; employ your time in such a manner as to make your improvement conspicuous. A boarding-school, I know, my dear Sister, is not like home, but reflect a moment, is it not necessary, *absolutely necessary*, to be more strict in the government of 20 or 30 young ladies, nearly of an age and different dispositions, than a private family?

You have been indulged, Octavia, so we have all. I was discontented when I first went from home.

The lofty tone did not last long. Late that evening Eliza wrote further to Octavia.

Tired, stupid, and sleepy, I feel that I can write nothing instructive or amusing. Oh these *summer balls* are not the thing, but it was much more comfortable than I expected. My ears were continually assailed with lamentations that you were not present. Mr. Kinsman would certainly have gone out for you—so he said—had he ever been at our house. He really asked one or two gentlemen to go. He is a frothy fellow. He rattles without a spark of fancy and stuns you with his volubility, as anything hollow or empty always makes the most noise. I told him I received a letter from you yesterday. He gave a pious ejaculation to heaven, turned gracefully on his heel and entreated in the most humble manner that I would grant him a sight of one line! I refused as I thought him too insignificant an animal to be so much honored.

Eliza wrote often to her cousin, Moses Porter, and used him as a sounding board for her social views.

My most charming Cousin! Most kind and condescending friend—teach me how I may express the grateful sense I have of the obligations I owe you; your many and long letters have chased away the spleen, they have rendered me cheerful and happy. O shame on you! Moses, you know I hate this formality among friends, you know how gladly I would throw all these fashionable forms from our correspondence; but you still oppose me, you adhere to them with as much scrupulosity as to the ten commandments, and for aught I know you believe them equally essential to the salvation of your soul. But, Eliza, you have not answered my last letter! True, and if I had not have answered it, would you never have written me again—and I confess I believe that you would not—yet I am mortified and displeased that you value my letters so little, that the exertions to continue the correspondence must all come from me, that if I relax my zeal in the smallest degree it may drop to the ground without your helping hand to raise it. I do think you are a charming fellow,—would not write because I am in debt, well, be it so, my ceremonious friend,—I submit, and though I transgress by sending a half sheet more than you ever did, yet I assure you 'twas to convince you of the violence of my anger which could *induce* me to forget the rules of politeness.

I may be censured for declaring it as my opinion that not one woman in a hundred marries for love. A woman of taste and sentiment will surely see but a very few whom she could love, and it is altogether uncertain whether either of them will particularly distinguish her. If they should, surely she is very fortunate, but it would be one of fortune's random favors and as such we have no right to expect. The female mind I believe is of a very pliable texture; if it were not we should be wretched indeed.

Gratitude is undoubtedly the foundation of the esteem we commonly feel for a husband. If his character is good—if he is not displeasing in his person or manners—what objection can we make that will not be thought frivolous by the greater part of the world? —yet I think there are many other things necessary for happiness, and the world should never compel me to marry a man because I could not give satisfactory reasons for not liking him. A single life is considered too generally as a reproach; but let me ask you, which is the most despicable—she who marries a man she scarcely thinks *well* of—to avoid the reputation of an old maid—or she, who with more delicacy, than marry one she could not highly esteem, preferred to live single all her life.

Every being who has contemplated human nature on a large scale will certainly justify me when I declare that the inequality of privilege between the sexes is very sensibly felt by us females, and in no instance is it greater than in the liberty of choosing a partner in marriage; true, we have the liberty of refusing those we don't like, but not of selecting those we do.

I could never love without being beloved, and I am confident in my own mind that no person whom I could love would ever think me sufficiently worthy to love me. But I congratulate myself that I am at liberty to refuse those I don't like, and that I have firmness enough to brave the sneers of the world and live an old maid, if I never find one I can love.

Scarborough, June 1, 1801

As to the qualities of mind peculiar to each sex, I agree with you that sprightliness is in favor of females and profundity of males. Their education, their pursuits would create such a quality even tho' nature had not implanted it. The business and pursuits of men require deep thinking, judgment, and moderation, while, on the other hand, females are under no necessity of digging deep, but merely 'skim the surface,' and we too commonly spare ourselves the exertion which deep researches require, unless they are absolutely necessary to our pursuits in life. Women who have not incentives to action suffer all the strong energetic qualities of the mind to sleep in obscurity. In this dormant state they become enervated and impaired, and at last die for *want of exercise.* The little airy qualities which produce sprightliness are left to flutter about like feathers in the wind, the sport of every breeze.

Women have more fancy, more lively imaginations than men. That is easily accounted for: a person of correct judgment and accurate discernment will never have that flow of ideas which one of a different character might,—every object has not the power to introduce into his mind such a variety of ideas, he rejects all but those closely connected with it. On the other hand, a person of small discernment will receive every idea that arises in the mind, making no distinction between those nearly related and those more distant, they are all equally welcome, and consequently such a mind abounds with fanciful, out-of-the-way ideas. Women have more imagination, more sprightliness, because they have less discernment.

The cultivation of the powers we possess, I have ever thought a privilege—or I may say duty—that belonged to the human species, and not man's exclusive prerogative.

I am aware of the censure that will ever await the female that attempts the vindication of her sex, yet I dare to brave that censure that I know to be undeserved. It does not follow [O what a pen!] that every female who vindicates the capacity of the sex is a disciple of Mary Wollstonecraft. Though I allow her to have said many things on which I cannot but approve, yet the very foundation on which she builds her work will be apt to prejudice us so against her that we will not allow her the merit she really deserves,—yet, prejudice set aside, I confess I admire many of her sentiments.

Portland, March 1, 1802

Such a frolic! Such a chain of adventures I never before met with.

Thursday it snowed violently, indeed for two days before it had been storming so much that the snow drifts were very large; however, as it was the last Assembly I could not resist the temptation of going, as I knew all the world would be there. About 7 I went downstairs and found young Charles Coffin, the minister, in the parlor. He stared awhile at my feathers and flowers, "Think, Miss Southgate," said he, after a long pause, "think you would go out to *meeting* in such a storm as this?" Then assuming a tone of reproof, he entreated me to examine well my feelings. I heard in silence, unwilling to begin an argument that I was unable to support. The stopping of the carriage roused me; I immediately slipt on my socks and coat, and met Horatio and Mr. Motley in the entry. The snow was deep, but Mr. Motley took me up in his arms and sat me in the carriage without difficulty.

I found a full assembly, many married ladies, and every one disposed to end the winter in good spirits. At one we left dancing and went to the card-room to wait for a coach. It stormed dreadfully. The hacks were all employed as soon as they returned, and we could not get one till 3 o'clock. It was the most violent storm I ever knew.

There were now 20 in waiting, the gentlemen scolding and fretting, the ladies murmuring and complaining. One hack returned; all flocked to the stairs to engage a seat. So many crowded down that 'twas impossible to get past; luckily I was one of the first. I stept in, found a young lady, almost a stranger in town, who keeps at Mrs. Jordan's, sitting in the back-seat. She immediately caught hold of me and beg'd if I could possibly accommodate her to take her home with me, as she had attempted to go to Mrs. Jordan's, but the drifts were so high, the horses could not get through. I was distres't, for I could not ask her home with me, for sister had so much company that I was obliged to go home with Sally Weeks and give my chamber to Parson Coffin. I told her this, and likewise that she should be provided for if my endeavors could be of any service.

None but ladies were permitted to get into the carriage; it presently was stowed in so full that the horses could not move; the door was burst open, for such a clamor as the closing of it occasioned I never heard before. The universal cry was—"a gentleman in the coach, let him come out!" We all protested there was none, as it was too dark to distinguish; but the little man soon raised his voice and bid the coachman proceed; a dozen voices gave contrary orders. 'Twas a proper riot, I was really alarmed. My gentleman, with a vast deal of fashionable independence, swore no power on earth should make him quit his seat; but a gentleman at the door jump't into the carriage, caught hold of him, and would have dragged him out if we had not all entreated them to desist. He squeezed again into his seat and the carriage at length started full of ladies except our lady man who had crept to us for shelter.

When we found ourselves in the street, the first thing was to find out who was in the carriage and where we were all going, who first must be left. Luckily two gentlemen had followed by

the side of the carriage, and when it stopt took out the ladies
as they got to their houses. Our sweet little, trembling, delicate,
unprotected fellow sat immovable whilst the two gentlemen that
were obliged to walk thro' all the snow and storm carried all the
ladies from the carriage.

We at length arrived at the place of our destination. The gentlemen then proceeded to take us out. My beau, unused to carrying
such a weight of sin and folly, sank under its pressure, and I was
obliged to carry my mighty self through the snow which almost
buried me. Such a time, I never shall forget it!

The storm continued till Monday, and I was obliged to stay;
but Monday I insisted on setting out. The horse and sleigh were
soon at the door, and again I sallied forth to brave the tempestuous
weather [for it still snowed] and surmount the many obstacles
I had to meet with. We rode on a few rods, when coming
directly upon a large drift, we stuck fast.

We could get neither forward nor turn round. After waiting
till I was most frozen, we got out, and with the help of a
truckman the sleigh was lifted up. We again went on, and at
length we arrived at Sister Boyd's door, and the drift before it was
the greatest we had met with; the horse was so exhausted that he
sunk down, and we really thought him dead. 'Twas some distance
from the gate and no path. The gentleman took me up in his
arms and carried me till my weight pressed him so far into the
snow that he had no power to move his feet. I rolled out of his
arms and wallowed till I reached the gate; then rising to shake
off the snow, I turned and beheld my beau fixed and immoveable;
he could not get his feet out to take another step. At length,
making a great exertion to spring his whole length forward, he
made out to reach the poor horse, who lay in a worse condition
than his master.

By this time all the family had gathered to the window, indeed
they saw the whole frolic; but 'twas not yet ended, for unluckily,
in pulling off the bonnet I had borrowed from Miss Weeks to send
to the sleigh to be carried back to her, I pulled off my wig and
left my head bare. I was perfectly convulsed with laughter.

Sometime in the Spring, 1802

I have often thought what profession I should choose were I a man. The *law* would be my choice. When I might hope to arrive at an eminence which would be gratifying to my feelings. I should then hope to be a public character, respected and admired. To be an eloquent speaker would be the delight of my heart. I thank Heaven I was *born* a woman. I have now only patiently to wait till some clever fellow shall take a fancy to me and place me in a situation, I am determined to make the best of it, let it be what it will. We ladies, you know, possess that "sweet pliability of temper." But remember, I desire to be thankful I am not a man. I should not be content with moderate abilities— nay, I should not be content with mediocrity in any thing, but as a woman I am equal to the generality of my sex, and I do not feel that great desire of fame I think I should if I was a man.

I hardly know what to say to you, Cousin. I can hardly believe you serious when you say that "the enlargement of the mind will inevitably produce superciliousness and a desire of ascendancy,"—I should much sooner expect it from an ignorant, uncultivated mind. We cannot enlarge and improve our minds without perceiving our weakness, and wisdom is always modest and unassuming,—on the contrary a mind that has never been exerted knows not its deficiencies and presumes much more on its powers than it otherwise would. You beg me to say no more about enlarging the mind, as it is disagreeable, and you are too much prejudiced ever to listen with composure to me when I write on the subject.

On what subjects shall I write you? I shall either fatigue and disgust you with feminine trifles, or shock you by stepping beyond the limits you have prescribed.

Last evening I spent in talking scandal [for which God forgive me] but was too tempting an occasion to be resisted. I wish you were acquainted with some of the ladies, I would then tell you many things that might amuse.

There were no further letters to Cousin Moses. He died suddenly of yellow fever, caught while boarding an infected vessel.

Salem, July 14, 1802

Dear Mother:

How is Uncle Porter's family? I cannot even now reconcile myself to the idea of leaving them so unexpectedly and so immediately, yet I know not how it could be avoided. I am in the midst of amusements and pleasure, they drive all melancholy reflection from my mind, but when alone, my feelings warmly pay a tribute to the merit of *our departed Moses;* yet I cannot,—do not realize, every thing contributes to make me think it a delusion, a mere dream; how is it possible I can realize it? Yet sometimes I feel it is, must be true. How soon do we reconcile ourselves to the loss of our dearest friends; what would most distract us in anticipation we meet with calmness when it approaches; strange, unaccountable. I surely loved Moses with sincerity. I knew of no person so distantly connected whom I felt so interested in,—yet he is dead,—he is gone, and I can speak of it without emotion. Adieu, I will write soon.

Salem, *later in July* 1802

What will you say, my Dear Mother, when you find I am gone with Mr. and Mrs. Hasket Derby to the Saratoga Springs? But I hasten to explain all.

Mr. and Mrs. Derby were going in their carriage alone. Mrs. Derby says she never travelled without some lady, and urged my accompanying her. Mr. and Mrs. Derby say I must tell you they will take *good* care of me and they shall take the full protection of me. Pray if you disapprove, do not tell me till I return, 'twill be too late to alter or retract, and I should be wretched if I thought you disapproved my going.

Salem, September 9, 1802

My Dearest Mother:

Once more I am safe in Salem and my first thoughts turn toward home. I arrived last night. The attention I have received from Mr. and Mrs. Derby has been of a kind that I shall look forward with delight to a time when I may be able to return it as

I wish. I am in perfect health and spirits and have enjoyed the journey more than I can express to you.

I have received more attentions at the Springs than in my whole life before, I know not why it was, but I went under every advantage. Mr. Derby is so well known and respected, and they are such charming people and treated me with so much affection, it could not be otherwise!

Among the many gentlemen I have become acquainted and who have been attentive, one I believe is serious. I know not, my dearest Mother, how to introduce this subject, yet as I fear you may hear it from others and feel anxious for my welfare, I consider it a duty to tell you all.

At Albany, on our way to Ballston, we put up at the same house with a *Mr. Bowne* from New York; he went on to the Springs the same day we did, and from that time was particularly attentive to me; he was always of our parties to ride, went to Lake George in company with us, and came on to Lebanon when we did,—for 4 weeks I saw him every day and probably had a better opportunity of knowing him than if I had seen him as a common acquaintance in town for years.

I felt cautious of encouraging his attentions, tho' I did not wish to *discourage* it,—there were so many *New Yorkers* at the Springs who knew him perfectly that I easily learnt his character and reputation; he is a man of *business*, uniform in his conduct and *very much respected*; all this we knew from report. Mr. and Mrs. Derby were very much pleased with him, but conducted towards me with peculiar *delicacy*, left me entirely to myself, as on a subject of so much importance they scarcely dared give an opinion. I left myself in a situation truly embarrassing.

At such a distance from all my friends,—my Father and Mother a perfect stranger to the person,—and prepossessed in his favor as much as so short an acquaintance would sanction,—his conduct was such as I shall ever reflect on with the greatest pleasure,—open, candid, generous, and delicate. He is a man in whom I could place the most unbounded confidence, nothing rash or impetuous in his disposition, but weighs maturely every circumstance;

he knew I was not at liberty to encourage his addresses without the approbation of my Parents, and appeared as solicitous that I should act with strict propriety as one of my most disinterested friends. He advised me like a friend and would not have suffered me to do anything improper.

He only required I would not discourage his addresses till he had an opportunity of making known to my Parents his character and wishes—this I promised and went so far as to tell him I approved him as far as I knew him, but the decision must rest with my Parents, their wishes were my Law. He insisted upon coming on immediately: that I absolutely refused to consent to.

But all my persuasion to wait till winter had no effect; the first of October he *will come*. I could not prevent it without a positive refusal; this I felt no disposition to give. And now, my dearest Mother, I submit myself wholly to the wishes of my Father and you, convinced that my happiness is your warmest wish, and to promote it has ever been your study. That I feel deeply interested in Mr. Bowne I candidly acknowledge, and from the knowledge I have of his heart and character I think him better calculated to promote my happiness than any person I have yet seen; he is a firm, steady, serious man, nothing light or trifling in his character, and I have every reason to think he has well weighed his sentiments towards me,—nothing rash or premature. I have referred him wholly to you, and you, my dearest Parents, must decide.

I wish my Father would write to Mr. Derby and know what he says of Mr. B.'s character. I long to hear from home. My love to all my friends, and believe me, with every sentiment of *duty* and *affection*,

                    Your daughter Eliza

                                        Boston, May 30, 1803
Here we are, my dear Octavia, at Mrs. Carter's Boarding House, and tho' we have endeavored to keep ourselves as much out of the way as possible, a great many people have called to pay their respects to Mr. and Mrs. Bowne.

When I hear an old acquaintance call me "Mrs. Bowne" it really makes me stare at first, it sounds so very odd.

New York, June 6, 1803

I am enraptured with New York. You cannot imagine anything half so beautiful as *Broadway*.

As to housekeeping, we don't begin to talk anything of it yet. I see Mr. B. now where he is universally known and respected, and every hour see some new proof how much he is honored and esteemed here.

New York, June 18, 1803

I am just going to set off for Long Island and therefore but a short letter. The fashions are *remarkably plain*, sleeves much longer, than ours, and half handkerchiefs are universally worn. At Mrs. Henderson's party there was but one lady except myself without a handkerchief,—dressed as plain as possible, the most fashionable women the plainest. I have got you a pretty India spotted muslin,—'tis fashionable here.

My husband sends a great deal of love, says we shall be traveling about all Summer, settle down soberly in October, and depend upon seeing you as soon as we are at housekeeping.

The City air has not stolen my *country bloom* yet, for every one says—"I need not ask you how you do, Mrs. Bowne, you look in such fine health."

New York, June 30, 1803

I returned from Long Island this morning: delightful sail, beautiful country, and pleasant visit. Malbone has finished my picture, but is unwilling we should have it as the likeness is not striking,—he says not handsome enough—so says Mr. B. But I think 'tis in some ways much flattered. It looks too serious, pensive, soft,—that's not *my* style at all. But perhaps 'twill look different; 'twas not quite finished when I saw it.

We are in expectation of great entertainment on fourth of July— *Independent* day! as they laugh at us Yankees for calling it,—the gardens, the Battery, and every thing to be illuminated, fireworks, music, etc., etc.

                                        New York, July 4, 1803

Dear Mother:

I have written generally to Octavia, but as I meant my letters for the family, 'tis not much matter to whom they were directed.

                                                        July 8

My letter will be an old date before I finish it. You must have perceived, my dear Mother, from my letters, that I am much pleased with New York. I was never in a place that I should prefer as a situation for life, and nothing but the distance from my friends can render it other than delightful. We have thus far spent the summer on a number of little excursions of 20 or 40 miles to see whatever is pleasant in the neighborhood.

Mr. Bowne's Quaker friends, tho' all very plain, are very amiable and affectionate, and I receive every attention from them I wish. I have a great many people call on me, and shall have it in my power to select just such a circle of acquaintances as suits my taste,—few people whose prospects of happiness exceed mine, which I often think of with grateful sensations.

'Tis very different here from most any place, for there is no article but you can find ready made to your taste, excepting table linen, bedding, etc., etc. One poor bed quilt is all I have towards housekeeping, and been married two months almost. I am sadly off, to be sure.

We have not yet found a house that suits us. Mr. Bowne don't like any of his own, and wishes to hire one for the present until he can *build*, which he intends doing next season; which I am very glad of, as I never liked living in a hired house and changing about so often.

How do all our friends at Saco and Topsham do? I often think of them, and Mr. Bowne and myself are talking of coming to see you next summer very seriously. Remember me to all the children. Dear little Mary,—I can't help crying sometimes, with all my pleasures and amusements; 'tis impossible to be at once reconciled to quitting all one's friends. I thought a great deal of the children. I never thought I loved them so much; I never pass a toy-shop or confectionery without wishing them here. How does Horatio succeed in business, as well as he expected? How comes on Father's turnpike and diking? Tell him I yesterday met a woman full broke out with the small-pox; I was within a yard of her before I perceived it; the first sensation was terror, and I ran several paces before I recollected myself. As soon as I arrived in town Doctor Moore examined my arm, enquired the particulars, and refused to inoculate me again; that he would venture to insure me from the small-pox; that he had inoculated hundreds and never had one take the small-pox after the kine-pox. Adieu.

Your affectionate daughter

Eliza S. Bowne

P.S. All the family desire to be remembered particularly. Mr. B. is out to dine.

To Octavia.

New York, July 23, 1803

I have sent a few sugar toys to the children, which you must divide,—the cradle for Mary, the basket for Arixene, etc., etc. A little frock I send as a pattern for Miranda, Arixene, and Mary, long or short sleeves as you please, whalebone in the back, laced. Two little fans for Arixene and Mary, with their names on them, you'll find in the bottom of the box.

I have some fine peaches and apricots on the table before me; Mr. Bowne brings me a pocketful of fruit every time he comes home. I have ate as many as I want to, and have been thinking how much I would give to get them to you, but this early fruit won't keep at all. I was at the theatre night before last—at Mount Vernon Garden. We commence our Southern journey in about 10 days. Love to all friends.

A son, Walter Bowne, Jr., was born in 1805 and is mentioned in this next letter to Eliza's young sister Miranda.

Jan. 14, 1806

My dear Miranda:

As to news—New York is not so gay as last Winter, few balls but a great many tea-parties.

You say I have said nothing of Walter in any of my recent letters; he is so hearty and well I hardly thought of him when I wrote; he has not had a day's sickness. I send him out walking frequently when 'tis so cold it quite makes the tears come; he trudges along with leading very well in the street, he never takes cold. He goes to bed at 6 o'clock, away in the room in the third story, without fire or candle, and there he sleeps. You know I am a great enemy to letting children sleep with a fire in the room; 'tis the universal practice here, and as long as I can avoid it I never mean to practice it; it subjects them to constant colds.

To Miranda.

Sunday, May 25, 1806

Walter grows such a playful little rogue, he is always in mischief; I am just leaving off his caps; I want his hair to grow before his Grandmamma sees him; he won't look so pretty without his caps. He creeps so much I find it impossible to keep him so nice as I used to.

Three more children were born to her: Octavia, Frederic, and Mary. Eliza, who had been in poor health for a while, found the New York winters severe, and it was decided that she should go to South Carolina for the winter of 1808–9.

New York, Dec. 27, 1808

You are anxious, my Dear Mother, to hear from my own hand how I am. My cough is extremely obstinate, I have occasionally a little fever, tho' quite irregular and sometimes a week without any.

I have a new Physician to attend me; he is a Frenchman of great celebrity, particularly in Pulmonary complaints, and has been wonderfully successful in the cure of coughs; he keeps me on a milk diet, but allows me to eat eggs and oysters. He does not give any opiates; Paregoric and Laudanum he entirely disapproves of; he gives no medicine but a decoction of Roots and Flowers; the *Iceland Moss* or *Lichen* made in a tea he gives a great deal of, and for cough I take a white Pectoral lotion he calls it, made principally of White Almonds, Gum Arabic, Gum Tragacanth [or something like it], the Syrup of Muskmelon seeds.

He thinks I am much better already. I have no pain at all, and have not had any. My cough seems to be all my disorder. He thinks he can cure that; indeed he speaks with perfect confidence, and says he has no doubt as soon as I get to warmer weather, my cough will soon leave me. We shall probably sail by Sunday at farthest.

You will hear from me, my Dear Mother, often,—at present my mind seems so occupied; leaving my children, preparing to go, making arrangements to shut up my house. 'Tis quite a trial to leave my little ones; I leave them at their Grandmother's. My little Mary has a wet-nurse; she is a fine, lively child, and thrives fast. Adieu, my Dear Mother; I did not think I could have written half as much; love to all my friends.

To her sister-in-law Caroline Bowne in New York.

Charleston, Jan. 28, 1809

Dear Caroline, I send a little pair of shoes for Mary, a little Cuckoo toy for Walter, and a tumbler of Orange Marmalade for Mother. I have had only one letter from New York since I have been here, and that from Mary Perkins, not one line from my husband. I can tell you nothing flattering of my health: I am very miserable; at present I have a kind of intermittent Fever; this afternoon I shall take an emetic, and hope a good effect.

How are my dear little ones? —I hope not too troublesome. I hardly trust myself to think of them,—precious children—how they bind me to life! Adieu. I have a bad headache and low-spirited today.

That was the last letter written by Eliza. Her husband wrote to her as follows, knowing nothing of how serious her illness had become.

To Mrs. Bowne.

New York, Feb'y 4, 1809

Your letter, my love, of the 13th and 14th has comforted me. You must keep up your spirits; you will do well, Dr. Bergere says; attacks similar to yours are not of the dangerous kind that some think; he approves of your taking the Lychen again. I have sent a bundle by Capt. Slocum, who sails tomorrow.

I am distressed I cannot go with him, but so it is. It is next to impossible I should leave here till about the 25th of this month. Mr. Jenkins, my assistant, is absent, and I cannot leave the office until he returns without relinquishing it altogether, and I have most of my houses to let this month, those I have lately built included, and which are not finished, but I am determined to leave here in all this month.

I hope you have a comfortable place now; what abominable lodgings the first were! Don't mind the expense: get everything and do everything you like, we can afford it. I wish my presence in this place could as well be dispensed with, but so it is. I think it right you should have a Physician. I will bring the things you mention; our children are well.

Ever,

Walter Bowne

Inscription on the monument in Archdale Churchyard, Charleston, South Carolina:

SACRED

To The Memory Of

ELIZA S. BOWNE

Wife of Walter Bowne of New York,

Daughter of Robert Southgate Esqr.,

of Scarborough, District of Maine,

who departed this life on the 19th

day of February, 1809, aged 25 years.

1. Abigail Adams at the age of 21.

2 and 3. Eliza Southgate, New England schoolgirl, became a New York wife at the age of 20, when she married Walter Bowne in 1803.

4. An eighteenth-century girl returning from school.

5. An antebellum Southern lady, ca. 1860.

Elizabeth Cady Stanton

EXCERPTS FROM HER AUTOBIOGRAPHY
EIGHTY YEARS AND MORE

ELIZABETH CADY STANTON
1815–1902

Perhaps more than any other single figure, Elizabeth Cady Stanton spans the great age of the woman's rights movement of the nineteenth century. More radical than any of the other founding mothers, she called for the granting of women's suffrage at the very first historic convention held at Seneca Falls in the summer of 1848. She remained a gadfly in the movement throughout her long life.

Married to an abolitionist who was sympathetic to the cause of women, she had seven children; her daughter Harriot became active with her in the suffrage movement, and her granddaughter Nora Stanton Barney continued the family tradition of feminism by becoming the first woman in the United States to receive a degree in civil engineering.

Published in 1898, her autobiography, Eighty Years and More, *is dedicated to Susan B. Anthony, "my steadfast friend for half a century," and bears the following quotation on the title page:*

"Social science affirms that woman's place in society marks the level of civilization."

A Political Beginning

I commenced the struggle of life under favorable circumstances on the 12th day of November, 1815, the same year that my father, Daniel Cady, a distinguished lawyer and judge in the state of New York, was elected to Congress.

Perhaps the excitement of a political campaign, in which my mother took the deepest interest, may have had an influence on my prenatal life and given me the strong desire that I have always felt to participate in the rights and duties of government.

My father, though gentle and tender, had such a dignified repose and reserve of manner that, as children, we regarded him with fear rather than affection.

My mother, Margaret Livingston, a tall, queenly looking woman, was courageous, self-reliant, and at her ease under all circumstances and in all places. She was the daughter of Colonel James Livingston, who took an active part in the War of the Revolution.

The first event engraved on my memory was the birth of a sister when I was four years old. I heard so many friends remark, "What a pity it is she's a girl!" that I felt a kind of compassion for the little baby. True, our family consisted of five girls and only one boy, but I did not understand at the time that girls were considered an inferior order of beings.

Our favorite resorts in the house were the garret and cellar. In the former were barrels of hickory nuts, and, on a long shelf, large cakes of maple sugar and all kinds of dried herbs and sweet flag; spinning wheels, as well as ancient costumes. Here we would crack the nuts, nibble the sharp edges of the maple sugar, chew some favorite herb, play ball, whirl the old spinning wheels, dress up in our ancestors' clothes, and take a birds'-eye view of the surrounding country from an enticing scuttle hole. This was forbidden ground; but we often went there on the sly, which only made the little escapades more enjoyable.

The cellar of our house was filled, in winter, with barrels of apples, vegetables, salt meats, cider, butter, pounding barrels and washtubs, offering admirable nooks for playing hide and seek. This cellar was on a level with a large kitchen where we played blind man's buff and other games when the day's work was done.

I can recall three colored men, Abraham, Peter, and Jacob, who acted as menservants in our youth. In turn they would sometimes play on the banjo for us and dance, taking real enjoyment in our games.

In the winter, outside the house, we had the snow with which to build statues and make forts, and huge piles of wood covered with ice, which we called the Alps, so difficult were they of ascent and descent. There we would climb up and down by the hour.

Johnstown was to me a gloomy-looking town. The middle of the streets was paved with large cobblestones, over which the farmers' wagons rattled from morning till night, while the sidewalks were paved with very small cobblestones, over which we carefully picked our way, so that free and graceful walking was out of the question. The streets were lined with solemn poplar trees, from which small yellow worms were continually dangling down.

Next to the Prince of Darkness, I feared these worms. They were harmless, but the sight of one made me tremble. So many people shared in this feeling that the poplars were all cut down and elms planted in their stead. The Johnstown academy and churches each had a doleful bell which seemed to be ever tolling for school, funerals, church, or prayer meetings. Next to the worms, those clanging bells filled me with the utmost dread; they seemed like so many warnings of an eternal future. Visions of the Inferno were strongly impressed on my childish imagination. It was thought that firm faith in hell and the devil was the greatest help to virtue. It certainly made me very unhappy whenever my mind dwelled on such teachings, and I have always had my doubts of the virtue that is based on the fear of punishment.

I have been told that I was a plump little girl, with very fair skin, rosy cheeks, good features, dark-brown hair, and laughing blue eyes. A student in my father's office told me one day, after conning my features carefully, that I had one defect which he could remedy. "Your eyebrows should be darker and heavier," said he, "and if you will let me shave them once or twice, you will be much improved."

I consented, and slight as my eyebrows were, they seemed to have had some expression, for the loss of them had a most singular effect on my appearance. Everybody, including the shaver, laughed at my odd-looking face, and I was in the depths of humiliation while my eyebrows were growing out again. Needless to say I never allowed the young man to repeat the experiment, although strongly urged to do so.

"You Should Have Been a Boy"

When I was eleven years old, my only brother, who had just graduated from Union College, came home to die. A young man of great talent and promise, he was the pride of my father's heart.

I recall going into the large darkened parlor and finding the casket, mirrors, and pictures all draped in white, and my father seated, pale and immovable. As he took no notice of me, after standing a long while, I climbed upon his knee, when he mechanically put his arm about me, and, with my head resting against his beating heart, we both sat in silence, he thinking of the wreck of all his hopes in the loss of a dear son, and I wondering what could be said or done to fill the void in his breast. At length he heaved a deep sigh and said: "Oh, my daughter, I wish you were a boy!"

Throwing my arms about his neck, I replied: "I will try to be all my brother was."

All that day and far into the night I pondered the problem of boyhood. I thought that the chief thing to be done in order to equal boys was to be learned and courageous. So I decided to study Greek and learn to manage a horse.

I learned to leap a fence and ditch on horseback.

I began to study Latin, Greek, and mathematics with a class of boys in the Academy, many of whom were much older than I. For three years one boy kept his place at the head of the class, and I always stood next. Two prizes were offered in Greek. I strove for one and took the second. One thought alone filled my mind. "Now," said I, "my father will be satisfied with me."

I rushed breathless into his office, laid the new Greek Testament, which was my prize, on his table and exclaimed: "There, I got it!" He took up the book, asked me some questions about the class, and, evidently pleased, handed it back to me. Then he kissed me on the forehead and exclaimed, with a sigh, "Ah, you should have been a boy!"

At Father's Office

As my father's office joined the house, I spent there much of my time, when out of school, listening to the clients stating their cases, talking with the students, and reading the laws in regard to woman.

The students, observing my interest, would amuse themselves by reading to me all the worst laws they could find, over which I would laugh and cry by turns. One Christmas morning I went into the office to show them, among others of my presents, a new coral necklace and bracelets. They all admired the jewelry and then began to tease me with hypothetical cases of future ownership.

"Now," said one, "if in due time you should be my wife, those ornaments would be mine; I could take them and lock them up, and you could never wear them except with my permission. I could even exchange them for a box of cigars, and you could watch them evaporate in smoke."

When, from time to time, my attention was called to these odious laws, I would mark them in my father's books with a pencil, and becoming more and more convinced of the necessity of taking some active measures against these unjust provisions, I resolved to seize the first opportunity, when alone in the office, to cut every one of them out of the books; supposing my father and his library were the beginning and end of the law.

However, this mutilation of his volumes was never accomplished, for without letting me know that he had discovered my secret, he explained to me one evening how laws were made, the large number of lawyers and libraries there were all over the State, and that if his library should burn up it would make no difference in woman's condition.

"When you are grown up, and able to prepare a speech," said he, "you must go down to Albany and talk to the legislators; tell them all you have seen in this office—the sufferings of women, robbed of their inheritance and left dependent on their unworthy sons, and, if you can persuade them to pass new laws, the old ones will be a dead letter." Thus was the future object of my life fore-shadowed and my duty plainly outlined by him who was most opposed to my public career when, in due time, I entered upon it.

Visits to Peterboro

The year, with us, was never considered complete without a visit to Peterboro, N.Y., the home of Gerrit Smith.

Every year representatives from the Oneida tribe of Indians visited him. His father had early purchased of them large tracts of land, and there was a tradition among them that, as an equivalent for the good bargains of the father, they had a right to the son's hospitality, with annual gifts of clothing and provisions.

The slaves, too, had heard of Gerrit Smith, the abolitionist, and of Peterboro as one of the safe points en route for Canada. His mansion was, in fact, one of the stations on the "underground railroad" for slaves escaping from bondage. Hence they, too, felt that they had a right to a place under his protecting roof. On such occasions the barn and the kitchen floor were utilized as chambers for the black man from the southern plantation and the red man from his home in the forest.

It was in Peterboro that I first met one who was then considered the most eloquent and impassioned orator on the anti-slavery plat-form, Henry B. Stanton. He was then in his prime, a fine-looking, affable young man, with remarkable conversational talent, and was ten years my senior, with the advantage that that number of years necessarily gives.

When she was almost twenty-five years old, she became engaged to Henry Stanton.

One outcome of those glorious days of October, 1839, was a marriage, in Johnstown, the 10th day of May, 1840, and a voyage to the Old World.

Wedding Journey

Mr. Stanton was going to Europe as a delegate to the World's Anti-slavery Convention, and we did not wish the ocean to roll between us. The Scotch clergyman who married us, being somewhat superstitious, begged us to postpone the ceremony to Saturday from Friday for fear of bad luck. But, as we were to sail early in the coming week, that was impossible. Next, we had to persuade him to leave out the word "obey" in the marriage ceremony. As I obstinately refused to obey one with whom I supposed I was entering into an equal relation, that point, too, was conceded.

They sailed for England, took up lodgings in London, in antici-pation of the convention that was to meet June 12, 1840, in Freemasons' Hall.

Excluding the Women Delegates

Delegates from all the anti-slavery societies were invited, yet, when they arrived, those representing associations of women were rejected.

The first female anti-slavery society had been formed in 1833.

Furthermore, though women were members of the National Anti-Slavery Society, accustomed to speak and vote in all its conventions, and to take an equally active part with men in the whole anti-slavery struggle, and were there as delegates from associations of men and women, as well as those distinctively of their own sex, yet all alike were rejected because they were women.

Women, according to English prejudices at the time, were ex-cluded by Scriptural texts from sharing equal dignity and authority with men in all reform associations; hence it was to English minds pre-eminently unfitting that women should be admitted as equal members of the World's Convention.

The question was hotly debated through an entire day. My husband made a very eloquent speech in favor of admitting the women delegates.

When we consider that Elizabeth Fry, Lucretia Mott, and many other remarkable women, speakers and leaders in the Society of Friends, were all compelled to listen in silence to the masculine platitudes on woman's sphere, one may form some idea of the indignation of such women as Lydia Maria Child, Maria Chapman, Angelina and Sarah Grimké, and Abby Kelly, who were impatiently waiting on this side of the Atlantic, in painful suspense, to hear how their delegates were received.

The clerical portion of the convention was most violent in its opposition. The women sat in a low curtained seat like a church choir, and modestly listened to the French, British and American Solons for twelve of the longest days in June, as did, also, our grand Garrison and others in the gallery. These men scorned a convention that ignored the rights of the very women who had fought, side by side, with them in the anti-slavery conflict. "After battling for so many long years," said Garrison, "for the liberties of African slaves, I can take no part in a convention that strikes down the most sacred rights of all women."

As Mrs. Mott and I walked home to our London lodgings, arm in arm, commenting on the incidents of the day, we resolved to hold a convention as soon as we returned home, and form a society to advocate the rights of women.

Return to the United States and Motherhood

The society to advocate the rights of women was not to be formed for a while. Henry Stanton, after consulting his wife's father, decided to commence the study of law.

As this arrangement kept me under the parental roof, I had two added years of pleasure, walking, driving, and riding on horseback with my sisters. These were pleasant and profitable years. I devoted them to reading law, history, and political economy, with occasional interruptions to take part in some temperance or anti-slavery excitement.

The puzzling questions that had occupied so much of my thoughts, now gave place to the practical one, "what to do with a baby."

In 1843 Henry Stanton was admitted to the bar. They moved to Boston, where he began the practice of law.

My second son was born in March, 1844, under more favorable auspices than the first, as I knew, then, what to do with a baby.

A new house, newly furnished, with beautiful views of Boston Bay, was all I could desire. Mr. Stanton announced to me, in starting, that his business would occupy all his time, and that I must take entire charge of the housekeeping. So, with two good servants and two babies under my sole supervision, my time was pleasantly occupied.

As Mr. Stanton did not come home to dinner, we made a picnic of our noon meals on Mondays, and all thoughts and energies were turned to speed the washing. No unnecessary sweeping or dusting, no visiting—it was held sacred to soap suds and clotheslines. I had all the most approved cook books, and spent half my time preserving, pickling, and experimenting in new dishes. I felt the same ambition to excel in all departments of the culinary art that I did at school in different branches of learning.

In the spring of 1847 we moved to Seneca Falls, New York. Here we spent sixteen years of our married life, and here our other children were born.

The New England winters had proved too severe for my husband, whose health was delicate, and so we had left Boston, with many regrets, to seek a more genial climate in central New York.

Seeds of Housewifely Rebellion

In Seneca Falls my life was comparatively solitary, and the change from Boston was somewhat depressing. There, all my immediate friends were reformers, I had near neighbors, a new home with all the modern conveniences, and well-trained servants.

Here, our residence was on the outskirts of the town, roads very often muddy and no sidewalks most of the way, Mr. Stanton was frequently away from home, I had poor servants, and an increasing number of children.* To keep a house and grounds in good order, purchase every article for daily use, keep the wardrobes of half a dozen human beings in proper trim, take the children to dentists, shoemakers, and different schools, or find teachers at home, altogether made sufficient work to keep one brain busy, as well as all the hands I could impress into service.

Then, too, the novelty of housekeeping had passed away, and much that was once attractive in domestic life was now irksome. I had so many cares that the company I needed for intellectual stimulation was a trial rather than a pleasure.

Up to this time life had glided by with comparative ease, but now the real struggle was upon me. My duties were too numerous and varied, and none sufficiently exhilarating or intellectual to bring into play my higher faculties. I suffered with mental hunger, which, like an empty stomach, is very depressing. I had books, but no stimulating companionship.

To add to my general dissatisfaction at the change from Boston, I found that Seneca Falls was a malarial region, and in due time all the children were attacked with chills and fever which lasted three months. The servants were afflicted in the same way. Cleanliness, order, my love of the beautiful and artistic, all faded away in the struggle to accomplish what was absolutely necessary from hour to hour. Now I understood, as I never had before, how women could

---

* *She wrote to her cousin, Elizabeth Smith Miller:*

Seneca Falls

Monday morning, February 11, 1851

Dear Liz—Laugh in your turn. I have actually got my fourth son! Yes, Theodore Stanton bounded upon the stage of life with great ease—comparatively!! He weighs ten and one-half pounds. I was sick but a few hours, and did not lie down until half an hour before he was born. This morning I got up, bathed myself in cold water, and have sat by the fire writing several letters.

sit down and rest in the midst of general disorder. Housekeeping, under such conditions, was impossible, so I packed our clothes, locked up the house, and went to that harbor of safety, my parents' home, as I did ever after in stress of weather.

I now fully understood the practical difficulties most women had to contend with in the isolated household, and the impossibility of woman's best development if in contact, the chief part of her life, with servants and children. Fourier's community life and co-operative households had a new significance for me.

Emerson says, "A healthy discontent is the first step to progress." The general discontent I felt with woman's portion as wife, mother, housekeeper, physician, and spiritual guide, the chaotic conditions into which everything fell without her constant supervision, and the wearied, anxious look of the majority of women impressed me with a strong feeling that some active measures should be taken to remedy the wrongs of society in general, and of women in particular.

My experience at the World's Anti-slavery Convention, all I had read of the legal status of women, and the oppression I saw everywhere, together swept across my soul, intensified now by many personal experiences. I could not see what to do or where to begin —my only thought was a public meeting for protest and discussion.

The First Woman's Rights Convention

In this tempest-tossed condition of mind I received an invitation to spend the day with Lucretia Mott, at Richard Hunt's, in Waterloo. There I met several members of different families of Friends, earnest, thoughtful women.

I poured out, that day, the torrent of my long-accumulating discontent, with such vehemence and indignation that I stirred myself, as well as the rest of the party, to do and dare anything. It moved us all to prompt action, and we decided, then and there, to call a "Woman's Rights Convention."

We wrote the call that evening and published it in the *Seneca County Courier* the next day, the 14th of July, 1848, giving only five days' notice, as the convention was to be held on the 19th and the 20th.

The call was inserted without signatures—in fact it was a mere announcement of a meeting—but the chief movers and managers were Lucretia Mott, Mary Ann McClintock, Jane Hunt, Martha C. Wright and myself.

The convention, which was held two days in the Methodist Church, was in every way a grand success. The house was crowded at every session, the speaking good, and a religious earnestness dignified all the proceedings.

These were the hasty initiative steps of "the most momentous reform that had yet been launched on the world—the first organized protest against the injustice which had brooded for ages over the character and destiny of one-half the race."

No words could express our astonishment on finding, a few days afterward, that what seemed to us so timely, so rational, and so sacred, should be a subject for sarcasm and ridicule to the entire press of the nation. With our Declaration of Rights and Resolutions for a text, it seemed as if every man who could wield a pen prepared a homily on "woman's sphere." All the journals from Maine to Texas seemed to strive with each other to see which could make our movement appear the most ridiculous.

The anti-slavery papers stood by us manfully and so did Frederick Douglass, both in the convention and in his paper, *The North Star*, but so pronounced was the popular voice against us, in the parlor, press, and pulpit, that most of the ladies who had attended the convention and signed the declaration, one by one, withdrew their names and influence and joined our persecutors. Our friends gave us the cold shoulder and felt themselves disgraced by the whole proceeding.

And the Second

If I had had the slightest premonition of all that was to follow that convention, I fear I should not have had the courage to risk it, and I must confess that it was with fear and trembling that I consented to attend another, one month afterward, in Rochester.

Fortunately, the first one seemed to have drawn all the fire, and of the second but little was said. But we had set the ball in motion, and now, in quick succession, conventions were held in Ohio, Indiana, Massachusetts, Pennsylvania, and in the City of New York, and have been kept up nearly every year since.

The Bloomer Dress

There was one bright woman among the many in our Seneca Falls literary circle to whom I would give more than a passing notice—Mrs. Amelia Bloomer, who represented three novel phases of woman's life. She was assistant postmistress; an editor of a reform paper, *The Lily*, advocating temperance and woman's rights; and an advocate of the new costume which bore her name!

Although she wore the bloomer dress, its originator was my cousin, Elizabeth Smith Miller, the only daughter of Gerrit Smith, the abolitionist.

In the winter of 1852 Mrs. Miller came to visit me in Seneca Falls, dressed somewhat in the Turkish style—short skirt, full trousers of fine black broadcloth; a Spanish cloak, of the same material, reaching to the knee; beaver hat and feathers and dark furs; altogether a most becoming costume and exceedingly convenient for walking in all kinds of weather.

To see my cousin, with a lamp in one hand and a baby in the other, walk upstairs with ease and grace, while, with flowing robes, I pulled myself up with difficulty, lamp and baby out of the question, readily convinced me that there was sore need of reform in woman's dress, and I promptly donned a similar attire. What incredible freedom I enjoyed for two years! Like a captive set free from his ball and chain, I was always ready for a brisk walk through sleet and snow and rain, to climb a mountain, jump over a fence, work in the garden, and, in fact, for any necessary locomotion.

Mrs. Bloomer having *The Lily* in which to discuss the merits of the new dress, the press generally took up the question, and much valuable information was elicited on the physiological results of woman's fashionable attire; the crippling effects of tight waists and long skirts, the heavy weight on the hips, and high heels, all combined to throw the spine out of plumb and lay the foundation for all manner of nervous diseases. But while all agreed that some change was absolutely necessary for the health of women, the press stoutly ridiculed those who were ready to make the experiment.

A few sensible women, in different parts of the country, adopted the costume, and farmers' wives especially proved its convenience. It was also worn by skaters, gymnasts, tourists, and in sanitariums. But, while the few realized its advantages, the many laughed it to scorn, and heaped such ridicule on its wearers that they soon found that the physical freedom did not compensate for the persistent persecution and petty annoyances suffered at every turn. To be rudely gazed at in public and private, and to be followed by crowds of boys in the streets, were exasperating. A favorite doggerel that our tormentors chanted ran thus:

> Heigh! ho! in rain and snow,
> The bloomer now is all the go.
> Twenty tailors take the stitches,
> Twenty women wear the breeches.
> Heigh! ho! rain or snow,
> The bloomer now is all the go.

The singers were generally invisible behind some fence or attic window.

The patience of most of us was exhausted in about two years; but our leader, Mrs. Miller, bravely adhered to the costume for nearly seven years. She was bravely sustained, however, by her husband, who never flinched in escorting his wife and her coadjutors. Mrs. Miller was also encouraged by the intense feeling of her father on the question of woman's dress. To him the whole revolution in woman's position turned on her dress. The long skirt was the symbol of her degradation.

Housekeeping Assistance

It was while living in Seneca Falls, and at one of the most despairing periods of my young life, that one of the best gifts of the gods came to me in the form of a good, faithful housekeeper. She was indeed a treasure, a friend and comforter, a second mother to my children, and understood all life's duties and gladly bore its burdens. She could fill any department in domestic life, and for thirty years was the joy of our household. But for this noble, self-sacrificing woman, much of my public work would have been quite impossible. If by word or deed I have made the journey of life easier for any struggling soul, I must in justice share the meed of praise accorded me with my little Quaker friend Amelia Willard.

Elizabeth became an eloquent public speaker as well as a chief writer for the cause of women's rights. At the very first woman's rights convention she had insisted on demanding the vote for women: encouraged only by Frederick Douglass in this boldness, even Lucretia Mott had protested, "Lizzie, thee wilt make us ridiculous." She was, for many years, the only woman to write and speak on the question of divorce. She was also an instigator of child-care reform and school reform. Together with Susan B. Anthony, she put out a newspaper, The Revolution, *for two and a half years and together with Matilda Gage they also worked to compile a history of the women's movement. She traveled all over the country, promoting the cause of woman suffrage. As the years went by, her energy never seemed to diminish.*

The Pleasures of Age

My suffrage sons and daughters through all the Northern and Western states decided to celebrate, on the 12th of November, 1885, my seventieth birthday, by holding meetings or sending me gifts and congratulations. I was invited to deliver an essay on "The Pleasures of Age," before the suffrage association in New

York City. It took me a week to think them up, but with the inspiration of Longfellow's "Morituri Salutamus," I was almost converted to the idea that "we old folks" had the best of it.

All during that autumn Miss Anthony and I looked forward to the spring, when we hoped to have completed the third and last volume of our History, and thus end the labors of ten years. We had neither the time nor eyesight to read aught but the imperative documents for the History. I was hungering for some other mental pabulum.

I had long heard so many conflicting opinions about the Bible—some saying it taught woman's emancipation and some her subjection—that the thought came to me that it would be well to collect every biblical reference to women in one small compact volume, and see on which side the balance of influence really was. To this end I proposed to organize a committee of competent women, with some Latin, Greek, and Hebrew scholars in England and the United States, for a thorough revision of the Old and New Testaments, and to ascertain what the status of woman really was under the Jewish and Christian religion. As the Church has thus far interpreted the Bible as teaching woman's subjection, it seemed to me pre-eminently proper and timely for women themselves to review the book.

"The Woman's Bible"

I laid the subject so near my heart before an English friend and my daughter, Mrs. Stanton Blatch. They responded promptly and heartily, and we immediately set to work. I wrote to every woman who I thought might join such a committee, and my English friend ran through the Bible in a few days, marking each chapter that in any way referred to women.

We found that the work would not be so great as we imagined, as all the facts and teachings in regard to women occupied less than one-tenth of the whole Scriptures. We purchased some cheap Bibles, cut out the texts, pasted them at the head of the page, and, underneath, wrote our commentaries as clearly and concisely as possible. We did not intend to have sermons or essays, but brief comments, to keep "The Woman's Bible" as small as possible.

As an example of her unflagging energy, there is this casual reference in her autobiography: "My seventy-third birthday I spent with my son Gerrit Smith Stanton, on his farm near Portsmouth, Iowa. I amused myself darning stockings and drawing plans for an addition to his house."

Later Birthdays and New Reforms

I celebrated my seventy-sixth birthday in New York City with my children. I had traveled about constantly for the last twenty years in France, England, and my own country, and had so many friends and correspondents, and pressing invitations to speak in clubs and conventions, that now I decided to turn over a new leaf and rest in an easy-chair. But so complete a change in one's life could not be easily accomplished.

On January 16, 1892, we held the Annual Suffrage Convention in Washington, and, as usual, had had a hearing before the Congressional Committee. My speech on the "Solitude of Self" was well received and was published in the Congressional Record. The *Woman's Tribune* struck off many hundreds of copies and it was extensively circulated.

Notwithstanding my determination to rest, I spoke to many clubs, wrote articles for papers and magazines, and two important leaflets, one on "Street Cleaning," another on "Opening the Chicago Exposition on Sunday." As Sunday was the only day the masses could visit that magnificent scene, with its great lake, extensive park, artificial canals, and beautiful buildings, I strongly advocated its being open on that day. One hundred thousand religious bigots petitioned Congress to make no appropriations for this magnificent Exposition, unless the managers pledged themselves to close the gates on Sunday, and hide this vision of beauty from the common people. Fortunately, this time a sense of justice outweighed religious bigotry. I sent my leaflets to every member of Congress and of the State legislatures, and to the managers of the Exposition, and made it a topic of conversation at every opportunity. The park and parts of the Exposition were kept open on Sunday, but some of the machinery was stopped as a concession to narrow Christian sects.

On December 21, 1892, we celebrated, for the first time, "Foremothers' Day."

Men had celebrated "Forefathers' Day" for many years, but as women were never invited to join in their festivities, the custom was now introduced of women having a dinner in celebration of that day, and gentlemen were to sit in the gallery just as ladies had done on similar occasions.

Part One of "The Woman's Bible" was finally published in November, 1895, and it created a great sensation. Some of the New York City papers gave a page to its review, with pictures of the commentators, of its critics, and even of the book itself.

The clergy denounced it as the work of *Satan*, though it really was the work of eight women.

Extracts from it, and criticisms of the commentators, were printed in the newspapers throughout America, Great Britain, and Europe. A third edition was found necessary, and finally an edition was published in England. The Revising Committee was enlarged, and Part Two scheduled for publication in 1898.

A Credo

During the winter of 1895–96 I was busy writing alternately on this autobiography and "The Woman's Bible," and articles for magazines and journals on every possible subject from Venezuela and Cuba to the bicycle. On the latter subject many timid souls were greatly distressed. Should women ride? What should they wear? What are "God's intentions" concerning them? Should they ride on Sundays?

These questions were asked in all seriousness. We had a symposium on these points in one of the daily papers. To me the answer to all these questions was simple—if woman could ride, it was evidently "God's intention" that she be permitted to do so. As to what she should wear, she must decide what is best adapted to her comfort and convenience. Those who prefer a spin of a few hours on a good road in the open air to a close church and a dull sermon, surely have the right to choose, whether with trees and flowers and singing birds to worship in "That temple not made with hands, eternal in the heavens," or within four walls to sleep during the intonation of that melancholy service that relegates us all, without distinction of sex or color, to the ranks of "miserable sinners." Let each one do what seemeth right in her own eyes, provided she does not encroach on the rights of others.

Without my knowledge or consent, my lifelong friend, Susan B. Anthony, made arrangements for the celebration of my eightieth birthday. In describing this occasion, I cannot do better than to reproduce in part, the account published in *The Arena:*

"What woman ever before sat silver-crowned, canopied with flowers, surrounded not by servile followers but by men and women who brought to her court the grandest service they had wrought, their best thought crystallized in speech and song."

Having been accustomed for half a century to blame rather than praise, I was surprised with such a manifestation of approval; I could endure any amount of severe criticism with complacency, but such an outpouring of homage and affection stirred me profoundly.

Naturally at such a time I reviewed my life, its march and battle on the highways of experience, and counted its defeats and victories. I remembered when a few women called the first convention to discuss their disabilities, that our conservative friends said: "You have made a great mistake, you will be laughed at from Maine to Texas and beyond the sea; God has set the bounds of woman's sphere and she should be satisfied with her position." That first convention, considered a "grave mistake" in 1848, is now referred to as "a grand step in progress."

When, in 1860, I demanded the passage of a statute allowing wives an absolute divorce for the brutality and intemperance of their husbands, this was also called a "mistake," and was regarded as "a step in progress" a few years later.

Again, I urged the same demands of the Church that we had already made of the State. There was objection, saying, "An attack on the Church would injure the suffrage movement." But I steadily made the demand, as opportunity offered, that women be ordained to preach the Gospel and to fill the offices as elders, deacons, and trustees. A few years later some of these suggestions were accepted. Thus was another "step in progress" taken.

In 1882 I tried to organize a committee to consider the status of women in the Bible, and the claim that the Hebrew Writings were the result of divine inspiration. When Part One of "The Woman's Bible" was published, again there was a general disapproval by press and pulpit, and even by women themselves, expressed in resolutions in suffrage and temperance conventions. Like other "mistakes," this too, in due time, will be regarded as "a step in progress."

Such experiences have given me confidence in my judgment, and patience with the opposition of my coadjutors, with whom on so many points I disagree. It requires no courage now to demand the right of suffrage, temperance legislation, liberal divorce laws, or for women to fill church offices—these battles have been fought and won. But it still requires courage to question the divine inspiration of the Hebrew Writings as to the position of woman. Why should the myths, fables, and allegories of the Hebrews be held more sacred than those of the Assyrians and Egyptians from whose literature most of them were derived? Seeing that the religious superstitions of women perpetuate their bondage more than all other adverse influences, I feel impelled to reiterate my demands for justice, liberty, and equality in the Church as well as in the State.

The birthday celebration was to me more than a beautiful pageant; more than a personal tribute. It was the dawn of a new day for the Mothers of the Race! The grand jubilee was a prophecy that with the exaltation of Womanhood would come new Life, Light, and Liberty to all mankind.

Ten years before, in 1885, there had been a celebration for Henry Stanton's eightieth birthday. His Random Recollections, a book of personal reminiscences, was published at that time and well received. Of this special occasion, his wife observed in her autobiography: "A dinner was given him on June 27th by the Press Club of New York City, with speeches and toasts by his lifelong friends. As no ladies were invited I can only judge from the reports in the daily papers, and what I could glean from the honored guest himself, that it was a very interesting occasion."

Elizabeth completed her autobiography in 1897, and introduced it with this somewhat ambivalent preface: "The story of my private life as the wife of an earnest reformer, as an enthusiastic housekeeper, proud of my skill in every department of domestic economy, and as the mother of seven children, may amuse and benefit the reader. The incidents of my public career as a leader in the most momentous reform yet launched upon the world—the emancipation of women—will be found in "The History of Woman Suffrage."

She died in New York City at the end of her eighty-seventh year, and was survived by six of her seven children.

Maria Mitchell

EXTRACTS FROM HER DIARY

MARIA MITCHELL
1818–1889

Maria Mitchell was born to Quaker parents on Nantucket Island, Massachusetts. Her father was devoted to astronomy, and all the children, as they grew old enough, were drafted into the service of counting seconds by the chronometer during his observations. Maria very early showed a talent for mathematics and an enthusiasm for the pursuit of astronomy herself.

Speaking of what special circumstances led her to a study of astronomy, she said in an interview with Julia Ward Howe:

"It was, in the first place, a love of mathematics, seconded by my sympathy with my father's love for astronomical observation. But the spirit of the place had also much to do with the early bent of my mind in this direction. In Nantucket people quite generally are in the habit of observing the heavens, and a sextant will be found in almost every house. The landscape is flat and somewhat monotonous, and the field of the heavens has greater attractions there than in places which offer more variety of view. In the days in which I lived there the men of the community were mostly engaged in sea-traffic of some sort, and 'when my ship comes in' was a literal, not a symbolical expression."

Leaving school at age sixteen, she tried a succession of teaching jobs until she found a nearly ideal situation as librarian of the Nantucket Atheneum. The library was open only afternoons and on Saturday evenings. As there were not many visitors, she had ample time for her own studies. Furthermore, she was a person of prodigious energies, as this excerpt from her early journal indicates.

"I was up before six, made the fire in the kitchen, and made coffee. Then I set the table in the dining-room, and made the fire there. Toasted bread and trimmed lamps. Rang the breakfast bell at seven. After breakfast, made my bed, and 'put up' the room. Then I came down to the Atheneum and looked over my comet computations till noon. Before dinner I did some tatting, and made seven button-holes for K. I dressed and then dined. Came back again to the Atheneum at 1.30, and looked over another set of computations, which took me until four o'clock. I was pretty tired by that time, and rested by reading 'Cosmos.' Lizzie E. came in, and I gossiped for half an hour. I went home to tea, and that over, I made a loaf of bread. Then I went up to my room and read through (partly writing) two exercises in German, which took me thirty-five minutes.

"It was stormy, and I had no observing to do, so I sat down to my tatting. Lizzie E. came in and I took a new lesson in tatting, so as to make the pearl-edged. I made about half a yard during the evening. At a little after nine I went home with Lizzie, and carried a letter to the post-office. I had kept steadily at work for sixteen hours when I went to bed."

On clear evenings, even if company had come to call, she would put on her "regimentals," carry a lantern, and ascend the rooftop of the Mitchell house to observe through her father's telescope. On October 1, 1847, she was "sweeping the sky" as usual when she believed she saw a comet. She hurried down to tell her father, who immediately came back up to the roof with her, verified her findings, and promptly wrote off to Professor Bond at Cambridge to announce his daughter's discovery. The king of Denmark had offered a gold medal to the first discoverer of a telescopic comet, and while the comet was viewed in Rome on October 3, in Kent, England, on October 7, and in Hamburg on October 11, Maria was the first. The gold medal was awarded to her, and the following year—1848—she was unanimously elected to the American Academy of Arts and Sciences as the first woman member—and for a long time thereafter the only one. As a small point of semantics, the secretary of the Academy deleted the usual word "Fellow" on her certificate and wrote in the phrase "Honorary Member."

For twenty years Maria stayed at her library post and then went to Vassar College as professor of astronomy and director of the observatory. She stayed on there for the next twenty years, and it was a boast of her later life that she had earned a salary without cease for over fifty years. She was also prideful of her good health, taking walks every day, no matter what the weather. A serious fall, however, put an end to her vigorous physical exercise, and she died some time later at her family's home in Lynn, Massachusetts.

The diary excerpts that follow give, I think, some indication of the tedium of the daily work as well as the glory of pursuing her chosen career. Further, they show that, despite her own early fame, she was ever conscious of the actual and psychological obstacles placed in the way of women becoming scientists.

Feb. 15, 1853. I think Dr. Hall in his "Life of Mary Ware" does wrong when he attempts to encourage the use of the *needle*. It seems to me that the needle is the chain of woman, and has fettered her more than the laws of the country.

Once emancipate her from the "stitch, stitch, stitch," the industry of which would be commendable if it served any purpose except the gratification of her vanity, and she would have time for studies which would engross as the needle never can. I would as soon put a girl alone into a closet to meditate as give her only the society of her needle. The art of sewing, so far as men learn it, is well enough; that is, to enable a person to *take the stitches*, and, if necessary, to make her own garments in a strong manner; but the dressmaker should no more be a universal character than the carpenter. Suppose every man should feel it is his duty to do his own mechanical work of *all* kinds, would society be benefited? would the work be well done? Yet a woman is expected to know how to do all kinds of sewing, all kinds of cooking, all kinds of any *woman's* work, and the consequence is that life is passed in learning these only, while the universe of truth beyond remains unentered.

Oct. 31, 1853. People have to learn sometimes not only how much the heart, but how much the head, can bear. My letter came from the Harvard Observatory and I had some work to do over. It was a wearyful job, but by dint of shutting myself up all day I did manage to get through with it. In the evening I was too tired to read, to listen, or to talk. . . .

Dec. 8, 1853. Last night we had the first meeting of the class in elocution. It was very pleasant, but my deficiency of ear was never more apparent to myself. We had exercises in the ascending scale, and I practiced after I came home, with the family as audience. . . . I am sure that I shall never say that if I had been properly educated I should have made a singer, a dancer, or a painter—I should have failed less, perhaps, in the last. . . . Coloring I might have been good in, for I do think my eyes are better than those of anyone I know.

Feb. 18, 1854. If I should make out a calendar by my feelings of fatigue, I should say there were six Saturdays in the week and one Sunday.

March 2, 1854. I "swept" last night two hours, by three periods. It was a grand night—not a breath of air, not a fringe of cloud, all clear, all beautiful. I really enjoy that kind of work, but my back soon becomes tired, long before the cold chills me. I saw two nebulae in Leo with which I was not familiar, and that repaid me for the time. I am always the better for open-air breathing, and was certainly meant for the wandering life of the Indian.

Sept. 22, 1854. On the evening of the 18th, while "sweeping," there came into the field the two nebulae in Ursa Major, which I have known for many a year, but which to my surprise now appeared to be three. . . . Had the nebula suddenly changed? Was it a comet, or was it merely a very fine night? Father decided at once for the comet; I hesitated, with my usual cowardice, and forbade his giving it a notice in the newspaper.

I watched it from 8.30 to 11.30 almost without cessation, and was quite sure at 11.30 that its position had changed with regard to the neighboring stars. I counted its distance from the known nebula several times, but the whole affair was difficult, for there were flying clouds, and sometimes the nebula and comet were too indistinct to be definitely seen.

The 19th was cloudy and the 20th the same, with the variety of occasional breaks, through which I saw the nebula, but not the comet.

On the 21st came a circular, and behold Mr. Van Arsdale had seen it on the 13th, but had not been sure of it until the 15th, on account of the clouds.

I was too well pleased with having really made the discovery to care because I was not first.

Let the Dutchman have the reward of his sturdier frame and steadier nerves!

Especially could I be a Christian because the 13th was cloudy, and more especially because I dreaded the responsibility of making the computations, *nolens volens,* which I must have done to be able to call it mine. . . .

I made observations for three hours last night, and am almost ill today from fatigue; still I have worked all day, trying to reduce the places, and mean to work hard again tonight.

Sept. 25, 1854. I began to recompute for the comet, with observations of Cambridge and Washington, today. I have had a fit of despondency in consequence of being obliged to renounce my own observations as too rough for use. The best that can be said of my life so far is that it has been industrious, and the best that can be said of me is that I have not pretended to what I was not.

October 17. I have just gone over my comet computations again, and it is humiliating to perceive how very little more I know than

I did seven years ago when I first did this kind of work. To be sure, I have only once in the time computed a parabolic orbit; but it seems to me that I know no more in general. I think I am a little better thinker, that I take things less upon trust, but at the same time I trust myself much less. The world of learning is so broad, and the human soul is so limited in power! We reach forth and strain every nerve, but we seize only a bit of the curtain that hides the infinite from us. . . .

Dec. 5, 1854. The comet looked in upon us on the 29th. It made a twilight call, looking sunny and bright, as if it had just warmed itself in the equinoctial rays. A boy on the street called my attention to it, but I found on hurrying home that father had already seen it, and had ranged it behind buildings so as to get a rough position. It was piping cold, but we went to work in good earnest that night, and the next night on which we could see it, was not until April.

I was dreadfully busy, and a host of little annoyances crowded upon me. I had a good star near it in the field of my comet-seeker, but *what* star?

On that rested everything, and I could not be sure even from the catalogue, for the comet and the star were so much in the twilight that I could get no good neighboring stars. We called it Arietes, or 707.

Then came a waxing moon, and we waxed weary in trying to trace the fainter and fainter comet in the mists of twilight and the glare of moonlight.

Next I broke a screw of my instrument, and found that no screw of that description could be bought in the town.

I started off to find a man who could make one, and engaged him to do so the next day. The next day was Fast Day; all the world fasted, at least from labor.

However, the screw was made, and it fitted nicely. The clouds cleared, and we were likely to have a good night. I put up my instrument, but scarcely had the screwdriver touched the new screw than out it flew from its socket, rolled along the floor of the "walk," dropped quietly through a crack into the gutter of the house-roof. I heard it click, and felt very much like using language un-becoming to a woman's mouth.

I put my eye down to the crack, but could not see it. There was but one thing to be done,—the floor-boards must come up. I got a hatchet, but could do nothing.

I called father; he brought a crowbar and pried up the board, then crawled under it and found the screw. I took good care not to lose it a second time.

The instrument was fairly mounted when the clouds mounted to keep it company, and the comet and I again parted.

In all observations, the blowing out of a light by a gust of wind is a very common and very annoying accident; but I once met with a much worse one, for I dropped a chronometer, and it rolled out of its box on to the ground. We picked it up in a great panic, but it had not even altered its rate, as we found by later observa-tions.

The glaring eyes of the cat, who nightly visited me, were at one time very annoying, and a man who climbed up a fence and spoke to me, in the stillness of the small hours, fairly shook not only my equanimity, but the pencil which I held in my hand. He was quite innocent of any intention to do me harm, but he gave me a great fright.

The spiders and bugs which swarm in my observing-houses I have rather an attachment for, but they must not crawl over my recording-paper. Rats are my abhorrence, and I learned with pleasure that some poison had been placed under the transit-house.

One gets attached (if the term may be used) to certain midnight apparitions. The Aurora Borealis is always a pleasant companion; a meteor seems to come like a messenger from departed spirits; and the blossoming of trees in the moonlight becomes a sight looked for with pleasure.

Aside from the study of astronomy, there is the same enjoyment in a night upon the housetop, with the stars, as in the midst of other grand scenery; there is the same subdued quiet and grateful seriousness; a calm to the troubled spirit, and a hope to the despond-ing. . . .

Dec. 26, 1854. They were wonderful men, the early astronomers. That was a great conception, which now seems to us so simple, that the earth turns upon its axis, and a still greater one that it revolves about the sun (to show this last was worth a man's lifetime, and it really almost cost the life of Galileo). Somehow we are ready to think that they had a wider field than we for speculation, that truth being all unknown it was easier to take the first step in its paths. But is the region of truth limited? Is it not infinite? . . .

We know a few things which were once hidden, and being known they seem easy; but there are the flashings of the Northern Lights; there is the conical zodiacal beam seen so beautifully in the early evenings of spring and the early mornings of autumn; there are the startling comets, whose use is all unknown; there are the brightening and flickering variable stars, whose cause is all unknown; and the meteoric showers—and for all of these the reasons are as clear 'as for the succession of day and night; they lie just beyond the daily mist of our minds, but our eyes have not yet pierced through it.

Jan. 1, 1855. I put some wires into my little transit this morning. I dreaded it so much, when I found yesterday that it must be done, that it disturbed my sleep. It was much easier than I expected. I took out the little collimating screws first, then I drew out the tube, and in that I found a brass plate screwed on the diaphragm which contained the lines. I was at first a little puzzled to know which screws held this diaphragm in its place, and, as I was very anxious not to unscrew the wrong ones, I took time to consider and found I need turn only two. Then out slipped the little plate with its three wires where five should have been, two having been broken. As I did not know how to manage a spider's web, I took the hairs from my own head, taking care to pick out white ones because I have no black ones to spare. I put in the two, after first stretching them over pasteboard, by sticking them with sealing-wax dissolved in alcohol into the little grooved lines which I found. When I had, with great labor, adjusted these, as I thought, firmly, I perceived that some of the wax was on the hairs and would make them yet coarser, and they were already too coarse; so I washed my little camel's-hair brush which I had been using, and began to wash them with clear alcohol. Almost at once I washed out another wire and soon another and another. I went to work patiently and put in the five perpendicular ones besides the horizontal one, which, like the others, had frizzled up and appeared to melt away. With another hour's labor I got in the five, when a rude motion raised them all again and I began over. Just at one o'clock I had got them all back in again. I attempted then to put the diaphragm back into its place. The sealing-wax was not dry, and with a little jar I sent the wires all agog. This time they did not come out of the little grooved lines into which they were put, and I hastened to take out the brass plate and set them in parallel lines. I gave up then for the day, but, as they looked well and were certainly in firmly, I did not consider that I had made an entire failure. I thought it nice ladylike work to manage such slight threads and turn such delicate screws; but fine as are the hairs of one's head, I shall seek something finer, for I can see how clumsy they will appear when I get on with the eyepiece and magnify their imperfections. They look parallel now to the eye, but with a magnifying power a very little crook will seem a billowy wave, and a faint star will hide itself in one of the yawning abysses.

January 15. Finding the hairs which I had put into my instrument not only too coarse, but variable and disposed to curl themselves up at a change of weather, I wrote to George Bond to ask him how I should procure spider lines. He replied that the web from the cocoons should be used, and that I should find it difficult at this time of year to get at them. I remembered at once that I had seen two in the library room of the Atheneum, which I had carefully refrained from disturbing. I found them perfect, and unrolled them. . . . Fearing that I might not succeed in managing them, I procured some hairs from C.'s head. C. being not quite a year old, his hair is remarkably fine and sufficiently long. . . . I made the perpendicular wires of the spider's webs, breaking them and doing the work over again a great many times. . . . I at length got all in,

crossing the five perpendicular ones with a horizontal one from
C.'s spinning-wheel. . . . After twenty-four hours exposure to the
weather, I looked at them. The spider-webs had not changed, they
were plainly used to a chill and made to endure changes of temperature; but C.'s hair, which had never felt a cold greater than that
of the nursery, nor a change more decided than from his mother's
arms to his father's, had knotted up into a decided curl!

*In addition to the American Academy of Arts and Sciences, Maria
was elected to the American Association for the Advancement of
Science, and often attended their annual conventions. This excerpt
from her diary refers to the one of the summer of 1855.*

August 23. It is really amusing to find one's self lionized in a
city where one has visited quietly for years; to see the doors of
fashionable mansions open wide to receive you, which never opened
before. I suspect that the whole corps of science laughs in its sleeves
at the farce.

The leaders make it pay pretty well. My friend Professor
Bache makes the occasions the opportunities for working sundry
little wheels, pulleys, and levers; the result of all which is that he
gets his enormous appropriations of $400,000 out of Congress, every
winter, for the maintenance of the United States Coast Survey.

For a few days Science reigns supreme,—we are feted and complimented to the top of our bent, and although complimenters and
complimented must feel that it is only a sort of theatrical performance, for a few days and over, one does enjoy acting the part of
greatness for a while! I was tired after three days of it, and glad to
take the cars and run away.

The descent into a commoner was rather sudden. I went alone
to Boston, and when I reached out my free pass, the conductor
read it through and handed it back, saying in a gruff voice, "It's
not worth nothing; a dollar and a quarter to Boston." Think what a
downfall! The night before, and

> One blast upon my bugle horn
> Were worth a hundred men!

1866. When we are chafed and fretted by small cares, a look at the stars will show us the littleness of our own interests.

. . . But star-gazing is not science. The entrance to astronomy is through mathematics. You must make up your mind to steady and earnest work. You must be content to get on slowly if you only get on thoroughly. . . .

The phrase "popular science" has in itself a touch of absurdity. That knowledge which is popular is not scientific.

1871. When astronomers compare observations made by different persons, they cannot neglect the constitutional peculiarities of the individuals, and there enters into these computations a quality called "personal equation." In common terms, it is that difference between two individuals from which results a difference in the *time* which they require to receive and note an occurrence. If one sees a star at one instant, and records it, the record of another, of the same thing, is not the same.

It is true, also, that the same individual is not the same at all times; so that between two individuals there is a mean or middle individual, and each individual has a mean or middle self, which is not the man of today, nor the man of yesterday, nor the man of tomorrow; but a middle man among these different selves. . . .

We especially need imagination in science. It is not all mathematics, nor all logic, but it is somewhat beauty and poetry.

There will come with the greater love of science greater love to one another. Living more nearly to Nature is living farther from the world and from its follies, but nearer to the world's people; it is to be of them, with them, and for them, and especially for their improvement. We cannot see how impartially Nature gives of her riches to all, without loving all, and helping all; and if we cannot learn through Nature's laws the certainty of spiritual truths, we can at least learn to promote spiritual growth while we are together, and live in a trusting hope of a greater growth in the future.

. . . The great gain would be freedom of thought. Women, more than men, are bound by tradition and authority. What the father, the brother, the doctor, and the minister have said has been received

undoubtingly. Until women throw off this reverence for authority
they will not develop. When they do this, when they come to truth
through their investigations, when doubt leads them to discovery, the
truth which they get will be theirs, and their minds will work on and
on unfettered.

1874. I am but a woman! For women there are, undoubtedly, great
difficulties in the path, but so much the more to overcome. First, no
woman should say "I am but a woman!" But a woman! What more
can you ask to be?

Born a woman—born with the average brain of humanity—born
with more than the average heart—if you are mortal, what higher
destiny could you have?

*In 1878, she traveled out to Denver, Colorado, to observe the solar
eclipse.*

We started from Boston a party of two; at Cincinnati a third
joined us; at Kansas City we came upon a fourth who was ready to
fall into our ranks, and at Denver two more awaited us; so we were
a party of six—"All good women and true."

All along the road it had been evident that the country was
roused to a knowledge of the coming eclipse; we overheard remarks
about it; small telescopes traveled with us, and our landlord at
Kansas City, when I asked him to take care of a chronometer, said
he had taken care of fifty of them in the previous fortnight. . . .

In sending out telescopes so far as from Boston to Denver, I had
carefully taken out the glasses, and packed them in my trunks. I
carried the chronometer in my hand.

It was only five hours' travel from Pueblo to Denver, and we
went on to that city. The trunks, for some unexplained reason,
or for no reason at all, chose to remain at Pueblo.

One telescope-tube reached Denver when we did; but a telescope-
tube is of no value without glasses. We learned that there was a
war between the two railroads which unite at Pueblo, and war, no
matter where or when it occurs, means ignorance and stupidity.

The unit of measure of value which the railroad man believes in is entirely different from that in which the scientist rests his faith.

A war between two railroads seemed very small compared with two minutes forty seconds of observation of a total eclipse. One was terrestrial, the other cosmic.

It was Wednesday when we reached Denver. The eclipse was to occur the following Monday.

We haunted the telegraph-rooms, and sent imploring messages. We placed ourselves at the station, and watched the trains as they tossed out their freight; we listened to every express-wagon which passed our door without stopping, and just as we were trying to find if a telescope could be hired or bought in Denver, the glasses arrived.

It was now Friday; we must put up tents and telescopes, and test the glasses.

It rained hard on Friday—nothing could be done. It rained harder on Saturday. It rained hardest of all on Sunday, and hail mingled with the rain. But Monday morning was clear and bright. . . .

As totality approached . . . all was silent, only the count, on and on, of the young woman at the chronometer. When totality came, even that ceased.

How still it was!

As the last rays of sunlight disappeared, the corona burst out all around the sun, so intensely bright near the sun that the eye could scarcely bear it; extending less dazzlingly bright around the sun for the space of about half the sun's diameter, and in some directions sending off streamers for millions of miles.

It was now quick work. Each observer at the telescopes gave a furtive glance at the un-sunlike sun, moved the dark eye-piece from the instrument, replaced it by a more powerful white glass, and prepared to see all that could be seen in two minutes forty seconds. They must note the shape of the corona, its color, its seeming substance, and they must look all around the sun for the "interior planet." . . . Our special artist, who made the sketch for my party, could not bear the light.

When the two minutes forty seconds were over, each observer left her instrument, turned in silence from the sun, and wrote down brief notes. Happily, someone broke through all rules of order, and shouted out, "The shadow! the shadow!" And looking toward the southeast we saw the black band of shadow moving from us, a hundred and sixty miles over the plain, and toward the Indian Territory. It was not the flitting of the closer shadow over the hill and dale: it was a picture which the sun threw at our feet of the dignified march of the moon in its orbit.

And now we looked around. What a strange orange light there was in the north-east! what a spectral hue to the whole landscape! Was it really the same old earth, and not another planet?

. . . we have a hunger of the mind which asks for knowledge of all around us, and the more we gain, the more is our desire; the more we see, the more are we capable of seeing.

Besides learning to see, there is another art to be learned,— *not to see* what is not.

If we read in today's paper that a brilliant comet was seen last night in New York, we are very likely to see it tonight in Boston, for we take every long, fleecy cloud for a splendid comet.

. . . The eye is as teachable as the hand. Everyone knows the most prominent constellations,—the Pleiades, the Great Bear, and Orion. . . . But common observers know these stars only as bright objects; they do not perceive that one star differs from another in glory; much less do they perceive that they shine with differently colored rays.

Those who know Sirius and Betel do not at once perceive that one shines with a brilliant white light and the other burns with a glowing red, as different in their brilliancy as the precious stones on a lapidary's table, perhaps for the same reason. And so there is an endless variety of tints of paler colors.

We may turn our gaze as we turn a kaleidoscope, and the changes are infinitely more startling, the combinations infinitely more beautiful; no flower garden presents such a variety and such delicacy of shades.

But beautiful as this variety is, it is difficult to measure it; it has a phantom-like intangibility—we seem not to be able to bring it under the laws of science.

. . . From age to age the colors of some prominent stars have certainly changed. This would seem more likely to be from change of place than of physical constitution.

Nothing comes out more clearly in astronomical observations than the immense activity of the universe. "All change, no loss, 'tis revolution all."

Observations of this kind are peculiarly adapted to women. Indeed, all astronomical observing seems to be so fitted. The training of a girl fits her for delicate work. The touch of her fingers upon the delicate screws of an astronomical instrument might become wonderfully accurate in results; a woman's eyes are trained to nicety of color. The eye that directs a needle in the delicate meshes of embroidery will equally well bisect a star with the spider-web of the micrometer. Routine observations, too, dull as they are, are less dull than the endless repetition of the same pattern in crochet-work.

Professor Cauvenet enumerates among "accidental errors in observing," those arising from imperfections in the senses, as "the imperfection of the eye in measuring small spaces; of the ear, in estimating small intervals of time; of the touch, in the delicate handling of an instrument."

A girl's eye is trained from early childhood to be keen. The first stitches of the sewing-work of a little child are about as good as those of the mature man. The taking of small stitches, involving minute and equable measurements of space, is a part of every girl's training; she becomes skilled, before she is aware of it, in one of the nicest peculiarities of astronomical observation.

The ear of a child is less trained, except in the case of a musical education; but the touch is a delicate sense given in exquisite degree to a girl, and her training comes in to its aid. She threads a needle almost as soon as she speaks; she touches threads as delicate as the spider-web of a micrometer.

Then comes in the girl's habit of patient and quiet work, peculiarly fitted to routine observations. The girl who can stitch from morning to night would find two or three hours in the observatory a relief.

March 16, 1885. In February, 1831, I counted seconds for father, who observed the annular eclipse at Nantucket. I was twelve and a half years old. In 1885, fifty-four years later, I counted seconds for a class of students at Vassar; it was the same eclipse, but the sun was only about half-covered. Both days were perfectly clear and cold.

Mary Ann Webster Loughborough

EXCERPTS FROM HER JOURNAL
MY CAVE LIFE IN VICKSBURG

MARY ANN WEBSTER
LOUGHBOROUGH
1836–1887

"A Lady"

Mary Ann Webster Loughborough, by-lined tersely and enigmatically as "A Lady" when her letters and journal were published in New York in 1864, was the wife of a Confederate officer and the mother of an infant girl. Following her husband from Tennessee to Missouri to Mississippi as the Civil War continued, she was a remarkably observant witness, with an eye for selective detail as keen as that of a painter.

At first, in 1862, she wrote of her experiences in letters to a friend:

"The hospital patients were removed; and I crossed the country to meet my husband, who was at Tupelo. Then when Tupelo was to be evacuated, my husband placed me in charge of the past quartermaster, who was to take me over the country with the wagon train.

"I gathered my baggage together, wrapped a shawl around my sleeping child, and then, with a hurried goodbye, we drove off, six miles through the woods, through what had been an impassable swamp.

"Soon we saw lights through the trees, then the rows of camp fires, and noise and bustle: cattle were driven through, with many a shout and halloo; wagons were passing rapidly; soldiers were cooking rations at the camp fires—a scene of busy preparation.

"We drove to the quartermaster's office, and the gentlemen conducted us in, regretting that they had been obliged to send for me in such a summary manner. The order to move had come at dark; and since then they had been employed constantly, as the town must be evacuated by daylight; for the Federal forces were advancing rapidly.

"The house was an unfinished building: one large, long room comprised the second story, with a small portion partitioned off, and dignified by the name of office. To this I, with my servant, was conducted through piles of mule collars, harness, bridles, etc.

"Here I was glad to find a little camp cot, on which I laid my child for the first time out of my arms. I took my knitting and sat by the window. The moon was low in the heavens; yet the tumult continued throughout the town. My child slept peacefully—her father many miles away, yet, I knew, filled with anxiety for our welfare.

"At dawn we were on our way. . . ."

Her journey continued, and that crude, cramped room where she had stayed overnight would come to seem in retrospect as spacious as a palace. Here is an excerpt from her last letter before the account of her cave life began:

"I know you are smiling, as you see Jackson written at the head of my letter—smiling to think how systematically I have bowed myself out of one town after another, as the Federal troops have bowed themselves in; yet you know the old saw, 'He that fights, and runs away,' etc.; though I can take no comfort in this, as fighting has been my abomination since the war began. I have always, in peaceful times, had an admiration for heroes in brilliant uniforms, and would now, if the hero could possibly assure me that the brilliant uniform would always be filled with life.

"You see, dear friend, that I am unlucky enough to be identified with some retreat or threatened city. . . ."

Her journal covers the period of time from mid-April 1863 to a few days after July 4, when the garrison at Vicksburg surrendered. Initially, the Union Army had attacked the bluffs above Vicksburg at the end of 1862 but had been repulsed. Caves had been dug for temporary shelter from the bombardments.

It was with a very happy heart and very little foreboding that I set off with a party of friends from Jackson for a pleasant visit to Vicksburg, on the fifteenth of April.

I had thought, during the first bombardment of Vicksburg, that the town must have been a ruin; yet very little damage has been done, though very few houses are without evidence of the first trial of metal. One, I saw, with a hole through the window; behind was one of corresponding size through the panel of the door, which happened to be open. The corner of the piano had been taken off, and on through the wall the shot passed; one, also, passed through another house, making a huge gap through the chimney. And yet the inhabitants live in their homes (those who have not lost some loved one) happy and contented, not knowing what moment the house may be rent over their heads by the explosion of a shell.

"Ah!" said I to a friend, "how is it possible you live here?"

"After one is accustomed to the change," she answered, "we do not mind it; but becoming accustomed, that is the trial."

I was reminded of the poor man in an infected district who was met by a traveller and asked, "How do you live here?" "Sir, we die," was the laconic answer. And this is becoming accustomed. I looked over this beautiful landscape, and in the distance plainly saw the Federal transports lying quietly at their anchorage. Was it a dream? Could I believe that over this smiling scene, in the bright April morning, the blight of civil warfare lay like a pall?

While standing and thinking thus, the loud booming of the guns in the water batteries startled me, the smoke showing that it was the battery just below me, that opened, I was told, on what was thought to be a masked battery on the opposite shore. No reply was elicited, however; and on looking through the glass, we saw in the line of levee, between the river and the Federal canal, a spot where new earth seemed to have been thrown up, and branches of trees to have been laid quite regularly in one place. This was all. General Lee, however, had ordered the spot to be fired on, and the firing continued some little time. Our ride that evening had been delightful. We sat long on the veranda in the pleasant air, with the soft melody and rich swell of music from the band floating around us, while ever and anon my eye sought the bend of the river, two miles beyond, where the Federal transports, brought out in bold relief by the waning, crimson light of the evening, lay in seeming quiet. Still, resting in Vicksburg seemed like resting near a volcano.

First Visit to a Cave

At night I was sleeping profoundly, when the deep boom of the signal cannon startled and awoke me. Another followed, and I sprang from my bed, drew on my slippers and robe, and went out on the veranda. Our friends were already there. The river was illuminated by large fires on the bank, and we could discern plainly the huge, black masses floating down with the current, now and then belching forth fire from their sides, followed by the loud report, and we could hear the shells exploding in the upper part of town. The night was one of pitchy darkness; and as they neared the glare thrown upon the river from the large fires, the gunboats could be plainly seen. Each one, on passing the track of the brilliant light on the water, became a target for the land batteries. We could hear the gallop, in the darkness, of couriers upon the paved streets; we could hear the voices of the soldiers on the riverside. The rapid firing from the boats, the roar of the Confederate batteries, and, above all, the screaming, booming sound of the shells, as they exploded in the air and around the city, made at once a new and fearful scene to me. The boats were rapidly nearing the lower batteries, and the shells were beginning to fly unpleasantly near.

Some of the gentlemen urged the ladies to go down into the cave at the back of the house, and insisted on my going, if alone. While I hesitated, fearing to remain, yet wishing still to witness the termination of the engagement, a shell exploded near the side of the house. Fear instantly decided me, and I ran, guided by one of the ladies, who pointed down the steep slope of the hill, and left me to run back for a shawl. While I was considering the best way of descending the hill, another shell exploded near the foot, and, ceasing to hesitate, I flew down, half sliding and running. Before I had reached the mouth of the cave, two more exploded on the side of the hill near me. Breathless and terrified, I found the entrance and ran in, having left one of my slippers on the hillside.

The cave was an excavation in the earth the size of a large room, high enough for the tallest person to stand perfectly erect, provided with comfortable seats, and altogether quite a large and habitable abode (compared with some of the caves in the city), were it not for the dampness and the constant contact with the soft earthy walls. We had remained but a short time, when one of the gentlemen came down to tell us that all danger was over, and that we might witness a beautiful sight by going upon the hill, as one of the transports had been fired by a shell, and was slowly floating down as it burned.

We returned to the house, and from the veranda looked on the burning boat, the only one, so far as we could ascertain, that had been injured, the other boats having all passed successfully by the city. We remained on the veranda an hour or more, the gentlemen speculating on the result of the successful run by the batteries. All were astonished and chagrined. It was found that very few of the Confederate guns had been discharged at all. Several reasons had been assigned; the real one was supposed to have been the quality of the fuses that were recently sent from Richmond, and had not been tried since their arrival. This night of all others they were found to be defective.

Back to Jackson

At breakfast on the morning of the 17th, we heard discussed the question, Whether there was a masked battery on the opposite shore or not? After some words on the subject, pro and con, we ranged the shore with the glass, seeing what the gentlemen believed to be a battery. They had been talking some moments, when I took the glass and saw a number of Federal soldiers walking on the levee toward the spot where the battery was supposed to be. Several others seemed to be engaged on this very place removing the branches. I called one of the gentlemen to look. I had given up the glass but a few moments, when a volume of smoke burst from the embankment, and two shells were sent, one after the other, exploding at the depot just below us. It was indeed a battery, with two guns, which commenced playing on the city vigorously.

We were to leave that morning, and were glad to, with the sound of the cannon and the noise of the shell still ringing in our ears.

How delighted I was with the quiet rest of our home in Jackson!

But our quiet was destined to be of short duration. We were startled one morning by hearing that Colonel Grierson, of the Federal army, was advancing on Jackson. The citizens applied to General Pemberton to protect them. He answered that there was no danger. Suddenly, the ladies' carriage and saddle horses were pressed, and the clerks and young men of the town were mounted on them, and started out to protect us (!). I was told that the first time they met the Federal troops most of them were captured, and we heard of them no more.

Again the rumor came that from Canton a large Federal force was advancing on Jackson. Jackson was to be defended!! which I doubted. Soon General Pemberton left and went to Vicksburg—Mrs. Pemberton to Mobile. Batteries were being erected in different parts of the town—one directly opposite the house I was in. I stood considering one morning where it was best to go, and what it was best to do, when a quick gallop sounded on the drive, and a friend rode hastily up and said, "Are you going to leave?" "Yes," I answered, "but I have not yet decided where to go." "Well, I assure you there is no time for deliberation; I shall take my family to Vicksburg, as the safest place, and, if you will place yourself under my charge, I will see you safely to your husband."

Very hurriedly we made our arrangements, packing with scarcely a moment to lose, not stopping to discuss our sudden move and the alarming news. Our friends, also, were in as great a panic and dismay as ourselves. Mrs. A. had some chests of heavy silver. Many of the pieces were such that it would have taken some time to bury them. Another friend feared to bury her diamonds, thinking in that case she might never see them more. Every tumult in the town caused us to fly to the doors and windows, fearing a surprise at any time; and not only ladies, with pale faces and anxious eyes, met us at every turn, but gentlemen of anti-military disposition were running hither and thither, with carpet bags and little valises, seeking conveyances, determined to find a safe place, if one could be found, where the sound of a gun or the smell of powder might never disturb them any more; and, as they ran, each had an alarming report to circulate; so that with the rush and roar of dray, wagon, and carriage, the distracting reports of the rapid advance of the Federal army, and the stifling clouds of dust that arose—with all, we were in a fair way to believe ourselves any being or object but ourselves.

To Vicksburg Again

Leaving the threatened, teeming town behind us, we moved slowly on—our friends, my little one, and myself—toward Vicksburg. I leaned my head against the window and looked into the darkness.

As we passed along nearing Vicksburg, we could see camps and camp fires, with the dim figures of men moving around them; we could see the sentinel guarding the Black River bridge; and farther, masses of men in the road marching quietly in the night time, followed by the artillery; long lines of wagons, too, passing through the ravines—now the white covers seen on the brow of the hill; losing sight of them again, we hear the shout of the teamsters, the crack of the whip—and again catch sight of a white top through trees—and the occasional song of a wagoner. At the depot soldiers were crowded, waiting to go out; and on our arrival at our friend's, we, so weary with the excitement and turmoil of the day, were glad to rest.

Upon reading the papers the next morning, almost the first article that caught my eye was an order from General Pemberton, insisting on all non-combatants leaving the city. "Heretofore," he said, "I have merely requested that it should be done; now I demand it." "Ah!" cried I, "have we no rest for the sole of our foot? Must we again go through the fright and anxiety of yesterday?" "We cannot leave here," replied my friend. "Where can we go? Here we are among our friends—we are welcome, and we feel in safety. Let us at least share the fate of those we love so much."

When the gentlemen came, we talked of the "order" with them. At first they said we must leave; but we entreated them to let us stay, representing our deplorable condition in a country overrun by soldiers, the great danger of trying to go to Mobile by railway, the track having been partly destroyed between Meridian and Jackson. We declared that we would almost starve—that we would meet any evil cheerfully in Vicksburg, where our friends were—where we were carefully housed, quiet, and contented. So, laughingly, they said they were completely overcome by our distress and would arrange it so that we could stay if we wished.

Settling In

We settled ourselves delightfully. With our sewing in the morning, and rides in the evening, our home was very pleasant—very happy and quiet. Rumors came to us of the advance of the Federal troops on the Black River; yet, so uncertain were the tidings, and so slow was the advantage gained, we began to doubt almost everything. My husband was stationed below at Warrenton, and came only occasionally to see us, as the gunboats were threatening that point. Still, we were in a manner already cut off from the outer world, for the cars had ceased running farther than the Black River bridge, where General Pemberton had stationed his forces, fortifying and waiting an attack; still, every morning the papers would tell us all was right, and our life passed on the same.

One night we heard heavy cannonading an hour or two, ceasing, and then commencing again quite early in the morning, undoubtedly from the vicinity of Warrenton. The next day we heard that the little village of Warrenton had been burned by shells thrown from the boats. My husband came in that evening, and told us that very little damage had been done, except setting fire to some of the cotton composing the fort, which was still smouldering and burning slowly under the earthworks.

Saturday came, and with it the news that a battle was going on between the Federal troops and General Pemberton's forces at Black River. Sunday, the 17th—the memorable seventeenth of May —as we were dressing for church, and had nearly completed the arrangement of shawls and gloves, we heard the loud booming of cannon.

Frightened, we walked down the street, hoping to find some friend that could tell us if it were dangerous to remain away from home at church. I feared leaving my little one for any length of time, if there were any prospect of an engagement. Still, as the bell of the Methodist church rang out loud and clear, my friend and I decided to enter, and were glad that we did so, for we heard words of cheer and comfort in this time of trouble. The speaker was a traveller, who supplied the pulpit this day, as the pastor was absent ministering to the wounded and dying on the battle field. After the blessing, he requested the ladies to meet and make arrangements for lint and bandages for the wounded.

As we returned home, we passed anxious groups of men at the corners; very few soldiers were seen; some battery men and officers, needed for the river defences, were passing hastily up the street. In all the dejected uncertainty, the stir of horsemen and wheels began, and wagons came rattling down the street—going rapidly one way, and then returning, seemingly, without aim or purpose; now and then a worn and dusty soldier would be seen passing with his blanket and canteen; soon, straggler after straggler came by, then groups of soldiers worn and dusty with the long march. "What can be the matter?" we all cried, as the streets and pavements became full of these worn and tired-looking men. We sent down to ask, and the reply was: "We are whipped; and the Federals are after us." We hastily seized veils and bonnets, and walked down the avenue to the iron railing that separates the yard from the street. We asked them if they did not want water; and some of them came into the yard to get it. The lady of the house offered them

some supper; and while they were eating, we were so much interested, that we stood around questioning them. Where these weary
and wornout men were going, we could not tell. I think they did not
know themselves.

Fresh Forces

At dark the fresh troops from Warrenton marched by, going out to
the intrenchments in the rear of the city about two miles. As the
troops passed by, the ladies waved their handkerchiefs, cheering
them and crying: "These are the troops that have not run. You'll
stand by us, and protect us, won't you? You won't *retreat* and bring
the Federals behind you."

And the men, who were fresh and lively, swung their hats, and
promised to die for the ladies—never to run—never to retreat; while
the poor fellows on the pavement, sitting on their blankets—lying
on the ground—leaning against trees, or anything to rest their
wearied bodies, looked on silent and dejected.

The ambulances had been passing with wounded and dead; and
one came slowly by with officers riding near it, bearing the dead
body of General Tilghman, the blood dripping slowly from it. We
were told, also of a friend who had been mortally wounded.

The next morning all was quiet; we heard no startling rumors;
the soldiers were being gathered together and taken out into the
rifle pits; Vicksburg was regularly besieged, and we were to stay
at our home and watch the progress of the battle. The rifle pits and
intrenchments were almost two miles from the city. We would be
out of danger, so we thought; but we did not know what was in
preparation for us around the bend of the river.

The day wore on; still all was quiet. At night our hopes revived,
but at three o'clock the artillery boomed from the intrenchments,
roar after roar, followed by the rattle of musketry: the Federal
troops were making their first attack. Looking out from the back
veranda, we could plainly see the smoke before the report of the guns
reached us.

The excitement was intense in the city. Groups of people stood on every available position where a view could be obtained of the distant hills, where the jets of white smoke constantly passed out from among the trees.

Some of our friends proposed going for a better view up on the balcony around the cupola of the court house. The view from there was most extensive and beautiful. Hill after hill arose in the distance, enclosing the city in the form of a crescent. Immediately in the centre and east of the river, the firing seemed more continuous, while to the left and running northly, the rattle and roar would be sudden, sharp, and vigorous, then ceasing for some time.

What a beautiful landscape lay out before us! Far in the distance lay the cultivated hills—some already yellow with grain, while on other hills and in the valleys the deep green of the trees formed the shadows in the fair landscape.

It was amid the clump of trees on the far distant hillside, that the Federal batteries could be discerned by the frequent puffings of smoke from the guns. Turning to the river, we could see a gunboat that had the temerity to come down as near the town as possible, and lay just out of reach of the Confederate batteries, with steam up.

Two more lay about half a mile above and nearer the canal; two or three transports had gotten up steam, and lay near the mouth of the canal. Below the city a gunboat had come up and landed, out of reach, on the Louisiana side, striving to engage the lower batteries of the town—firing about every fifteen minutes. While we were looking at the river, we saw two large yawls start out from shore, with two larger boats tied to them, and full of men.

We learned that they were the Federal prisoners that had been held in the town, and today paroled and sent over to the Federal encampment, so that the resources of the garrison might be husbanded as much as possible, and the necessity of sustaining them avoided.

The idea made me serious. We might look forward truly now to perhaps real suffering.

Yet, I did not regret my resolution to remain, and would have left the town more reluctantly than ever before, for we felt that now, indeed, the whole country was unsafe, and that our only hope of safety lay in Vicksburg.

The little boats, with their prisoners, had gained the opposite shore, and we could see the liberated men walking along the river bank; we could see, also, the little steamtug coming down, and stopping at the gunboat near the city; it, also, visited the transports and the gunboats near the canal, and then, leaving, steamed with much swiftness up the river toward the mouth of the Yazoo.

In looking again with a glass in the rear of the city, we could see the Southern soldiers working at their guns, and walking in the rear of a fort on a hill nearer by. The Federal troops were too distant to discern.

We saw an officer coming in with his head bound up and his arm in a sling, his servant walking by his side leading his horse. Aside from the earnest groups of spectators moving from one place to another, the town seemed perfectly quiet.

Into the Cave

Next day, two or three shells were thrown from the battle field, exploding near the house. This was our first shock, and a severe one. We did not dare go in the back part of the house all day.

Some of the servants came and got down by us for protection, while others kept on with their work as if feeling a perfect contempt for the shells.

In the evening we were terrified and much excited by the loud rush and scream of mortar shells; we ran to the small cave near the house, and were in it during the night, by this time wearied and almost stupefied by the loss of sleep.

The caves were plainly becoming a necessity, as some persons had been killed on the street by fragments of shells. The room that I had so lately slept in had been struck by a fragment of a shell during the first night, and a large hole made in the ceiling. Terror stricken, we remained crouched in the cave, while shell after shell followed each other in quick succession. I endeavored by constant prayer to prepare myself for the sudden death I was almost certain awaited me. My heart stood still as we would hear the report from the guns, and the rushing and fearful sound of the shell as it came toward us. As it neared, the noise became more deafening; the air was full of the rushing sound; pains darted through my temples; my ears were full of the confusing noise; and, as it exploded, the report flashed through my head like an electric shock, leaving me in a quiet state of terror the most painful that I can imagine—cowering in a corner, holding my child to my heart—the only feeling of my life being the choked throbs of my heart, that rendered me almost breathless. As singly they fell short, or beyond the cave, I was aroused by a feeling of thankfulness that was of short duration. Again and again the terrible fright came over us in that night.

Morning found us more dead than alive, with blanched faces and trembling lips. We were not reassured on hearing, from a man who took refuge in the cave, that a mortar shell in falling would not consider the thickness of earth above us a circumstance.

Some of the ladies, more courageous by daylight, asked him what he was in there for, if that was the case. He was silenced for an hour, when he left. As the day wore on, and we were still preserved, though the shells came as ever, we were somewhat encouraged.

So constantly dropped the shells around the city, that the inhabitants all made preparations to live under the ground during the siege. My husband sent over and had a cave made in a hill near by. We seized the opportunity one evening, when the gunners were probably at their supper, for we had a few moments of quiet, to go over and take possession.

We were under the care of a friend of my husband, who was paymaster of the staff of the same General with whom my husband was Adjutant. We had neighbors on both sides of us; and it would have been an amusing sight to a spectator to witness the domestic scenes presented by the number of servants preparing the meals under the high bank containing the caves.

Daily Life Underground

Our dining, breakfasting, and supper hours were quite irregular. When the shells were falling fast, the servants came in for safety, and our meals waited for completion some little time; again they would fall slowly, with the lapse of many minutes between, and out would start the cooks to their work.

Some families had light bread made in large quantities, and subsisted on it with milk (provided their cows were not killed from one milking to another), without any more cooking, until called on to replenish. Though most of us lived on corn bread and bacon, served three times a day, the only luxury of the meal consisting in its warmth, I had some flour, and frequently had some hard, tough biscuit made from it, there being no soda or yeast to be procured. At this time we could, also, procure beef.

A gentleman friend was kind enough to offer me his camp bed, a narrow spring mattress, which fitted within the contracted cave very comfortably; another had his tent fly stretched over the mouth of our residence to shield us from the sun; and thus I was the recipient of many favors, and under obligations to many gentlemen of the army for delicate and kind attentions.

And so I went regularly to work, keeping house under ground. Our new habitation was an excavation made in the earth, and branching six feet from the entrance, forming a cave in the shape of a T. In one of the wings my bed fitted; the other I used as a kind of dressing room; in this the earth had been cut down a foot or two below the floor of the main cave; I could stand erect here; and when tired of sitting in other portions of my residence, I bowed myself into it, and stood impassively resting at full height—one of the variations in the still shell-expectant life. My husband's servant cooked for us under protection of the hill. Our quarters were close, indeed; yet I was more comfortable than I expected I could have been made under the earth in that fashion.

We were safe at least from fragments of shell—and they were flying in all directions; though no one seemed to think our cave any protection, should a mortar shell happen to fall directly on top of the ground above us. We had our roof arched and braced, the supports of the bracing taking up much room in our confined quarters. The earth was about five feet thick above, and seemed hard and compact; yet, my poor husband, every time he came in, examined it, fearing, amid some of the shocks it sustained, that it might crack and fall upon us.

One night, after my little one had been laid in bed, I sat at the mouth of the cave, with the servants drawn around me, watching the brilliant display of fireworks the mortar boats were making —the passage of the shell, as it travelled through the heavens, looking like a swiftly moving star. As it fell, it approached the earth so rapidly, that it seemed to leave behind a track of fire.

This night we kept our seats, as they all passed rapidly over us, none falling near. The incendiary shells were still more beautiful in appearance. As they exploded in the air, the burning matter and balls fell like large, clear blue-and-amber stars, scattering hither and thither.

Each day, as the couriers came into the city, my husband would write me little notes, asking after our welfare, and telling me of the progress of the siege. I, in return, would write to him of our safety, but was always careful in speaking of the danger to which we were exposed. I thought he had enough to try him, without suffering anxiety for us; so I made light of my fears, which were in reality wearing off rapidly. Every week he came in to make inquiries in person. In his letters he charged me particularly to be careful of the provisions—that no one could tell what our necessities might be.

One morning, after breakfast, the shells began falling so thickly around us, that they seemed aimed at the particular spot on which our cave was located. Two or three fell immediately in the rear of it, exploding a few moments before reaching the ground, and the fragments went singing over the top of our habitation. I, at length, became so much alarmed—as the cave trembled excessively —for our safety, that I determined, rather than be buried alive, to stand out from under the earth; so, taking my child in my arms, and calling the servants, we ran to a refuge near the roots of a large fig tree, that branched out over the bank, and served as a protection from the fragments of shells. As we stood trembling there—for the shells were falling all around us—some of my gentlemen friends came up to reassure me, telling me that the tree would protect us, and that the range would probably be changed in a short time. While they spoke, a shell, that seemed to be of enormous size, fell, screaming and hissing, immediately before the mouth of our cave, within a few feet of the entrance, sending up a huge column of smoke and earth, and jarring the ground most sensibly where we stood. What seemed very strange, the earth closed in around the shell, and left only the newly up-turned soil to show where it had fallen.

Long it was before the range was changed, and the frightful missiles fell beyond us—long before I could resolve to return to our sadly threatened home.

I found on my return that the walls were seamed here and there with cracks, but the earth had remained firm above us. I took possession again, with resignation, yet in fear and trembling.

Fire by Night

This night, as a few nights before, a large fire raged in the town. I was told that a large storehouse, filled with commissary stores, was burning, casting lurid lights over the devoted city; and amid all, fell—with screams and violent explosions, flinging the fatal fragments in all directions—our old and relentless enemies, the mortar shells.

The night was so warm, and the cave so close, that I tried to sit out at the entrance, our servant George saying that he would keep watch and tell when they were falling toward us. Soon the report of the gun would be heard, and George, standing on the hillock of loose earth, near the cave, looked intently upward; while I, with suspended breath, would listen anxiously as he cried, "Here she comes! going over!" then again, "Coming—falling—falling!" Then I would spring to my feet, and for a moment hesitate about the protection of the cave. Suddenly, as the rushing descent was heard, I would beat a precipitate retreat into it, followed by the servants.

That night I could scarcely sleep, the explosions were so loud and frequent. Fearing to retire, I sat in the moonlight at the entrance, the square of light that lay in the doorway causing our little bed, with the sleeping child, to be set out in relief against the dark wall of the cave—causing the little mirror and a picture or two I had hung against the wall to show misshaped lengths of shadow—tinting the crimson shawl that draped the entrance of my little dressing room, with light on the outer folds, and darkening in shadow the inner curves;—beautifying all, this silvery glow of moonlight, within the darkened earth—beautifying my heart with lighter and more hopeful thoughts.

Days wore on, and the mortar shells had passed over continually without falling near us; so that I became quite at my ease, in view of our danger, when one of the Federal batteries opposite the intrenchments altered their range; so that, at about six o'clock every evening, Parrott shells came whirring into the city, frightening the inhabitants of caves woefully.

Our policy in building had been to face directly away from the river, and all caves were prepared, as near as possible, in this manner. As the fragments of shells continued with the same impetus after the explosion, in but one direction, onward, they were not likely to reach us, fronting in this manner with their course.

But this was unexpected—guns throwing shells from the battle field directly at the entrance of our caves. Really, was there to be no mental rest for the women of Vicksburg?

The cave we inhabited was about five squares from the levee. A great many had been made in a hill immediately beyond us; and near this hill we could see most of the shells fall. Caves were the fashion—the rage—over besieged Vicksburg. Negroes, who understood their business, hired themselves out to dig them, at from thirty to fifty dollars, according to the size. Many persons, considering different localities unsafe, would sell them to others, who had been less fortunate, or less provident; and so great was the demand for cave workmen, that a new branch of industry sprang up and became popular.

On to the Battle Field

It was about four o'clock, one Wednesday evening—the shelling during the day had gone on about as usual—I was reading in safety, I imagined, when the unmistakable whirring of Parrott shells told us that the battery we so much feared had opened from the intrenchments. I ran to the entrance to call the servants in; and immediately after they entered, a shell struck the earth a few feet from the entrance, burying itself without exploding. I ran to the little dressing room, and could hear them striking all around us. I crouched closely against the wall, for I did not know at what moment one might strike within the cave. A man came in much frightened, and asked to remain until the danger was over. The servants stood in the little niche by the bed, and the man took refuge in the small ell where I was stationed. He had been there but a short time, standing in front of me, and near the wall, when a Parrott shell came whirling in at the entrance, and fell in the centre of the cave before us all, lying there smoking. Our eyes were fastened upon it, while we expected every moment the terrible explosion would ensue.

I pressed my child closer, and drew nearer to the wall. Our fate seemed almost certain. The poor man who had sought refuge within was most exposed of all. With a sudden impulse, I seized a large double blanket that lay near, and gave it to him for the purpose of shielding him from the fragments; and thus we remained for a moment, with our eyes fixed in terror on the missile of death, when George, the servant boy, rushed forward, seized the shell, and threw it into the street, running swiftly in the opposite direction. Fortunately, the fuse had become nearly extinguished and the shell fell harmless—remaining near the mouth of the cave, as a trophy of the fearlessness of the servant and our remarkable escape.

Shortly after, I received a note from my husband, saying that he was very much troubled in regard to our safety in the city. Therefore, he had decided to have a home made for me near the battle field, where he was stationed—one that would be entirely out of reach of the mortar shells. I was positively shocked at the idea—going to the battle field! where ball and shell fell without intermission. Was he in earnest? I could scarcely believe it.

The next evening, about four o'clock, my husband's dear face appeared. He wished us to go out as soon as possible. As at this hour in the evening, for the last week, the Federal guns had been quiet until almost sundown, he urged me to be ready in the shortest time possible; so soon we were in the ambulance, driving with great speed toward the rifle pits.

O the beautiful sunlight and the fresh evening air! How glowing and delightful it all seemed after my incarceration under the earth! I turned to look again and again at the setting sun and the brilliant crimson glow that suffused the atmosphere.

The road we were travelling was graded out through the hills; and on every side we could see, thickly strewn among the earthy cliffs, the never-to-be-lost sight of caves—large caves and little caves—some cut out substantially, roomy, and comfortable, with braces and props throughout—many only large enough for one man to take refuge in, standing;—again, at a low place in the earth was a seat for a passer-by in case of danger.

Driving on rapidly, we reached the suburbs of the city, where the road became shady and pleasant—still with caves at every large road excavation, reminding one very much of the numberless holes that swallows make in summer; for both the mortar and Parrott shells disputed this district; and a cave, front in whatever direction it might, was not secure from fragments. My husband impatiently urged on the driver, fearing that when the firing recommenced we would still be on the road. Suddenly, a turn of the drive brought in sight two large forts on the hills above us; and passing down a ravine near one of these, the ambulance stopped. We were hastily taken out and started for our home, when I heard a cutting of the air—the most expressive term I can use for that peculiar sound—above my head; and the balls dropped thickly around me, bringing leaves and small twigs from the trees with them.

I felt a sudden rush to my heart; but the soldiers were camped near, and many stood cautiously watching the effect of the sudden fall of metal around me. I would not for the world have shown fear; so, braced by my price, I walked with a firm and steady pace, notwithstanding the treacherous suggestions of my heart that beat a loud "Run, run."

My husband, fearing every moment that I might fall by his side, hurried me anxiously along. Within a short distance was the adjutant's office, where we took refuge until the firing became less heavy.

The "office" was a square excavation made in the side of the hill, covered over with logs and earth, seemingly quite cool and comfortable. I had been confined for so long a time in a narrow space of earth, that daylight, green trees, and ample room became a new pleasure to me. At sundown there was a cessation in the rapid fall of balls and shells; and we again started for our home.

The New Abode

I was taken up a little footpath that led from the ravine up under a careless, graceful arch of wild grape vines, whose swinging branchlets were drawn aside; and a low, long room, cut into the hillside and shaded by the growth of forest trees around, was presented to my view as our future home. What a pleasant place, after the close little cave in the city!—large enough for two rooms—the back and sides solid walls of earth, the sloping of the hill bringing down the wall to about four feet at the entrance, leaving the spaces above, between the wall and roof, for light; the side, looking out on the road through the ravine, was entirely open, yet shaded from view by the clustering vines over the pathway.

I took possession delightedly. A blanket, hung across the centre, made us two good-sized rooms; the front room, with a piece of carpet laid down to protect us from the dampness of the floor, and two or three chairs, formed our little parlor; and the back room, quiet and retired, the bedroom. Over the top of the earth, or our house, held up by huge forked props, were the trunks of small trees laid closely across together; over that, brush, limbs, and leaves, and covering all this the thickness of two or three feet of earth beaten down compactly and thought perfectly safe from Minié balls and Parrott or shrapnell shells.

Our little home stood the test nobly. We were in the first line of hills back of the heights that were fortified; and, of course, we felt the full force of the very energetic firing that was constantly kept up; and being so near, many that passed over the first line of hills would fall directly around us.

One morning our servant George made an important discovery—a newly made stump of sassafras, very near the cave, with large roots extending in every direction, affording us an inexhaustible vein of tea for future use. We had been drinking water with our meals previous to this disclosure. We, however, were more fortunate than many of the officers, having access to an excellent cistern near us; while many of our friends used muddy water, or river water, which, being conveyed so great a distance, became extremely warm and disagreeable.

Fruits and vegetables were not to be procured at any price. Already the men in the rifle pits were on half rations—flour or meal enough to furnish bread equivalent in quantity to two biscuits in two days; many of them ate it all at once, and the next day fasted, preferring, as they said, to have one good meal.

So they sat cramped up all day in the pits—their rations cooked in the valley and brought to them—scarcely daring to change their positions and stand erect, for Federal sharpshooters were watching for the heads; and to rise above the breastworks was almost certain death.

They amused themselves, while lying in the pits, by cutting out little trinkets from the wood of the parapet and the Minié balls that fell around them. Major Fry, from Texas, excelled in skill and ready invention, I think; he sent me one day an arm chair that he had cut from the Minié ball—the most minute affair of the kind I ever saw, yet perfectly symmetrical. At another time, he sent me a diminutive plough made from the parapet wood, with traces of lead, and a lead point made from a Minié ball.

I am told by my friends who call, that I am looking worn and pale, and frequently asked if I am not weary of this cave life. I parry the question as well as possible, for I do not like to admit it for my husband's sake; yet I *am* tired and weary—ah! so weary! I never was made to exist under ground; and when I am obliged to, what wonder that I vegetate, like other unfortunate plants— grow wan, spindling, and white! Yet, I must reason with myself: I had chosen this life of suffering with one I love; and what suffering, after all, have I experienced?—privations in the way of good and wholesome food, not half what the poor people around us are experiencing. I will not be unnerved—I have no right to complain.

To reason with myself in this time of danger was one of the chief employments of my cave life. Time passes on, and all say the siege cannot last much longer.

A Sad Accident

A soldier, named Henry, had noticed my little two-year-old girl often, bringing her flowers at one time, an apple at another, and again a young mocking bird, and had attached her to him much by these little kindnesses. Frequently, on seeing him pass, she would call his name, and clap her hands gleefully, as he rode the general's handsome horse for water, causing him to prance past the cave for her amusement. She called my attention to him one morning, saying: "O mamma, look at Henny's horse how he plays!" He was riding a small black horse that was exceedingly wild, turning in his saddle to grasp something from the ground as he moved speedily on. Soon after, he rode the horse for water; and I saw him return and fasten it to a tree.

Afterward I saw him come down the hill opposite, with an unexploded shrapnell shell in his hand. In a few moments I heard a quick explosion in the ravine, followed by a cry—a sudden, agonized cry. I ran to the entrance, and saw a courier, whom I had noticed frequently passing by, roll slowly over into the rivulet of the ravine and lie motionless. And at a little distance: Henry—oh, poor Henry!—holding out his mangled arms—the hands torn and hanging from the bleeding, ghastly wrists—a fearful wound in his head—the blood pouring from his wounds. Shot, gasping, wild, he staggered around, crying piteously, "Where are you, boys? O boys, where are you? Oh, I am hurt! I am hurt! Boys, come to me!—come to me! God have mercy! Almighty God have mercy!"

My little girl clung to my dress, saying, "O mamma, poor Henny's killed! Now he'll die, mamma. Oh, poor Henny!" I carried her away from the painful sight.

My first impulse was to run down to them with the few remedies I possessed. Then I thought of the crowd of soldiers around the men; and if my husband should come and see me there—the only lady—he might think I did wrong; so I sent my servant, with camphor and other slight remedies I possessed, and turned into my cave, with a sickened heart.

Nearing the End

We were now swiftly nearing the end of our siege life: the rations had nearly all been given out. For the last few days I had been sick; still I tried to overcome the languid feeling of utter prostration. My little one had swung in her hammock, reduced in strength, with a low fever flushing in her face. My husband was all anxiety, I could plainly see. A soldier brought up, one morning, a little jaybird, as a plaything for the child. After playing with it for a short time, she turned wearily away. "Miss Mary," said the servant, "she's hungry; let me make her some soup from the bird."

At first I refused; the poor little plaything should not die; then, as I thought of the child, I half consented. With the utmost haste, Cinth disappeared; and the next time she appeared, it was with a cup of soup, and a little plate, on which lay the white meat of the poor little bird.

On Saturday a painful calm prevailed: there had been a truce proclaimed; and so long had the constant firing been kept up, that the stillness now was absolutely oppressive.

At ten o'clock General Bowen passed by, dressed in full uniform, accompanied by Colonel Montgomery, and preceded by a courier bearing a white flag. My husband came by, and asked me if I would like to walk out; so I put on my bonnet and sallied forth beyond the terrace, for the first time since I entered. The grass seemed deadened—the ground ploughed into furrows in many places; while scattered over all, like giants' pepper, in numberless quantity, were the shrapnell balls.

I could now see how very near to the rifle pits my cave lay; only a small ravine between the two hills separated us.

No one knew, or seemed to know, why a truce had been made; but all believed that a treaty of surrender was pending.

The next morning my husband came up, with a pale face, saying: "It's all over! The white flag floats from our forts! Vicksburg has surrendered!"

He put on his uniform coat, silently buckled on his sword, and prepared to take out the men, to deliver up their arms in front of the fortification.

I felt a strange unrest, the quiet of the day was so unnatural. I walked up and down the cave until my husband returned. The day was extremely warm; and he came with a violent headache. He told me that the Federal troops had acted splendidly; they were stationed opposite the place where the Confederate troops marched up and stacked their arms; and they seemed to feel sorry for the poor fellows who had defended the place for so long a time. Far different from what he had expected, not a jeer or taunt came from any of the Federal soldiers. Occasionally, a cheer would be heard; but the majority seemed to regard the poor unsuccessful soldiers with a generous sympathy.

The next morning, Monday, as I was passing through the cave, I saw something stirring at the base of one of the supports of the roof: taking a second look, I beheld a large snake curled between the earth and the upright post. I went quickly and sent one of the servants for my husband, who, coming up immediately, took up his sword and fastened one of the folds of the reptile to the post. It gave one quick dart toward him, with open jaws. Fortunately, the length of the sword was greater than the upper length of body; and the snake fell to the earth a few inches from my husband, who set his heel firmly on it, and severed the head from the body with the sword. I have never seen so large a snake; it was fully as large round the body as the bowl of a good-sized glass tumbler, and over two yards long.

The Confederate troops were being marched into Vicksburg to take the parole that the terms of the treaty of surrender demanded. In a few days they would leave the city they had held so long.

On Friday they began their march toward the South; and on Saturday poor George came to me, and said he had put on a pair of blue pants and, thinking they would take him for a Federal soldier, had tried to slip through after my husband, but he was turned back; so he came, begging me to try and get him a pass: the effort was made; and to this day I do not know whether he ever reached my husband or not.

Saturday evening, Vicksburg, with her terraced hills—with her pleasant homes and sad memories, passed from my view in the gathering twilight.

Arvazine Angeline Cooper

FROM HER UNPUBLISHED MANUSCRIPT
JOURNEY ACROSS THE PLAINS

6. (*Above*) Astronomer Maria Mitchell, the first woman member of the American Academy of Arts and Sciences, with her father, William Mitchell.

7. A dedicated scientist, Maria Mitchell studied prodigiously for twenty years, while working as the librarian of the Nantucket Atheneum. For the next twenty years she served as professor of astronomy and director of the observatory at Vassar.

8. A leading figure in the women's rights movement of the nineteenth century, Elizabeth Cady Stanton called for the granting of women's suffrage at the Seneca Falls Convention of 1848.

9. Young Elizabeth Cady Stanton

10. Three generations of feminists: Elizabeth Cady Stanton, her daughter Harriot, also active in the suffrage movement, and her granddaughter Nora Stanton Barney, the first woman in the United States to receive a degree in civil engineering.

11. "A Madonna of the Prairies" painted by P. V. E. Ivory.

12. A pioneer of the plains gathering buffalo chips.

ARVAZINE ANGELINE COOPER
1845–1929

Mrs. Arvazine Angeline Cooper, the mother of fifteen children, wrote down the account (here somewhat abridged) of her trip across the plains from Missouri to Oregon in 1863. She traveled with her husband, Daniel Jackson Cooper, the "Pa" of the narrative, who had been to California six years earlier. With them were her husband's parents—Grandpa, also known as "Pap," and Grandma Cooper—and her husband's young unmarried brothers and sisters— Sarah, Riley, John, Bud, and Paty. At the time of the journey Mrs. Cooper was eighteen years old, the mother of a sixteen-month-old daughter and pregnant with her second child, who was born during the trip.

Starting Out

We made our start April 8, 1863. The cause of our leaving at that time was the very unsatisfactory manner, in our immediate section, of conducting the war of the great Rebellion. It seemed to us that we were left almost without a status in our beloved Government.

At that time we had no thought of being abolitionist; the rebels, though, treated us as such, and while it was true the union men were organized into companies scattered over the state, called Enrolled Militia, they were not uniformed or equipped by the government, but had to shift for themselves.

They were stationed near their homes, and were commonly known as home guards, but were in a very poor fix to guard anything. As they were in that dreadful borderline that was raided continually by guerilla bands and "bush whackers," it seemed we were doing no good toward aid in suppressing the rebellion, so we longed exceedingly to get away.

We had but little hope, however, of getting safely out of the country, as one old man had the year before traded his land to his rebel neighbors for such stock as they cared to spare and started to Kansas; before he got many miles on the way these same neighbors overtook him and robbed him of almost everything. And, too, Pa being in this military organization made it doubtful if he could get permission to leave. Still, he said if I was willing, and he could get a transfer to the Pacific Coast (he having been to California knew more about that state than any other), we would try to get away. I felt as if I would venture anything to live where law and order reigned again, and was eager to make the attempt.

Well, Pa was successful in getting his transfer, and when Grandpa Cooper heard of our intentions he decided to make the attempt, too. In three weeks' time we were ready, after a fashion, to start.

The country was so devastated we had to go fifty miles to get tin cups and plates, as they were deemed almost a necessity on the long, rough journey, then could get only two or three cups and no plates, so we had to use our Delft ware, but I might as well state right here that there did not much of it survive the trip.

We traded our land for a few head of stock, mostly unbroken steers, which were to be our team. We were fortunate enough to procure very good wagons.

We had to take such provision as we could get, not such as we would choose, it being almost impossible to get any dried fruit or beans. However, we had plenty of bacon and flour and milk on the start.

All this time of preparation I was too bewildered to think much about the partings there would be for me, but when the day for starting came so quickly, I began to realize that little backwoodsy corner of Southwest Missouri was all the world to me, and I was not only leaving my native land, but every single tie of blood relations, for something so far away and vague that it seemed very unreal, and I had not the remotest idea that I would ever see any of my kindred again.

Very few of my kinfolks or neighbors came to bid me goodbye, for in that troublous time there was no knowing what the war fiend would do to their homes in their absence. In brooding over all this, I let a kind of wordless grief take possession of me, I kept it all to myself, and shed my tears when others were asleep, and kept up appearances so well that no one suspected I was not reasonably happy.

I was very inexperienced in every way, especially was it so about camping out, and the very first night was a very trying one. I was morbidly shy, and a strange man was traveling with us, and too my dear little baby Belle was just learning to walk, and would cling to my skirts, or if left to herself would get into things. Her favorite pursuit was washing the dish rag in the water bucket, which proved a rather serious matter when we got farther on to where water was a very scarce article.

Somehow I got the supper ready and sprawled around on the ground among our pots and pans and dishes, and began our first meal of many that followed in uncomfortable circumstances. One good thing was that little Belle never cried and was supremely happy all the time. In fact, she was almost too self-assured, for she would go anywhere her little stumbling feet could carry her, and take anything her bright little eyes spied, provided it was not too cumbersome for her little hands. At this first meal, in her busy stumbling efforts, she put her foot into a big cup of thick sorghum molasses, and when I spied her she was making strenuous efforts to keep at her work with her foot in the cup. And thus ended our first day's travel.

Crossing

The second day, soon after leaving camp, we crossed a small stream called Spring River. It was the first water course we had come to; consequently our team did not know it was their duty to keep right on and out on the other side. They disposed themselves in as promiscuous attitudes as their yokes and chains would permit, and halted for an indefinite time to soak their feet.

I thought we would have to wait their pleasure, or Pa would have to get into the water and lead them out, as all the urging seemed to have no effect on them. But in the nick of time a burly fellow came down on the other side and said "Throw me that whip," and presto! that whip began to pop like a volley of musketry, and the woods fairly roared with the oaths he rolled out, and those oxen lined up on that bank as if they meant to cross the plains that day.

The man handed back the whip with the remark, "You don't know how to drive cattle, you must swear at them," which greatly discouraged me, for the man was not going with us, and I thought if the team had to be sworn at every time we had a stream to cross, I had rather the rebels would murder us all and be done with our troubles. However, those same cattle pulled us all the way to Oregon, and that was the only time I heard them sworn at.

This crossing was near the post where Pa's company was stationed, and it seemed rather significant that they were just making up a scouting party to go out in the direction we were heading. This would afford us some protection, but I felt very apprehensive till we were well out of the state. Their very presence kept it always before me that we might be raided and get into a fight, for which I had no desire whatever.

When we got safely over this dangerous first part of our journey, it began to feel as if we were really on the way to California. We traveled very slowly most of the first half of our journey, in order to let our stock get in good condition by the time we came to the mountains and poor feed.

Among the Indians

We had to cross the Kaw River by ferry, and our stock was very hard to get onto the boat. It took the best part of a half day to get across.

The people that kept the ferry were Cherokee Indians. Their women came down to the river, and politely invited us up to their house to wait till everything was across, and as I was very tired standing round I accepted their invitation. I found them very well fixed with household affairs, and very kind and sociable.

One woman had a young babe, and had a handy contrivance she called an Indian cradle for it. It was what we call a hammock now, adapted to the size of an infant, and hung between two bed posts. I thought it very ingenious, but I came so near losing caste by visiting with the Indians that I never dared imitate it, though it was much more convenient than makeshifts I used afterwards.

So we fared along, through Kansas and Nebraska, over rolling country covered with buffalo grass, seeing less and less of anything that looked like timber till we came to South Platte, where we began to see more people traveling West. We met several Mormon freight trains going back East for supplies, and passed overland stage stations occasionally, where there were always a lot of friendly Indians, who at times annoyed us considerably by begging. They were very anxious to have us know they were friendly, and would come and shake hands with us, saying "How, how," meaning "Howdy," and Belle learned it right away and would always run to meet them and How-how with them which pleased them greatly.

At Fort Laramie they got rather aggressive in their demands, till an officer came over from the fort and told them in their own language that we would need all of what seemed to them our over-abundant supplies to keep us from starving on our exceedingly long journey. By the way, this same gallant officer was inquiring if some of us white families would take his two half-breed children and raise them. He said he would rather have them raised by white people than by their Indian mother. Although there were several families laying by there that day, he found no one willing to take them. Half-breeds were a new species to us then.

Deeper into Indian Territory

By this time we had left all settlements far behind, and the country seemed more and more in possession of the Indians. After we crossed the North Platte, we passed a place where there had been a large Indian camp a short time before. They had left a number of lodge poles, and in looking around the boys found a scalp they had lost. It was an Indian scalp, which did not seem quite so personal as if it had been a white person's. It was skillfully framed into a bent willow twig with sinew, one end of which was left about ten inches long, as if it were for a handle.

All the way over these lonely stretches, there had never been a single day that I can remember that we were not cheered by the music of the cheerful meadow larks. I say we, but in truth I must except myself, for I heard without heeding, though to outward appearances I was normal. Yet my inward gloom was so unnatural and morbid that nothing penetrated it to any ameliorating extent.

Ever since we began to leave the settlements, we had seen drove after drove of antelope. They seemed curious about us and would travel along beside us for hours, but always at a safe distance. At first we tried to stalk them, or lure them up with a red flag, as a man at a stage station had told us wonderful tales of how he had killed them that way. However, although they would walk round and round as long as we displayed the flag, they seemed to know perfectly how far away to keep to be safe from a gun.

But the buffalo we had heard so much about and rather dreaded encountering some stampeding herd—those we saw nothing of except dead ones and two little calves that hunters had captured and taken to the settlements, and were raising with their cattle. But the ubiquitous buffalo chips were our only fuel for many days, and were much more satisfactory than one would think who had never tried them.

Joining Forces

After finding that scalp, and noting other indications, such as the stock being nervous and easily frightened, and the Indians not coming to "how" with us, we began to think seriously of making up a train for mutual protection.

We began selecting our crowd by consulting with whom we liked best of those we had become acquainted with, among them being several outfits of miners going to Montana. They were more desirable because they had no families to look after, consequently would be stronger if we had trouble with the Indians.

One of these men, named Deckert, had crossed the plains sixteen times, and by tacit consent we looked upon him as captain and guide, and it was well we did, for his knowledge of the country and willingness to help saved us much hardship and loss of stock. He would go on ahead with his horse and find good water, and also guard us against the alkali water, which was fatal if stock drank of it. We saw many dead animals all along the worst section, while we did not lose one.

There were fourteen wagons of us now, and we got along so pleasantly we did not like to swell our crowd.

We had left the Platte rivers by now and started up Sweetwater, the streams generally being our geographical guides. This led us into a country where there were no stations of any kind, but all held by the Indians. It was said they would be more hostile than any we had seen, which seemed strange to me, as they had entirely quit bothering us by begging, in fact we did not even see any. This, however, was said by the knowing ones to be a sign that they were not friendly. So before we left the Sweetwater, we stopped a few days to collect a large, strong train. When we had collected about twenty-seven wagons, another train came along calling themselves the Johnson train. With their wagons that was enough to make seventy-three in all, and as neither party was considered strong enough to go alone through this most dangerous part of all our journey, we concluded to go together.

With the Johnson Train

We started on, seventy-three wagons strong, on a new road built a few years before by the government. It was said that feed and water were better on this road than any other, and also that there was less desert country; all of which we found true.

But the Johnson train were not well pleased with this decision. None of them had ever crossed the plains before, and were afraid we would get lost. But we were all satisfied, as our captain Deckert had said it was the best, and we trusted him implicitly.

We were getting into the mountains now, and it was cold and disagreeable. I had to wear my shawl the first day of July, and was uncomfortably cold then, even while I was cooking over the fire.

And, as large bodies are usually more ponderous in their movements, our large train proved no exception. It was our aim to get along as fast as possible, but the Johnson train had the worst old ramshackle wagons mostly that ever crossed the plains, I think, and in the rough mountain road one would break down almost every day. It delayed the whole train till it was repaired, and it began to seem like we would have to winter in the Rocky Mountains.

And as idle hands are prone to mischief, these idle times of waiting gave great opportunity for mischief making, and there was no lack of material with which to make it, for the Johnson train were mostly rebel and ours mostly union.

The complaints and dissensions waxed hotter. The Johnson train had the whooping-cough among their children, and we were afraid we would get it. We stipulated that they should form on one side of the corral and we the other, and each keep our children on our own side. But we were afraid that was not sufficient safeguard, and we were annoyed greatly by so much delay, of which they were mostly the cause, and they were loud in their denunciations of us for insisting on coming this new road, declaring it would lead us into some kind of ambush where the Indians would kill us all.

Well, this state of things kept getting no better fast, till there happened a catastrophe so dire as to drive everything else out of our minds.

The Stampede

We had camped in a beautiful valley at the foot of the east side of the Rocky Mountains, and everything seemed peaceful and quiet. Most all the people were gone to bed, when the cattle got scared and stampeded, running out at the side where our wagon stood.

There were about four hundred head, and they made a noise like thunder. It was not quite dark yet, and I got up to get out of the wagon, but in front of our wagon was a mighty torrent of cattle. They had pressed against our wagon till it was turned half way round.

So I sat and waited with the composure of bewilderment, terror, and astonishment. Pa had got out and gone I knew not where, so I thought I best stay where I was. When the roaring, surging mass of cattle passed on, then the human element of the disturbance became apparent, and it was no less terrorizing than the other. Such wailings and howlings, especially of some of those would-be brave warriors of the Johnson train I hope I shall never hear again, for the first impression among them was that the Indians had come sure enough.

Men that I should judge had never used the Divine name except in profanity, were calling earnestly on the Lord for help, and very naturally I suppose, feeling that He was a long way off, they used the utmost power of their lungs. And the poor women were screaming, and all those poor whooping coughy children, of whom there were seventy-five in the Johnson train alone, had to take a turn at coughing. And dogs! This train had evidently started out with the idea that dogs were scarce where they were going, and they had big dogs, little dogs, mother dogs and their puppies, and dogs of all nondescript varieties, which added not a little to the unearthly racket.

So I sat and listened, thinking I would surely hear the traditional war whoop if it were Indians, which I imagined would be even more terrible than this pandemonium.

There was but little rest for anyone that night, for it required the united efforts of all the men to keep the cattle from running over the corral and destroying everything, themselves included.

When morning came we were a perplexed and woebegone lot. The Johnson train were clamorous to go on, thinking if they stayed there another night, the Indians would surely massacre us. They could not get the Indian idea out of their heads.

Our side was willing to do whatever Deckert advised, and he thought as it was almost an impossibility to hitch up the wild frightened steers, we had better wait till they were pretty well tired out.

But before the matter was settled, it became evident that I was in a poor fix to travel, so when our guide learned about that, he said that settled the matter as far as he was concerned, and anybody that insisted on a woman going on in the fix I was in ought to be hung, and that he would stay with Cooper if no one else did.

The Baby Is Born

So our train all decided to stay, and were hoping the Johnsonites would go on. Although they never said so, we thought they were afraid to go on without us, and, too, the wagon mender belonged to our train.

As all remained, Deckert recommended the experiment of each man taking his team and caring for it separately through the day, as it might have a tendency to allay their panic. The scheme succeeded admirably all through the day, and the people became cheerful again. At two o'clock a little blue-eyed brother came to our wagon, to share the honors and favors with the little black-eyed Belle; and at five o'clock a couple took advantage of the layby to get married, and as Grandpa was the only clergyman, they came to his wagon, which was close to ours. I raised my wagon cover a little bit, and can virtually claim that I was at the wedding, as I heard the ceremony distinctly.

By sundown we were all feeling that the calamity was over, and we could resume our journey in our usual manner the next day. But alas! and alas! when we collected the cattle for the night they were worse, if possible, than the night before. We saw that it was not safe to put them in the corral, but dangerous even to keep them in sight of it.

So twenty men on horseback took them about two miles away, and decided to take turn about, ten watching at a time, and so get a little rest. But there was no rest for any of them, for it was a hard task for all to keep them from getting away entirely.

The camp had a good rest, and as the cattle were too far away to disturb us, we thought they were getting along all right. We found out our mistake when they came in in the morning, but as it seemed a necessity we essayed to make a start.

Our guide Deckert sent the women and children on ahead with what horse teams there were, to get along as best they could till it could be seen what could be done with the still restless ox teams.

From now on as my narrative will necessarily be so personal as to seem egotistical, I will write in the third person.

A Change of Style

Our guide also told the father of the little stranger to get his wagon out of danger of the commotion at the camp. With much maneuvering and much help he succeeded in getting three-fourths of his team hitched up, and dragged his worldly possessions forth for a space on the road. All, that is, except little Belle, whom Grandma had taken. He stopped to wait for the others, standing by his team.

The young mother with her babe lay quietly listening to the commotion at the corral, which she could not hear very distinctly, and wondering if they would ever all get safely started, when suddenly at a loud crash back at the corral, the team started with her as quick as the flash of a gun, at their utmost speed, leaving the father far behind.

The mother had long since resigned herself to the inevitable, and made no outcry, thinking if she only knew which way the wagon would turn when it went over, as surely it must, she might somehow be able to keep her baby more safe, till she became sensible that the movement was decidedly slower.

Presently she heard her husband's breathless voice, demanding if she was frightened. She answered "no," but was wondering why the team was going so slowly. He said that two-fourths more of the team had broken loose and run off, which left only one-fourth of the team which was one span of oxen to continue. They were physically unable to make much headway, though they were full of panic, and trying with all their might.

The husband got help and got the two yoke back, and once more got his team in traveling order, putting on an additional brake of quite a different sort, which consisted of a stout young man with a club sufficient to fell an ox if need be.

The others, too, got into line fortunately with no more damage than ruining one wagon. They moved forward, and by judicious use of said club, had no more runaways or other casualties except the lead pair of steers breaking their yoke and getting away. They let them go, however, and rushed on with two yoke.

I will state right here that this father and mother did not think what the name of the territory might be for many a day, and are not sure yet what it was then, or what it is now, where their first son was born.

The Ascent

Not long after leaving this memorable camp, they entered a rocky cavern, continuing up, up, for two days before gaining the summit. The wagon of that poor weary mother of the young babe was stood on such slanting ground that her feet were considerably higher than her head, and she was too weary and distracted to think of changing her head to the other side of the bed. The father was too tired and sleepy, with his two days and nights chasing insane cattle, to notice that all was not comfortable.

By the time they got to the summit the oxen were so jaded that they were not quite so hard to control, for they had let them travel at a lively gait. Although the young mother had controlled herself admirably, she had received a severe nervous shock, and when she was dropping off to sleep with such weariness as no one who had never been in such a situation could begin to imagine, she would be certain she heard that terrifying roar the cattle made when starting on a stampede. She even routed out her husband to help when all was quiet.

On account of her rest being broken by this terrifying hallucination and the weariness of the rough road, and also proper diet could not be had, the fountain that every child born into this world has an inherent right to, began to diminish. The little fellow began to complain of short rations. The motion of the wagon soothed him in the daytime, so he entered his protest mainly at night, and as the poor mother was not able to sleep a wink while the wagon was in motion, she was in exceeding sore straits, for there was nothing in the limited variety of food available that the baby would eat. However, she was saved from utter despair by another mother whose sick baby would eat very little, and so the good woman conceived the idea of feeding her baby for her.

Descent

If it was hard getting on top of that mountain, it was but a hint of what it was getting down.

The first day of the descent, the young mother's bed slipped clear out from under her, and she had hard work to keep herself and babe from following it into the front part of the wagon box.

The cattle were mean and unruly on the down grade, too. The second day her husband tied her bed to the wagon bows before starting. Then sometimes she had hard work to keep from slipping off the bed, and the cattle got worse and worse till

the father and club man had all they could do to keep them just
from tearing down that mountain and smashing everything.

Everyone got so tired out, and little Belle got sleepy, so in the
afternoon they put her on her mother's bed. Soon after the road
was so steep and rough that she pitched off the bed, and was
caught balancing on the front gate of the wagon. The mother
screamed, but the uproar was so great that no one heard her,
and the dust was so thick that the father, who was not more
than ten feet away, could not see her, and if she had fallen out,
no one but the mother would have known it.

Well, she rose to the occasion and hauled her in, though she
had been warned with many solemn shakes of the head by the
good old mothers of the train that the consequences would be
dire if she ventured even to lift her head while the wagon was
moving, and she was such a foolish impressionable young thing
she thought she might drop dead in consequence of her rash
act. However, she thought she would rather die than have her
daughter mangled under the hoofs of these horrible cattle.

Soon after this a little girl did get run over, but as she was at
the side of the road, only one wheel went over her, and it was a
very light wagon, but she was hurt bad enough anyway. Her
lower jaw was split right in front. There was a young dentist
along who tied the two front teeth together firmly, and she soon
got well.

Incident in the Valley

When we did get down the mountain it was into the most
beautiful valley I have ever seen. The level, rich soil was covered
with luxuriant grass that had the appearance of an immense
wheat field. It was about twenty-five miles long by ten wide,
with a clear mountain stream fringed with willows and alive with
trout winding through it.

We camped early and were cooking and eating a meal once
more in peace, and some were wishing we had implements and
seed, so we could stop and settle in this very paradise of a place,

when the guards came tearing around a bend in the stream screaming "Indians! Indians!"

At the cry, pandemonium broke loose again, and every one that could carry a stick, if it was only for a staff to help him along, started as fast as they could go to meet the hostile band.

The young mother was left alone with her babe and little Belle who might have carried a stick, but did not even get up from the ox yoke where she was sitting eating her supper. The cry of "Indians" had no terrors for her, for all of them she had seen were friendly, and she loved to tell them "How, how."

The poor mother was longing frantically to get her into the wagon so she could clasp her once more to her bosom before she was scalped, but was dreading the scolding she might possibly get if she got out and fetched her, when the young man that was traveling with them came back for his ammunition which he had forgotten in his haste, so she had him put Belle in the wagon. Then she lay there listening for the war-whoop and slaughter, but heard nothing except the yelling, screaming, and praying that had grown so familiar since the stampede began.

Soon the redoubtable Captain Angell of the Johnson train returned to camp, saying it was no use for him to stay out there as he had no gun. Then the young mother remembered hearing him urging some one that he had a gun in his wagon for some one to take, and loudly proclaiming its merits. She thought at the time that he must have an extra gun, but he was only trying to be left without a gun so he would not have to fight.

Well, after all the hubbub and double-quick charge of little, big, young and old, they met four Indians coming to camp with fish to sell! The people had got almost as scary as the cattle.

I will add in defense, though, that it was rather smoky, which kept them from seeing clearly. Some were for slaying these four Indians right away, saying they were nothing but spies. Our guide Deckert advised moderation, only forbidding any one selling them any ammunition, which they were exceedingly anxious to buy, offering a good pony for four loads for a shot gun.

On to the Coast

After this false alarm, we pushed on. There was little comfort or peace, though, for the mother of the new baby, for by this time he had the habit firmly fixed of howling most of the time the wagon was stopped, and she was still unable to sleep when it was moving. Then, too, she took cold in her breast, and as all the remedies of all kinds, and all the delicacies of all the train, and all the patience and kindness of everybody had been severely taxed by a woman who had got a fish hook fast in her finger way back on Platte River and had it cut out, and the poor young mother had heard so much about her exactions, she did not ask for attentions, but mostly bore her sufferings in grim silence, and her ailment came to its own conclusion in its own way almost unaided. It was at the worst about Boise City, and her sufferings were so great that her recollections are not very distinct for quite a space along there. It all seems like a jumble and confusion of jolting wagon, crying baby, dust, sage-brush, and passing and being passed with friendly greetings by those we had traveled so far with, and the never ceasing pain and suffering which was not greatly diminished till we were way up Burnt River.

By this time we were meeting droves of people going to the mines around Boise. They told us wonderful tales about big red apples and all manner of other good things in the Willamette Valley. We thought it strange that they were getting away from there in such numbers, and that they would advise us to go to a land of such great plenty when provisions were so scarce and high along there. We soon concluded, though, that they were gold crazy. As we were not, we would get to this goodly land as soon as possible.

So we plodded on, meeting many freight teams, and pack trains, and bands of cattle. The folks we met all agreed about the terrible state of the road over the Cascade Mountains, which we found to our sorrow they did not exaggerate. But by dint of sticking to it, and tying logs to our wagons down hill, and digging footholds for our steers up hill, we arrived on the west side of the mountains, and oh! joy, we found the big red apples! and we found something else we had not expected.

The Arrival

We found a welcome that a long lost brother might envy.

The people ministered to us personally, with the products of their own labor.

They did not wait for us to go to them and ask, but seeing us afar off, they ran with buckets, with baskets and pans, and failing these, ran with aprons and hats full of good things till we were threatened with overloading. Soon, seeing we were in such a hospitable land, and believing it would grieve their generous souls if we did not take all that was offered, we conceived the idea of putting what we could not eat in the brush by the road side, and so make the people at the next house happy by finding us unsupplied.

And everywhere we went we were treated with such kindly consideration that we felt amply paid for our persistent struggle to reach this goodly land of peace and plenty.

And the stampede baby, with all his trials and tribulations, at about two months old when carried into the first house he was ever in, noticed the difference and cried to be taken out where he could see the sky which was so familiar to him. And the poor, weary mother still had life enough to appreciate the "Beautiful Willamette."

But her toils and troubles did not entirely cease with her long journey, for she is now an old mother of a large family, and in apology for this peculiar and inadequate account, will say that it all happened in time of the War of the Rebellion, when suspicion, discord, and anger were rife in the land; and that she has written it entirely from memory in the year nineteen hundred and one.

Dr. Anna Howard Shaw

EXCERPTS FROM HER AUTOBIOGRAPHY
THE STORY OF A PIONEER

DR. ANNA HOWARD SHAW
1847–1919

Of Scottish parentage, Anna Shaw was born in Newcastle-on-Tyne, England. When she was two years old her father sailed for America, hoping to make a living for his family. Two years later, in 1851, his wife followed with the six children, Anna being the next to youngest. They lived at first in Massachusetts, where one more child was born. Then, when Anna was twelve, they moved to Michigan.

When Dr. Shaw was in her late sixties she wrote her autobiography, entitling it The Story of a Pioneer.

First Memories

In 1859 Father preceded us to the Michigan woods, and there, with his oldest son, James, took up a claim.

They cleared a space in the wilderness just large enough for a log cabin, and put up the bare walls of the cabin itself. Then father returned to Lawrence, Massachusetts, and his work, leaving James behind.

A few months later, my mother, my two sisters, Eleanor and Mary, my youngest brother, Henry, eight years of age, and I,

then twelve, went to Michigan to work on and hold down
the claim while father, for eighteen months longer, stayed on in
Lawrence, sending us such remittances as he could. His second
and third sons, John and Thomas, remained in the East with
him.

In the Wilderness

When he took up his claim of three hundred and sixty acres
of land in the wilderness of northern Michigan, and sent my
mother and five young children to live there alone until he could
join us, he gave no thought to the manner in which we were
to make the struggle and survive the hardships before us.

He had furnished us with land and the four walls of a log
cabin. Some day, he reasoned, the place would be a fine estate,
which his sons would inherit and in the course of time pass on
to their sons—always an Englishman's most iridescent dream. That
for the present we were one hundred miles from a railroad, forty
miles from the nearest post-office, and half a dozen miles from
any neighbors save Indians, wolves, and wildcats; that we were
wholly unlearned in the ways of the woods as well as in the
most primitive methods of farming; that we lacked not only every
comfort, but even the bare necessities of life; and that we must
begin, single-handed and untaught, a struggle for existence in
which some of the severest forces of nature would be arrayed
against us—these facts had no weight in my father's mind.

Even if he had witnessed my mother's despair on the night of
our arrival in our new home, he would not have understood it.
From his viewpoint, he was doing a man's duty. He was working
steadily in Lawrence, and, incidentally, giving much time to the
Abolition cause and to other big public movements of his day
which had his interest and sympathy. He wrote to us regularly
and sent us occasional remittances, as well as a generous supply
of improving literature for our minds. It remained for us to
strengthen our bodies, to meet the conditions in which he had
placed us, and to survive if we could.

We faced our situation with clear and unalarmed eyes the morning after our arrival. The problem of food, we knew, was at least temporarily solved. We had brought with us enough coffee, pork, and flour to last for several weeks; and the one necessity father had put inside the cabin walls was a great fireplace, made of mud and stones, in which our food could be cooked.

The problem of our water-supply was less simple, but my brother James solved it for the time by showing us a creek a long distance from the house; and for months we carried from this creek, in pails, every drop of water we used, save that which we caught in troughs when the rain fell.

Building the House

We held a family council after breakfast, and in this, though I was only twelve, I took an eager and determined part. I loved work—it has always been my favorite form of recreation—and my spirit rose to the opportunities of it which smiled on us from every side.

Obviously the first thing to do was to put doors and windows into the yawning holes father had left for them, and to lay a board flooring over the earth inside our cabin walls, and these duties we accomplished before we had occupied our new home a fortnight.

There was a small saw-mill nine miles from our cabin, on the spot that is now Big Rapids, and there we bought our lumber. The labor we supplied ourselves, and though we put our hearts into it and the results at the time seemed beautiful to our partial eyes, I am forced to admit, in looking back upon them, that they halted this side of perfection. We began by making three windows and two doors; then, inspired by these achievements, we ambitiously constructed an attic and divided the ground floor with partitions, which gave us four rooms.

The general effect was temperamental and sketchy. The boards which formed the floor were never even nailed down; they were fine, wide planks without a knot in them, and they looked so well that we merely fitted them together as closely as we could and light-heartedly let them go at that.

Neither did we properly chink the house. Nothing is more comfortable than a log cabin which has been carefully built and finished; but for some reason—probably because there seemed always a more urgent duty calling to us around the corner—we never plastered our house at all.

The result was that on many future winter mornings we awoke to find ourselves chastely blanketed by snow, while the only warm spot in our living-room was that directly in front of the fireplace, where great logs burned all day. Even there our faces scorched while our spines slowly congealed, until we learned to revolve before the fire like a bird upon a spit.

No doubt we would have worked more thoroughly if my brother James, who was twenty years old and our tower of strength, had remained with us; but when we had been in our new home only a few months he fell ill and was forced to go East for an operation. He was never able to return to us, and thus my mother, we three young girls, and my youngest brother—Harry, who was only eight years old—made our fight alone until father came to us, more than a year later.

Dividing the Labor

Mother was practically an invalid. She had a nervous affliction which made it impossible for her to stand without the support of a chair. But she sewed with unusual skill, and it was due to her that our clothes, notwithstanding the strain to which we subjected them, were always in good condition. She sewed for hours every day, and she was able to move about the house, after a fashion, by pushing herself around on a stool which James made for her as soon as we arrived. He also built for her a more comfortable chair with a high back.

The division of labor planned at the first council was that mother should do our sewing, and my older sisters, Eleanor and

Mary, the housework, which was far from taxing, for of course we lived in the simplest manner.

My brothers and I were to do the work out of doors, an arrangement that suited me very well, though at first, owing to our lack of experience, our activities were somewhat curtailed. It was too late in the season for plowing or planting, even if we had possessed anything with which to plow, and moreover, our so-called "cleared" land was thick with sturdy tree-stumps.

Even during the second summer plowing was impossible; we could only plant potatoes and corn, and follow the most primitive method in doing even this. We took an ax, chopped up the sod, put the seed under it, and let the seed grow. The seed did grow, too—in the most gratifying and encouraging manner. Our green corn and potatoes were the best I have ever eaten. But for the present we lacked these luxuries.

We had, however, in their place, large quantities of wild fruit—gooseberries, raspberries, and plums which Harry and I gathered on the banks of our creek. Harry also became an expert fisherman. We had no hooks or lines, but he took wires from our hoop-skirts and made snares at the ends of poles. My part of this work was to stand on a log and frighten the fish out of their holes by making horrible sounds, which I did with impassioned earnestness. When the fish hurried to the surface of the water to investigate the appalling noises they had heard, they were easily snared by our small boy, who was very proud of his ability to contribute in this way to the family table.

During our first winter we lived largely on cornmeal, making a little journey of twenty miles to the nearest mill to buy it; but even at that we were better off than our neighbors, for I remember one family in our region who for an entire winter lived solely on coarse-grained yellow turnips, gratefully changing their diet to leeks when these came in the spring.

Such furniture as we had we made ourselves. In addition to my mother's two chairs and the bunks which took the place of beds, James made a settle for the living-room, as well as a table and several stools. At first we had our tree-cutting done for us, but we soon became expert in this gentle art, and I developed such skill that in later years, after father came, I used to stand with him and "heart" a log.

Winter Days

During the winter life offered us few diversions and many hardships. Our creek froze over, and the water problem became a serious one, which we met with increasing difficulty as the temperature steadily fell. We melted snow and ice, and existed through the frozen months, but with an amount of discomfort which made us unwilling to repeat at least that special phase of our experience.

In the spring, therefore, I made a well. Long before this, James had gone, and Harry and I were now the only outdoor members of our working-force. Harry was still too small to help with the well; but a young man, who had formed the neighborly habit of riding eighteen miles to call on us, gave me much friendly aid. We located the well with a switch, and when we had dug as far as we could reach with our spades, my assistant descended into the hole and threw the earth up to the edge, from which I in turn removed it. As the well grew deeper we made a half-way shelf, on which I stood, he throwing the earth on the shelf, and I shoveling it up from that point. Later, as he descended still farther into the hole we were making, he shoveled the earth into buckets and passed them up to me, I passing them on to my sister, who was now pressed into service. When the excavation was deep enough we made the wall of slabs of wood, roughly joined together.

I recall that well with calm content. It was not a thing of beauty, but it was a thoroughly practical well, and it remained the only one we had during the twelve years the family occupied the cabin.

During our first year there was no school within ten miles of us, but this lack failed to sadden Harry or me. We had brought with us from Lawrence a box of books, in which, in winter months, when our outdoor work was restricted, we found much comfort. They were the only books in that part of the country, and we read them until we knew them all by heart. Moreover, father sent us regularly the *New York Independent,* and with this admirable literature, after reading it, we papered our walls. Thus, on stormy days, we could lie on the settle or the floor and read the *Independent* over again with increased interest and pleasure.

The following year a school was opened only three miles from the Shaw home, and Anna attended it for several months. Her reading and previous schoolwork in Lawrence, however, had apparently put her on a higher intellectual level than the teacher; this made for acrimony, and after a while Anna was requested to leave. She continued her studies at home, "where," as she wryly phrases it, "I was a much more valuable economic factor than I had been in school."

The next year, when she was fourteen, she began to have a bent for her future career as a minister. There was no suddenly dramatic, mystical call, but somehow the longings were taking shape. As she notes in her autobiography, "For some reason I wanted to preach—to talk to people, to tell them things. Just why, just what, I did not yet know—but I had begun to preach in the silent woods, to stand up on stumps and address the unresponsive trees, to feel the stir of aspiration within me."

But the calling was not to be pursued immediately.

Becoming a Teacher

When I was fifteen years old I was offered a situation as schoolteacher. By this time the community was growing around us with the rapidity characteristic of these Western settlements, and we had nearer neighbors whose children needed instruction.

I passed an examination before a school-board consisting of three nervous and self-conscious men whose certificate I still hold, and I at once began my professional career on the modest salary of two dollars a week and my board. The school was four miles from my home, so I "boarded round" with the families of my pupils, staying two weeks in each place, and often walking from three to six miles a day to and from my little log school-house in every kind of weather.

During the first year I had about fourteen pupils, of varying ages, sizes, and temperaments, and there was hardly a book in the school-room except those I owned. One little girl, I remember, read from an almanac, while a second used a hymn-book.

In winter the school-house was heated by a wood-stove, to which the teacher had to give close personal attention. I could not depend on my pupils to make the fires or carry in the fuel; and it was often necessary to fetch the wood myself, sometimes for long distances through the forest. Again and again, after miles of walking through winter storms, I reached the school-house with my clothing wet through, and in these soaked garments I taught during the day.

In "boarding round" I often found myself in one-room cabins, with bunks at the end and the sole partition a sheet or blanket, behind which I slept with one or two of the children. It was the custom on these occasions for the man of the house to delicately retire to the barn while we women got to bed, and to disappear again in the morning while we dressed. In some places the meals were so badly cooked that I could not eat them, and often the only food my poor little pupils brought to school for their noonday meal was a piece of bread or a bit of raw pork.

A First Suitor

I earned my two dollars a week that year, but I had to wait for my wages until the dog tax was collected in the spring. When the money was thus raised, and the twenty-six dollars for my thirteen weeks of teaching were graciously put into my hands, I went "outside" to the nearest shop and joyously spent almost the entire amount for my first "party dress." The gown I bought was, I considered, a beautiful creation. In color it was a rich magenta, and the skirt was elaborately braided with black cable-cord. My admiration for it was justified, for it did all a young girl's eager heart could ask of any gown—it led to my first proposal.

The youth who sought my hand was about twenty years old, and by an unhappy chance he was also the least attractive young person in the countryside—the laughing-stock of the neighbors, the butt of his associates. The night he came to offer me his heart there were already two young men at our home calling on my sisters, and we were all sitting around the fire in the living-room when my suitor appeared.

His costume, like himself, left much to be desired. He wore a blue flannel shirt and a pair of trousers made of flour-bags. Such trousers were not uncommon in our region, and the boy's mother, who had made them for him, had thoughtfully selected a nice clean pair of sacks. But on one leg was the name of the firm that made the flour—A. and G. W. Green—and by a charming coincidence A. and G. W. Green happened to be the two young men who were calling on my sisters! On the back of the bags, directly in the rear of the wearer, was the simple legend, *"96 pounds"*; and the striking effect of the young man's costume was completed by a bright yellow sash which held his trousers in place.

The vision fascinated my sisters and their two guests. They gave it their entire attention, and when the new-comer signified with an eloquent gesture that he was calling on me, and beckoned me into an inner room, the quartet arose as one person and followed us to the door. Then, as we inhospitably closed the door, they fastened their eyes to the cracks in the living-room wall, that they might miss none of the entertainment.

When we were alone my guest and I sat down in facing chairs and in depressed silence. The young man was nervous, and I was both frightened and annoyed. I had heard suppressed giggles on the other side of the wall, and I realized, as my self-centered visitor failed to do, that we were not enjoying the privacy the situation seemed to demand. At last the youth informed me that his "dad" had just given him a cabin, a yoke of steers, a cow, and some hens. When this announcement had produced its full effect, he straightened up in his chair and asked, solemnly, "Will ye have me?"

An outburst of chortles from the other side of the wall greeted the proposal, but the ardent youth ignored it, if indeed he heard it. With eyes staring straight ahead, he sat rigid, waiting for my answer; and I, anxious only to get rid of him and to end the strain of the moment, said the first thing that came into my head. "I can't," I told him. "I'm sorry, but—but—I'm engaged."

He rose quickly, with the effect of a half-closed jack-knife that is suddenly opened, and for an instant stood looking down upon me. He was six feet two inches tall, and extremely thin. I am very short, and, as I looked up, his flour-bag trousers seemed to join his yellow sash somewhere near the ceiling of the room. He put both hands into his pockets and slowly delivered his valedictory. "That's darned disappointing to a fellow," he said, and left the house.

After a moment devoted to regaining my maidenly composure I returned to the living-room, where I had the privilege of observing the enjoyment of my sisters and their visitors. Helpless with mirth and with tears of pleasure on their cheeks, the four rocked and shrieked as they recalled the picture my gallant had presented. For some time after that incident I felt a strong distaste for sentiment.

She continued to teach, and by the end of the Civil War, she was earning the largest salary possible: one hundred and fifty-six dollars a year, for two terms of thirteen weeks each. For years she had been longing to go to college; it still seemed a distant dream.

High-School Days

The dollars for an education accumulated very, very slowly, until at last, in desperation, weary of seeing the years of my youth rush past, bearing my hopes with them, I took a sudden and radical step. I gave up teaching, left our cabin in the woods, and went to Big Rapids to live with my sister Mary, who had married a successful man and who generously offered me a home.

There, I had decided, I would learn a trade of some kind, of any kind; it did not greatly matter what it was. The sole essential was that it should be a money-making trade, offering wages which would make it possible to add more rapidly to my savings. In those days, in a small pioneer town, the fields open to women were few and unfruitful. The needle at once presented itself, but at first I turned with loathing from it. I would have preferred the digging of ditches or the shoveling of coal; but the needle alone persistently pointed out my way, and I was finally forced to take it.

Fate, however, as if weary at last of seeing me between her paws, suddenly let me escape. Before I had been working a month at my uncongenial trade Big Rapids was favored by a visit from a Universalist woman minister, the Reverend Marianna Thompson, who came there to preach. Her sermon was delivered on Sunday morning, and I was, I think, almost the earliest arrival of the great congregation which filled the church. It was a wonderful moment when I saw my first woman minister enter her pulpit; and as I listened to her sermon, thrilled to the soul, all my early aspirations to become a minister myself stirred in me with cumulative force. After the services I hung for a time on the fringes of the group that surrounded her, and at last, when she was alone and about to leave, I found courage to introduce myself and pour forth the tale of my ambition. Her advice was as prompt as if she had studied my problem for years.

"My child," she said, "give up your foolish idea of learning a trade, and go to school. You can't do anything until you have an education. Get it, and get it *now*."

Her suggestion was much to my liking, and I paid her the compliment of acting on it promptly, for the next morning I entered the Big Rapids High School, which was also a preparatory school for college. There I would study, I determined, as long as my money held out.

The preceptress of the high school put me into the speaking

and debating classes, where I was given every opportunity to hold forth to helpless classmates when the spirit of eloquence moved me.

As an aid to public speaking I was taught to "elocute," and I remember in every mournful detail the occasion on which I gave my first recitation.

The selection I intended to recite was a poem entitled "No Sects in Heaven," but when I faced my audience (which included parents and friends as well as classmates) I was so appalled by its size and by the sudden realization of my own temerity that I fainted during the delivery of the first verse.

Sympathetic classmates carried me into the anteroom and revived me, after which they naturally assumed that the entertainment I furnished was over for the evening. I, however, felt that if I let that failure stand against me I could never afterward speak in public; and within ten minutes, notwithstanding the protests of my friends, I was back in the hall and beginning my recitation a second time. The audience gave me its eager attention. Possibly it hoped to see me topple off the platform again, but nothing of the sort occurred. I went through the recitation with self-possession and received some friendly applause at the end.

Stage Fright and Stage Presence

Strangely enough, those first sensations of "stage fright" have been experienced, in a lesser degree, in connection with each of the thousands of public speeches I have made since that time. I have never again gone so far as to faint in the presence of an audience; but I have invariably walked out on the platform feeling the sinking sensation at the pit of the stomach, the weakness of the knees, that I felt in the hour of my debut.

From that night I took part in all our debates, recited yards of poetry to any audience, and even shone mildly in amateur theatricals. It was probably owing to all this activity that I attracted the interest of the presiding elder of our district—Dr. Peck, a man of progressive ideas.

There was at that time a movement on foot to license women

to preach in the Methodist Church, and Dr. Peck was ambitious to be the first presiding elder to have a woman ordained for the Methodist ministry. Gently but persistently, the preceptress of my high school directed the attention of Dr. Peck to me, and immediately things began to happen.

Without telling me to what it might lead, she finally arranged a meeting at her home by inviting Dr. Peck and me to dinner. Being unconscious of any significance in the occasion, I chatted light-heartedly about the large issues of life and probably settled most of them to my personal satisfaction. Dr. Peck drew me out and led me on, listened and smiled. When the evening was over and we rose to go, he turned to me with sudden seriousness:

"My quarterly meeting will be held at Ashton," he remarked, casually. "I would like you to preach the quarterly sermon."

I stared at him in utter stupefaction. Then slowly I realized that, incredible as it seemed, the man was in earnest.

"Why," I stammered, "*I* can't preach a sermon!"

Dr. Peck smiled at me. "Have you ever tried?" he asked.

I started to assure him vehemently that I never had. Then, as if Time had thrown a picture on a screen before me, I saw myself as a little girl preaching alone in the forest, as I had so often preached to a congregation of listening trees. I qualified my answer. "Never," I said, "to human beings."

Dr. Peck smiled again. "Well," he told me, "the door is open. Enter or not, as you wish."

She was then twenty-three years old.

The First Pulpit

I had six weeks in which to prepare my sermon, and I gave it most of my waking hours as well as those in which I should have been asleep.

There was no church in Ashton, so I preached in its one little school-house, which was filled with a curious crowd, eager to look at and hear the girl who was defying all conventions by getting out of the pew and into the pulpit. There was much whispering and suppressed excitement before I began, but when I gave out my text silence fell upon the room, and from that moment until I had finished my hearers listened quietly. A kerosene-lamp stood on a stand at my elbow, and as I preached I trembled so violently that the oil shook in its glass globe; but I finished without breaking down.

The next day Dr. Peck invited me to follow him around in his circuit; he wished me to preach in each of the thirty-six places, as it was desirable to let the various ministers hear and know me before I applied for my license as a local preacher.

The sermon also had another result, less gratifying. It brought out, on the following morning, the first notice of me ever printed in a newspaper. This was instigated by my brother-in-law, and it was brief but pointed. It read:

"A young girl named Anna Shaw preached at Ashton yesterday. Her real friends deprecate the course she is pursuing."

The little notice had something of the effect of a lighted match applied to gunpowder. The entire community arose in consternation, and I became a bone of contention over which friends and strangers alike wrangled until they wore themselves out. The members of my family, meeting in solemn conclave, sent for me. They had a proposition to make, and they lost no time in putting it before me. If I gave up my preaching they would send me to college and pay for my entire course.

We had a long evening together, and it was a very unhappy one. At the end of it I was given twenty-four hours in which to decide whether I would choose my people and college, or my pulpit and the arctic loneliness of a life that held no family circle. It did not require twenty-four hours of reflection to convince me that I must go my solitary way.

That year I preached thirty-six times, at each of the presiding elder's appointments; and the following spring, at the annual Methodist Conference of our district, held at Big Rapids, my name was presented to the assembled ministers as that of a candidate for a license to preach.

Two years later, when she was twenty-five, Anna entered Albion College in Michigan. To eke out her expenses, she gave a series of public lectures on temperance, and continued to preach in country schoolhouses and churches. In the summer after her first year of college she went to a Northern lumber camp to preach in the pulpit of a minister who was away on his honeymoon.

Dark Journey

The stage took me within twenty-two miles of my destination. To my dismay, however, when I arrived Saturday evening, I found that the rest of the journey lay through a dense woods, and that I could reach my pulpit in time the next morning only by having someone drive me through the woods that night.

It was not a pleasant prospect, for I had heard appalling tales of the stockades in this region and of the women who were kept prisoners there. But to miss the engagement was not to be thought of, and when, after I had made several vain efforts to find a driver, a man appeared in a two-seated wagon and offered to take me to my destination, I felt that I had to go with him, though I did not like his appearance.

He was a huge, muscular person, with a protruding jaw and a singularly evasive eye; but I reflected that his forbidding expression might be due, in part at least, to the prospect of the long night drive through the woods, to which possibly he objected as much as I did.

It was already growing dark when we started, and within a few moments we were out of the little settlement and entering the woods. With me I had a revolver I had long since learned to use, but which I very rarely carried. I had hesitated to bring it now—had even left home without it; and then, impelled by some impulse I never afterward ceased to bless, had returned for it and dropped it into my hand-bag.

I sat on the back seat of the wagon, directly behind the driver, and for a time, as we entered the darkening woods, his great shoulders blotted out all perspective as he drove on in stolid silence. Soon the darkness folded around us like a garment. I could see neither the driver nor his horses. I could hear only the sibilant whisper of the trees and the creak of our slow wheels in the rough forest road.

Suddenly the driver began to talk, and at first I was glad to hear the reassuring human tones, for the experience had begun to seem like a bad dream. I replied readily, and at once regretted that I had done so, for the man's choice of topics was most unpleasant. He began to tell me stories of the stockades—grim stories with horrible details, repeated so fully and with such gusto that I soon realized he was deliberately affronting my ears. I told him I could not listen to such talk.

He replied with a series of oaths and shocking vulgarities, stopping his horses that he might turn and fling the words into my face. He ended by snarling that I must think him a fool to imagine he did not know the kind of woman I was. What was I doing in that rough country, and why was I alone with him in those dark woods at night?

I tried to answer him calmly. "You know perfectly well who I am," I reminded him. "And you understand that I am making this journey to-night because I am to preach to-morrow morning and there is no other way to keep my appointment."

He uttered a laugh which was a most unpleasant sound. "Well," he said, coolly, "I'm damned if I'll take you. I've got you here, and I'm going to keep you here!"

I slipped my hand into the satchel in my lap, and it touched my revolver. No touch of human fingers ever brought such comfort. With a deep breath of thanksgiving I drew it out and cocked it, and as I did so he recognized the sudden click.

"Here! What have you got there?" he snapped.

"I have a revolver," I replied, as steadily as I could. "And it is cocked and aimed straight at your back. Now drive on. If you stop again, or speak, I'll shoot you."

For an instant or two he blustered. "By God," he cried, "you wouldn't dare."

"Wouldn't I?" I asked. "Try me by speaking just once more."

Even as I spoke I felt my hair rise on my scalp with the horror of the moment, which seemed worse than any nightmare a woman could experience. But the man was conquered by the knowledge of the waiting, willing weapon just behind him. He laid his whip savagely on the backs of his horses and they responded with a leap that almost knocked me out of the wagon.

He did not speak again, nor stop, but I dared not relax my caution for an instant. Hour after hour crawled toward day, and still I sat in the unpierced darkness, the revolver ready. I knew he was inwardly raging, and that at any instant he might make a sudden jump and try to get the revolver away from me. I decided that at his slightest movement I must shoot.

Daylight

But dawn came at last, and just as its bluish light touched the dark tips of the pines we drove up to the log hotel in the settlement that was our destination. Here my driver spoke. "Get down," he said gruffly. "This is the place."

I sat still. Even yet I dared not trust him. Moreover, I was so stiff after my vigil that I was not sure I could move.

"You get down," I directed, "and wake up the landlord. Bring him out here."

He sullenly obeyed and aroused the hotel-owner, and when the latter appeared I climbed out of the wagon with some effort but without explanation.

That morning I preached in my friend's pulpit as I had promised to do, and the rough building was packed with lumber-men who had come in from the neighboring camp. Their appearance caused a great surprise, as they had never attended a service before. They formed a most picturesque congregation, for they all wore brilliant lumber-camp clothing—blue or red shirts with yellow scarfs twisted around their waists, and gay-colored jackets and logging-caps. There were forty or fifty of them, and when we took up our collection they responded with much liberality and cheerful shouts to one another.

"Put in fifty cents!" they yelled across the church. "Give her a dollar!"

The collection was the largest that had been taken up in the history of the settlement, but I soon learned that it was not the spiritual comfort I offered which had appealed to the lumber-men. My driver of the night before, who was one of their number, had told his pals of his experience, and the whole camp had poured into town to see the woman minister who carried a revolver.

"Her sermon?" said one of them to my landlord, after the meeting. "Huh! I dunno what she preached. But, say, don't make no mistake about one thing: the little preacher has sure got grit!"

From Albion College, Anna went on to theological school at Boston University, then took up the pastorate of a church at East Dennis on Cape Cod. After four years there, while still officiating as minister, she went into Boston several times a week to study medicine and obtained a medical degree from Boston University three years later. It was never her intention to become a practicing physician but—in her own words—"I had merely wished to add a certain amount of medical knowledge to my mental equipment."

Branching out still further, she began to lecture for the Massachusetts Woman Suffrage Association, then under the leadership of Lucy Stone. After a time the association offered her a salary of one hundred dollars a month to become a full-time lecturer and organizer. She resigned her pastorate and devoted her future efforts to the cause, eventually becoming president of the National American Woman Suffrage Association, succeeding Susan B. Anthony and Carrie Chapman Catt in that office.

During the First World War she was appointed chairman of the Women's Committee of the National Council of National Defense, and received the Distinguished Service Medal for that work. At the end of the war she toured the country on behalf of the League of Nations and treaty of peace. It is said that she surpassed the eloquence of all her former speaking and drew vast crowds. Exhausting herself, she developed pneumonia and died at her home in Moylan, Pennsylvania, in the summer of 1919.

Susie King Taylor

❧

EXCERPTS FROM HER AUTOBIOGRAPHY
REMINISCENCES OF MY LIFE IN CAMP

SUSIE KING TAYLOR
1848–1912

Susie King Taylor was born a slave on one of the Sea Islands of Georgia. Her mother, married at the age of thirteen, bore nine children, three of them dying in infancy. Susie, the eldest child, was raised by her grandmother in Savannah, and learned—illegally —to read and write.

During the Civil War, when the Sea Islands were taken over by Union forces, Susie, then fourteen, escaped to freedom, and some months later she married Edward King, a liberated slave, who joined the earliest Negro regiment to be organized by the Grand Army of the Republic—the First South Carolina Volunteers (later known as the 33rd United States Colored Troops) under Colonel T. W. Higginson.

Mrs. King became the regimental laundress, and also served as a nurse and teacher. When her husband died after the war, she supported herself for a number of years by teaching at a freedmen's school in Savannah.

Moving north to Boston when she was twenty-six, she worked in domestic service for five years until her marriage to Russell Taylor. She became a founder of the Boston branch of the Women's Relief Corps, and, remaining devoted to veterans' organizational work, she also became increasingly concerned with inequities in the treatment of black and white citizens in the United States.

In 1902 she published her Reminiscences of My Life in Camp.

My Childhood

I was born under the slave law in Georgia. I was born on the Grest Farm (which was on an island known as the Isle of Wight), Liberty County, about thirty-five miles from Savannah, on August 6, 1848, my mother being waitress for the Grest family.

I have often been told by mother of the care Mrs. Grest took of me. She was very fond of me, and I remember when my brother and I were small children, and Mr. Grest would go away on buisness, Mrs. Grest would place us at the foot of her bed to sleep and keep her company. Sometimes he would return home earlier than he had expected to; then she would put us on the floor.

When I was about seven years old, Mr. Grest allowed my grandmother to take me to live with her in Savannah. There was no railroad connection in those days; all travel was by stage-coach. I remember, as if it were yesterday, the coach which ran in from Savannah, with its driver, whose beard nearly reached his knees. His name was Shakespeare, and often I would go to the stable where he kept his horses, just to look at his wonderful beard.

There were three of us with my grandmother, my younger sister and brother. My grandmother went every three months to see my mother. She would hire a wagon to carry bacon, tobacco, flour, molasses, and sugar. These she would trade with people in the neighboring places, for eggs, chickens, or cash, if they had it. These, in turn, she carried back to the city market, where she had a customer who sold them for her. The profit from these, together with laundry work and care of some bachelors' rooms, made a good living for her.

Clandestine School

My brother and I being the two eldest, we were sent to a friend of my grandmother, Mrs. Woodhouse, a widow, to learn to read and write. She was a free woman and lived on Bay Lane, about half a mile from my house.

We went every day about nine o'clock, with our books wrapped in paper to prevent the police or white persons from seeing them.

We went in, one at a time, through the gate, into the yard to the L kitchen, which was the schoolroom. She had twenty-five or thirty children whom she taught, assisted by her daughter, Mary Jane. The neighbors would see us going in sometimes, but they supposed we were there learning trades, as it was the custom to give children a trade of some kind.

After school we left the same way we entered, one by one, when we would go to a square, about a block from the school, and wait for each other. We would gather laurel leaves and pop them on our hands, on our way home.

I remained at her school for two years or more, when I was sent to a Mrs. Mary Beasley, where I continued until May, 1860, when she told my grandmother she had taught me all she knew, and grandmother had better get some one else who could teach me more, so I stopped my studies for a while.

I had a white playmate about this time, named Katie O'Connor, who lived on the next corner of the street from my house, and who attended a convent. One day she told me, if I would promise not to tell her father, she would give me some lessons. On my promise not to do so, and getting her mother's consent, she gave me lessons about four months, every evening. At the end of this time she was put into the convent permanently, and I have never seen her since.

A month after this, James Blouis, our landlord's son, was attending the High School, and was very fond of grandmother, so she asked him to give me a few lessons, which he did until the middle of 1861, when the Savannah Volunteer Guards, to which he and his brother belonged, were ordered to the front. In the first battle of Manassas, his brother was killed, and he deserted over to the Union side, and at the close of the war went to Washington, D.C., where he has since resided.

The Uses of Literacy

I often wrote passes for my grandmother, for all colored persons, free or slaves, were compelled to have a pass; free colored people having a guardian in place of a master. These passes were good until 10 or 10:30 P.M. for one night or every night for one month. The pass read as follows:—

Savannah, Ga., March 1, 1860.

Pass the bearer _____ from 9 to 10:30 P.M.

VALENTINE GREST

Every person had to have this pass, for at nine o'clock each night a bell was rung, and any colored persons found on the street after this hour were arrested by the watchman, and put in the guard-house until next morning, when their owners would pay their fines and release them.

I knew a number of persons who went out at any time at night and were never arrested, as the watchman knew them so well he never stopped them, and seldom asked to see their passes, only stopping them long enough, sometimes, to say "Howdy," and then telling them to go along.

About this time I had been reading so much about the "Yankees" I was very anxious to see them. The whites would tell their colored people not to go to the Yankees, for they would harness them to carts and make them pull the carts around, in place of horses.

I asked grandmother one day if this was true. She replied, "Certainly not!" that the white people did not want slaves to go over to the Yankees, and told them these things to frighten them. "Don't you see those signs pasted about the streets? one reading, 'I am a rattlesnake; if you touch me I will strike!' Another reads, 'I am a wild-cat! Beware,' etc. These are warnings to the North; so don't mind what the white people say."

I wanted to see these wonderful "Yankees" so much, as I heard my parents say the Yankee was going to set all the slaves free. Oh, how those people prayed for freedom! I remember, one night, my grandmother went out into the suburbs of the city to a church meeting, and they were fervently singing this old hymn,—

> Yes, we shall all be free,
> Yes, we shall all be free,
> Yes, we shall all be free,
> When the Lord shall appear,—

when the police came in and arrested all who were there, saying they were planning freedom, and sang "The Lord," in place of "Yankee," to blind any one who might be listening.

Grandmother never forgot that night, although she did not stay in the guard-house, as she sent to her guardian, who came at once for her; but this was the last meeting she ever attended out of the city proper.

Seeing the "Yankee" First Hand

On April 1, 1862, about the time the Union soldiers were firing on Fort Pulaski, I was sent out into the country to my mother. I remember what a roar and din the guns made. They jarred the earth for miles. The fort was at last taken by them. Two days after, my uncle took his family of seven and myself to St. Catherine Island. We landed under the protection of the Union fleet, and remained there two weeks, when about thirty of us were taken aboard a gunboat to be transferred to St. Simon's Island; and at last, to my unbounded joy, I saw the "Yankee."

After we were all settled aboard and started on our journey, the captain asked me where I was from. I told him Savannah, Georgia. He asked if I could read; I said, "Yes!"

"Can you write?" he next asked.

"Yes, I can do that also," I replied, and as if he had some doubts of my answers he handed me a book and a pencil and told me to write my name and where I was from.

I did this; then he wanted to know if I could sew.

On hearing I could, he asked me to hem some napkins for him. He was surprised at my accomplishments (for they were such in those days), for he said he did not know there were any Negroes in the South able to read or write.

He said, "You seem to be so different from the other colored people who came from the same place you did."

"No!" I replied, "the only difference is, they were reared in the country and I in the city."

That seemed to satisfy him, and we had no further conversation that day on the subject.

In the afternoon the captain observed a boat in the distance, and as it drew nearer he noticed it had a white flag hoisted, but before it reached us he ordered all passengers between decks so we could not be seen, for he thought they might be spies. The boat finally drew alongside, and had Mr. Edward Donegall on board, who wanted his two servants, Nick and Judith.

He wanted these, as they were his own children. Our captain told him he knew nothing of them, which was true, for at the time they were on St. Simon's Island, and not, as their father supposed, with us. After the boat left, we were allowed to come up on deck again.

On St. Simon's Island

Next morning we arrived at St. Simon's, and after a few days I was asked to take charge of a school for the children on the island. I said I would gladly do so if I could have some books, and in a week or two I received two large boxes of books and testaments from the North.

I had about forty children to teach, beside a number of adults who came to me nights, all of them so eager to learn to read, to read above anything else. A chaplain from Boston would come to the school sometimes and lecture to the pupils on Boston and the North.

About the first of June we were told that there was going to be a settlement of the war. Those who were on the Union side would remain free, and those in bondage were to work three days for their masters and three for themselves. It was a gloomy time for us all, and we were to be sent to Liberia. The chaplain from Boston asked me would I rather go back to Savannah or go to Liberia. I told him the latter place by all means. We did not know when this would be, but we were prepared in case this settlement should be reached. However, the Confederates would not agree to the arrangement, or else it was one of the many rumors flying about at the time, as we heard nothing further of the matter.

There were a number of communities on the island, just like little villages, and we would go from one to the other on business, to call, or only for a walk.

There were about six hundred men, women, and children on St. Simon's, the women and children being in the majority, and we were afraid to go very far from our own quarters in the daytime, and at night even to go out of the house for a long time, although the men were on watch all the time; for there were not any soldiers on the island, only the marines who were on the gunboats along the coast. The rebels, knowing this, could steal by them under cover of the night, and getting on the island would capture any persons venturing out alone and carry them to the mainland. Several of the men disappeared, and as they were never heard from we came to the conclusion they had been carried off in this way.

In October an order came to evacuate the island, and we boarded a transport for Beaufort, South Carolina.

With the First Colored Troops

At the camp in Beaufort, I was enrolled as a laundress.

The first suits worn by the boys were red coats and pants, which they disliked very much, for, they said, "The rebels see us, miles away."

The first colored troops did not receive any pay for eighteen months, and the men had to depend wholly on what they received from the commissary. A great many of these men had large families, and as they had no money to give them, their wives were obliged to support themselves and children by washing for the officers of the gunboats and the soldiers, and making cakes and pies which they

sold to the boys in camp. Finally, in 1863, the government decided
to give them half pay, but the men would not accept this. They
wanted "full pay" or nothing. They preferred rather to give their
services to the state, which they did until 1864, when the government granted them full pay, with all the back pay due.

I remember hearing Captain Heasley telling his company, one
day, "Boys, stand up for your full pay! I am with you, and so are all
the officers." This captain was from Pennsylvania, and was a very
good man; all the men liked him.

I had a number of relatives in this regiment,—several uncles,
some cousins, and my husband was a sergeant in Company E.

Proclamation and After

On the first of January, 1863, we held services for the purpose
of listening to the reading of President Lincoln's proclamation.
It was a glorious day for us all, and we enjoyed every minute of it,
and as a fitting close and the crowning event of this occasion we had
a grand barbeque.

A number of oxen were roasted whole, and we had a fine feast.
Although not served as tastily or correctly as it would have been at
home, yet it was enjoyed with keen appetites and relish. The soldiers
sang or shouted "Hurrah!" all through the camp, and seemed over-
flowing with fun and frolic until taps were sounded, when many,
no doubt, dreamed of this memorable day.

In February, several cases of varioloid broke out among the boys
which caused some anxiety in camp. One man from Company E
(the company my husband and I were with) had it very badly. He
was put into a tent apart from the rest of the men, and only the
doctor and the camp steward were allowed to see or attend him;
but I went to see this man every day and nursed him. The last
thing at night, I always went to see that he was comfortable, but
in spite of the good care and attention he received, he succumbed
to the disease.

I was not in the least afraid of the small-pox. I had been vaccinated, and I drank sassafras tea constantly, which kept my blood purged and prevented me from contracting this dread scourge.

I taught a great many of the comrades in Company E to read and write, when they were off duty. Nearly all were anxious to learn. My husband taught some also when it was convenient for him. I was very happy to know my efforts were successful in camp, and also felt grateful for the appreciation of my services. I gave my services willingly for four years and three months without receiving a dollar. I was glad, however, to be allowed to go with the regiment, to care for the sick and afflicted comrades.

I learned to handle a musket very well while in the regiment, and could shoot straight and often hit the target. I assisted in cleaning the guns and used to fire them off, to see if the cartridges were dry, before cleaning and reloading, each day. I thought this great fun. I was also able to take a gun all apart, and put it together again.

In winter, when it was very cold, I would take a mess-pan, put a little earth in the bottom, and go to the cook-shed and fill it nearly full of coals, carry it back to my tent and put another pan over it; so when the provost guard went through camp after taps, they would not see the light, as it was against the rules to have a light after taps. In this way I was heated and kept very warm.

When at camp, I visited the hospital in Beaufort, where I met Clara Barton. There were a number of sick and wounded soldiers there, and I went often to see the comrades. Miss Barton was always very cordial toward me, and I honored her for her devotion and care of those men.

Fort Wagner being only a mile from our camp, I went there two or three times a week, and would go up on the ramparts to watch the gunners send their shells into Charleston—which they did every fifteen minutes—and had a full view of the city from that point. Outside of the fort were many skulls lying about; I have often moved them one side out of the path. The comrades and I would have quite a debate as to which side the men fought on. Some thought they were the skulls of our boys; others thought they were the enemy's; but as there was no definite way to know, it was never decided which could lay claim to them.

They were a gruesome sight, those fleshless heads and grinning jaws, but by this time I had become accustomed to worse things and did not feel as I might have earlier in my camp life.

The regiment was ordered to various islands, and she accompanied them. Then, when her husband was sent out on a mission that took him away for an extended period, she wanted to get back to Beaufort where it would be possible to get news from him.

Survival

On November 23 I got a pass for Beaufort. There was a yacht that carried passengers from Hilton Head, where I was, to Beaufort. The only people at Hilton Head, beside the soldiers, were a woman who came over on a permit to see her husband who was very ill (he died while she was there), a corporal's wife with her two-year-old child, and one other soldier's wife. . . . As soon as we could get the yacht, they, together with a comrade just discharged, an officer's boy, and myself, took passage on it for Beaufort.

It was nearly dark before we had gone any distance, and about eight o'clock we were cast away and were only saved through the mercy of God.

I remember going down twice. As I rose the second time, I caught hold of the sail and managed to hold fast. The mother held on to her child with one hand, while with the other she managed to hold fast to some part of the boat, and we drifted and shouted as loud as we could, trying to attract the attention of some of the government boats which were going up and down the river. But it was in vain, we could not make ourselves heard, and just when we gave up all hope, and in the last moment—as we thought—gave one more despairing cry, we were heard.

Two boats were put off and a search was made, to locate our distressed boat. They found us at last, nearly dead from exposure. In fact, the poor little baby was dead, although her mother still held her by her clothing, with her teeth. The soldier was drowned, having been caught under the sail and pinned down. The rest of us were saved.

I had to be carried bodily, as I was thoroughly exhausted. We were given the best attention that we could get at this place where we were picked up. We were capsized about 8:15 P.M. and it was near midnight when they found us. Next day, they kept a sharp lookout on the beach for anything that might be washed in from the yacht, and got a trunk and several other things. Had the tide been going out, we should have been carried to sea and lost.

I was very ill and under the doctor's care for many weeks in Beaufort. The doctor said I ought to have been rolled, as I had swallowed so much water. In January I went back to the island where I could be treated by my own doctor, who did all in his power to alleviate my suffering, for I was swollen very much. This he reduced and I recovered, but had a severe cough for a long time afterward.

A New Life

On February 9, 1866, the regiment was mustered out. My husband and I returned to Savannah, a number of the comrades returning at the same time. A new life was before us now, all the old life left behind. After getting settled, I opened a school at my home, as there was not any public school for Negro children.

I had twenty children at my school, and received one dollar a month for each pupil. I also had a few older ones who came at night. There were several other private schools besides mine, one on the same street I lived on. I taught almost a year, when a free school opened, which took a number of my scholars.

My husband, Sergeant King, was a boss carpenter, but being just mustered out of the army, and the prejudice against his race being still too strong to insure much work at his trade, he took contracts for unloading vessels, and hired a number of men to assist him.

On September 16, 1866, he died, leaving me soon to welcome a little stranger alone.

In December, I was obliged to give up teaching, but in April, 1867, I opened a school in Liberty County, Georgia, and taught there one year; but country life did not agree with me, so I returned to the city, and a friend took charge of my school.

On my return to Savannah, I found that the free school had by now taken all my former pupils, so I opened a night school, where I taught a number of adults.

This, together with other things I could get to do and the assistance of my brother-in-law, supported me. I taught this school until the fall of 1868, when a free night school opened, and again my scholars left me, and I had to close my school.

From Teacher to Domestic

I put my baby with my mother and entered in the employ of a family, where I lived quite a while, but had to leave, as the work was too hard.

In 1872 I put in a claim for my husband's bounty and received one hundred dollars, some of which I put in the Freedmen's Savings Bank. In the fall of that year I went to work for a very wealthy lady, Mrs. Charles Green, as laundress. In the spring of 1873, Mr. and Mrs. Green came North to Rye Beach for the summer, and as their cook did not care to go so far from home, I went with them in her place. While there, I won a prize for excellent cooking at a fair which the ladies who were summering there held to raise funds to build an Episcopal Church.

I returned South with Mrs. Green, and soon after, she went to Europe. Then I went to Boston and entered the service of Mr. Thomas Smith's family, where I remained until the death of Mrs. Smith. I next lived with Mrs. Gorham Gray, Beacon Street, where I remained until I was married, in 1879, to Russell L. Taylor.

Remembering Old Comrades

All this time my interest in the boys in blue had not abated. I was still loyal and true, whether they were black or white. My hands have never left undone anything they could do towards their aid and comfort in the twilight of their lives.

In 1886 I helped to organize Corps 67, Women's Relief Corps, auxiliary to the Grand Army of the Republic, and it is a very flourishing corps today. I have been Guard, Secretary, Treasurer for three years, and in 1893 I was made President.

I helped to furnish and pack boxes to be sent to the soldiers and hospitals during the first part of the Spanish war; there were black soldiers there too. At the battle of San Juan Hill, they were in the front, just as brave, loyal, and true as those other black men who fought for freedom and the right; and yet their bravery and faithfulness were reluctantly acknowledged, and praise grudgingly given. All we ask for is "equal justice," the same that is accorded to all other races who come to this country, of their free will—not forced to, as we were—and are allowed to enjoy every privilege, unrestricted, while we are denied what is rightfully our own in a country which the labor of our forefathers helped to make what it is.

The Work of Colored Women During the War

There are many people who do not know what some of the colored women did during the war. There were hundreds of them who assisted the Union soldiers by hiding them and helping them to escape.

Many were punished for taking food to the prison stockades for the prisoners. When I went into Savannah, in 1865, I was told of one of these stockades which was in the suburbs of the city.

The Union soldiers were in it, worse than pigs, without any shelter from sun or storm, and the colored women would take food there at night and pass it to them, through the holes in the fence. The soldiers were starving, and these women did all they could towards relieving those men, although they knew the penalty, should they be caught giving them aid.

Others assisted in various ways the Union army. These things should be kept in history before the people. There has never been a greater war in the United States than the one of 1861, where so many lives were lost,—not men alone, but noble women as well.

Let us not forget that terrible war, or our brave soldiers who were thrown into Andersonville and Libby prisons, the awful agony they went through, and the most brutal treatment they received in those loathsome dens, the worst ever given human beings; and if the white soldiers were subjected to such treatment, what must have been the horrors inflicted on the Negro soldiers in their prison pens? Can we forget those cruelties?

Injustice, Present and Past

I read an article, which said the ex-Confederate Daughters had sent a petition to the managers of the local theatres in Tennessee to prohibit the performance of "Uncle Tom's Cabin," claiming it was exaggerated—that is, the treatment of the slaves—and would have a very bad effect on the children who might see the drama.

I paused and thought back a few years of the heart-rending scenes I have witnessed; I have seen many times, when I was a mere girl, thirty or forty men, handcuffed, and as many women and children, come every first Tuesday of each month from Mr. Wiley's trade office to the auction blocks. The route was down our principal street to the court-house, which was only a block from where I resided.

All people in those days got all their water from the city pumps, which stood about a block apart throughout the city. The one we used to get water from was opposite the court-house. I remember, as if it were yesterday, seeing droves of Negroes going to be sold, and I often went to look at them, and I could hear the auctioneer very plainly from my house, auctioning these poor people off.

Do these Confederate Daughters ever send petitions to prohibit the atrocious lynchings and wholesale murdering and torture of the Negro?

Do you ever hear of them fearing this would have a bad effect on the children?

It does not seem as if our land is yet civilized. I do not condemn all the Caucasian race because the Negro is badly treated by a few of the race. No! for had it not been for the true whites, assisted by God and the prayers of our forefathers, I should not be here today.

A Visit to Louisiana

The inevitable always happens. On February 3, 1898, I was called to Shreveport, La., to the bedside of my son, who was very ill. He had been traveling on business when he fell ill, and had been sick two weeks when they sent to me. I tried to have him brought home to Boston, but they could not send him, as he was not able to sit and ride this long distance; so on the sixth of February I left Boston to go to him.

I reached Cincinnati on the eighth, where I took a train for the south. I asked a white man standing near—before I got my train—what car I should take. "Take that one," he said, pointing to one.

"But that is a smoking car!"

"Well," he replied, "that is the car for colored people."

I went to this car, and on entering it all my courage failed me. I have ridden in many coaches, but I was never in such as these. I wanted to return home again, but when I thought of my sick boy I said, "Well, others ride in these cars and I must do likewise," and tried to be resigned, for I wanted to reach my boy, as I did not know whether I should find him alive.

I arrived in Chattanooga at eight o'clock in the evening, where the porter took my baggage to the train which was to leave for Marion, Miss. Soon after I was seated, just before the train pulled out, two tall men with slouch hats on walked through the car, and on through the train.

Finally they came back to our car and stopping at my seat said, "Where are those men who were with you?"

I did not know to whom they were speaking, as there was another woman in the car, so I made no reply.

Again they asked me, standing directly in front of my seat, "Where are those men who came in with you?"

"Are you speaking to me?" I said.

"Yes!" they said.

"I have not seen any men," I replied.

They looked at me a moment, and one of them asked where I was from. I told him Boston; he hesitated a minute and walked out of our car to the other car.

When the conductor came around I told him what these men had said, and asked him if they allowed persons to enter the car and insult passengers. He only smiled.

Later, when the porter came in, I mentioned it to him. He said, "Lady, I see you do not belong here; where are you from?" I told him. He said, "I have often heard of Massachusetts. I want to see that place."

"Yes!" I said, "you can ride there on the cars, and no person would be allowed to speak to you as those men did to me." He explained that those men were constables, who were in search of a man who had eloped with another man's wife.

"That is the way they do here," he said. "Each morning you can hear of some Negro being lynched"; and on seeing my surprise, he said, "Oh, that is nothing; it is done all the time. We have no rights here. I have been on this road for fifteen years and have seen some terrible things."

I was a little surprised at the way the poor whites were made to ride on this road. They put them all together by themselves in a car, between the colored people's coach and the first-class coach, and it looked like the "laborers' car" used in Boston to carry the different day laborers to and from their work.

I got to Marion, Miss., at two o'clock in the morning, arrived at Vicksburg at noon, and at Shreveport about eight o'clock in the evening, and found my son just recovering from a severe hemorrhage. He was very anxious to come home, and I tried to secure a berth for him on a sleeper, but they would not sell me one, and he was not strong enough to travel otherwise.

If I could only have gotten him to Cincinnati, I might have brought him home, but as I could not I was forced to let him remain where he was. It seemed very hard, when his father fought to protect the Union and our flag, yet his boy was denied, under this same flag, a berth to carry him home to die, because he was a Negro.

"Incidents" in Shreveport

I found that the people who had lived in Massachusetts and were settled in Shreveport were very cordial to me and glad to see me. There was a man murdered in cold blood for nothing. He was a colored man and a "porter" in a store in this town. A clerk had left his umbrella at home. It had begun to rain when he started for home, and on looking for the umbrella he could not, of course, find it.

He asked the porter if he had seen it. The porter said no, he had not. "You answer very saucy," said the clerk, and drawing his revolver, he shot the colored man dead. He was taken up the street to an office where he was placed under one thousand dollars bond for his appearance and released, and that was the end of the case.

I was surprised at this, but I was told by several white and colored persons that this was a common occurrence, and the persons were never punished if they were white, but no mercy was shown to Negroes.

I met several comrades, white and colored, there, and noticed that the colored comrades did not wear their buttons. I asked one of them why this was, and was told, should they wear it, they could not get work. Still some would wear their buttons in spite of the feeling against it. I met a newsman from New York on the train. He was a veteran, and said that Sherman ought to come back and go into that part of the country.

Shreveport is a horrid place when it rains. The earth is red and sticks to your shoes, and it is impossible to keep rubbers on, for the mud pulls them off.

After the death of my son, while on my way back to Boston, I came to Clarksdale, one of the many stations on the road from Vicksburg.

At Clarksdale, I saw a man hanged. It was a terrible sight, and I felt alarmed for my own safety down there.

When I reached Memphis I found conditions of travel much better. The people were mostly Western and Northern here; the cars were nice, but separate for colored persons until we reached the Ohio River, when the door was opened and the porter passed through, saying "The Ohio River! change to the other car."

I thought, "What does he mean? We have been riding all this distance in separate cars, and now we are all to sit together."

It certainly seemed a peculiar arrangement.

Thoughts on Present Conditions

Living here in Boston where the black man is given equal justice, I must say a word on the general treatment of my race, both in the North and South, in this twentieth century. I wonder if our white fellow men realize the true sense or meaning of brotherhood?

For two hundred years we had toiled for them; the war of 1861 came and was ended, and we thought our race was forever freed from bondage, and that the two races could live in unity with each other, but when we read almost every day of what is being done to my race by some whites in the South, I sometimes ask, "Was the war in vain? Has it brought freedom, in the full sense of the word, or has it not made our conditions more hopeless?"

In this "land of the free" we are burned, tortured, and denied a fair trial, murdered for any imaginary wrong conceived in the brain of the Negro-hating white man. There is no redress for us from a government which promised to protect all under its flag.

It seems a mystery to me. They say, "One flag, one nation, one country indivisible."

Is this true? Can we say this truthfully, when one race is allowed to burn, hang, and inflict the most horrible torture weekly, monthly, on another? No, we cannot sing, "My country, 'tis of thee, Sweet land of Liberty"! It is hollow mockery. The Southland laws are all on the side of the white, and they do just as they like to the Negro, whether in the right or not.

I do not uphold my race when they do wrong. They ought to be punished, but the innocent are made to suffer as well as the guilty, and I hope the time will hasten when it will be stopped forever.

Prospects for the Future

While in Shreveport, I had visited ex-Senator Harper's house. He is a colored man, and owns a large business block, besides a fine residence and several good building lots. Another family, the Pages, living on the same street, were quite wealthy, and a large number of colored families owned their own homes, and were industrious, refined people; and if they were only allowed justice, the South would be the only place for our people to live.

In 1861 the Southern papers were full of advertisements for "slaves," but now, despite all the hindrances and "race problems," my people are striving to attain the full standard of all other races born free in the sight of God, and in a number of instances have succeeded.

Justice we ask,—to be citizens of these United States, where so many of our people have shed their blood with their white comrades, that the stars and stripes should never be polluted.

"Mother" Mary Jones

EXCERPTS FROM HER AUTOBIOGRAPHY

"MOTHER" MARY JONES
May 1, 1830–November 30, 1930

Mary Harris Jones is one of the most remarkable figures in American labor history. At the age of fifty the widow Jones changed her style of living completely. From having worked as a teacher and dressmaker, she became a full-time union organizer.

In her widow's weeds and black bonnet, with an umbrella for a sword, she traveled on foot from one workers' community to another, through the coal towns of West Virginia and Pennsylvania all the way west to the copper mines of Colorado.

She worked in the cotton mills of the South to gather material for a series of meetings against child labor. Later she supported the garment and streetcar strikes in New York City.

The only dangerous weapon in her possession was the hatpin that attached the flat-top bonnet to her curly white hair, yet more than one state governor called out the militia against her. What right, they demanded, had she to be organizing in their areas, to be interfering with private ownership's ways of conducting business? Who was she? Could she prove that she was a resident of the state? Where was her identification?

"Here," Mother Jones would reply in her high falsetto voice, her gray eyes flashing behind her spectacles, "right here," and she

would rap the point of her umbrella against her worn and dusty shoes. "My feet are my passport; they take me where my children call for help." The miners, the miners' wives, and the miners' children, all these were her brood and many thousands more.

In Pittsburgh to support a strike in the steel mills, she was asked by the local judge if she had a permit to speak on the streets. "Yes, your honor," she answered, "I have." "Who issued it to you?" the judge demanded. She answered, "Patrick Henry; Thomas Jefferson; John Adams!"

The last great struggle she engaged in actively was the steel strike of 1919. At the age of ninety-three, however, she was still working among the striking coal miners in West Virginia.

She also attended the convention of the Farmer-Labor Party, where she stirred the delegates with her words: "The producer, not the meek, shall inherit the earth. Not today perhaps, nor tomorrow, but over the rim of the years my old eyes can see the coming of another day."

On her one hundredth birthday, on May Day 1930, congratulations poured in from all over the world, from labor unions, from friends and acquaintances, even from John D. Rockefeller, Jr. On the lawn of her modest home in Silver Spring, Maryland, where friends were caring for her, she made a vigorous speech for the talking-picture cameras. Six months later she died of old age.

Her funeral was not somber. The crowd of mourners remembered her words and applied them. "Pray for the dead," was what salty old Mother Jones had taken for her motto, "and fight like hell for the living."

Here are extracts from Mother Jones's own life story.

Early Years

I was born in the city of Cork, Ireland, in 1830. My father, Richard Harris, came to American in 1835, and as soon as he had become an American citizen he sent for his family. His work as a laborer with railway construction crews took him to Toronto, Canada. Here I was brought up, but always as the child of an American citizen. Of that citizenship I have ever been proud.

After finishing the common schools, I attended the Normal school with the intention of becoming a teacher. Dress-making too, I learned proficiently. My first position was teaching in a convent in Monroe, Michigan. Later, I came to Chicago and opened a dress-making establishment. I preferred sewing to bossing little children.

However, I went back to teaching again, this time in Memphis, Tennessee. Here I was married in 1861. My husband was an iron moulder and a staunch member of the Iron Moulders' Union.

In 1867, a yellow fever epidemic swept Memphis. Its victims were mainly among the poor and the workers. The rich and the well-to-do fled the city. Schools and churches were closed. People were not permitted to enter the house of a yellow fever victim without permits. The poor could not afford nurses. Across the street from me, ten persons lay dead from the plague. The dead surrounded us. They were buried at night quickly and without ceremony. All about my house I could hear weeping and the cries of delirium.

One by one, my four little children sickened and died. I washed their little bodies and got them ready for burial.

My husband caught the fever and died. I sat alone through nights of grief. No one came to me. No one could. Other homes were as stricken as mine. All day long, all night long, I heard the grating of the wheels of the death cart.

After the union had buried my husband, I got a permit to nurse the sufferers. This I did until the plague was stamped out.

I returned to Chicago and went again into the dress-making business with a partner. We were located on Washington Street near the lake.

In October, 1871, the great Chicago fire burned up our establishment and everything that we had. The fire made thousands homeless. We stayed all night and the next day without food on the lake front, often going into the lake to keep cool.

Old St. Mary's church at Wabash Avenue was thrown open to the refugees and there I camped until I could find a place to go.

Near by in an old, tumbled down, fire scorched building the Knights of Labor held meetings. I used to spend my evenings at their meetings, listening to splendid speakers. Sundays we went out to the woods and held meetings.

I became acquainted with the labor movement. I learned that in 1865, after the close of the Civil War, a group of men met in Louisville, Kentucky. They came from the North and from the South; they were the "blues" and the "greys" who a year or two before had been fighting each other over the question of chattel slavery. They decided that the time had come to formulate a program to fight another brutal form of slavery—industrial slavery. Out of this decision had come the Knights of Labor.

From the time of the Chicago fire I became more and more engrossed in the labor struggle and I decided to take an active part in the efforts of the working people to better the conditions under which they worked and lived. I became a member of the Knights of Labor.

One of the first strikes that I remember occurred in the Seventies. The Baltimore and Ohio Railroad employees went on strike and they sent for me to come help them. I went.

In the Movement

From 1880 on, I became wholly engrossed in the labor movement.

Before 1899 the coal fields of Pennsylvania were not organized. Immigrants poured into the country and they worked cheap. Hours of work down under ground were cruelly long. Fourteen hours a day was not uncommon, thirteen, twelve. The life or limb of the miner was unprotected by any laws. Families lived in company owned shacks that were not fit for their pigs. Children died by the hundreds due to the ignorance and poverty of their parents.

Often I have helped lay out for burial the babies of the miners, and the mothers could scarce conceal their relief at the little ones' deaths. Another was already on its way, destined, if a boy, for the breakers; if a girl, for the silk mills where the other brothers and sisters already worked.

The United Mine Workers decided to organize these fields and work for the human conditions for human beings. Organizers were put to work. Whenever the spirit of the men in the mines grew strong enough a strike was called.

In Arnot, Pennsylvania, a strike had been going on four or five months. The men were becoming discouraged. The coal company sent the doctors, the school teachers, the preachers and their wives to the homes of the miners to get them to sign a document that they would go back to work.

The President of the district, Mr. Wilson, and an organizer, Tom Haggerty, got despondent. The signatures were overwhelmingly in favor of returning to work Monday morning.

Haggerty suggested that they send for me and on Saturday they telephoned to Barnesboro where I was organizing to come at once or they would lose the strike. I told him that I was holding a meeting that night but I would leave early the next morning.

I started Sunday at daybreak. At Roaring Branch, the nearest train connection with Arnot, the secretary of the Arnot Union, a young boy, William Bouncer, met me with a horse and buggy. We drove sixteen miles over rough mountain roads. It was biting cold.

In the afternoon I held a meeting. "You've got to take the pledge," I said. "Rise and pledge to stick to your brothers and the union till the strike's won! The meeting stands adjourned till ten o'clock tomorrow morning. Everyone come and see that the slaves that think to go back to their masters come along with you."

I returned to my room at the hotel. It was the only one in town, and owned by the coal company. At eleven o'clock that night the housekeeper knocked at my door and told me that I had to give up my room; that she was told it belonged to a teacher. "It's a shame, Mother," she whispered, as she helped me into my coat.

I found little Bouncer sitting on guard down in the lobby. He took me up the mountain to a miner's house. A cold wind

almost blew the bonnet from my head. At the miner's shack I
knocked. A light came in the tiny window. The door opened.
"And did they put you out, Mother?"

"They did that."

The miner held the oil lamp with the thumb and his little
fingers and I could see that the others were off. His face was
young but his body was bent over.

He insisted on my sleeping in the only bed, with his wife.
He slept with his head on his arms on the kitchen table. Early
in the morning his wife rose to keep the children quiet, so that
I might sleep a little later as I was very tired.

At eight o'clock she came into my room, crying. "You must
get up, Mother. The sheriff is here to put us out for keeping you.
This house belongs to the company."

The family gathered up all their earthly belongings, which
weren't much, took down all the holy pictures, and put them in
a wagon, and they with all their neighbors went to the meeting.
The sight of that wagon with the sticks of furniture and the
holy pictures and the children, with the father and mother and
myself walking along through the streets, turned the tide. It made
the men so angry that they decided not to go back that morning
to the mines.

The Dishpan Brigade

Then the company tried to bring in scabs. I told the men to
stay home with the children for a change and let the women
attend to the scabs.

I organized an army of women housekeepers.

On a given day they were to bring their mops and brooms and
"the army" would charge the scabs up at the mines. The general
manager, the sheriff and the corporation hirelings heard of our
plans and were on hand. The day came and the women came
with the mops and brooms and pails of water.

I decided not to go up to the Drip Mouth myself, for I
knew they would arrest me and that might rout the army. I

selected as leader an Irish woman who had a most picturesque appearance. She had slept late and her husband had told her to hurry up and get into the army. She had grabbed a red petticoat and slipped it over a thick cotton nightgown. She wore a black stocking and a white one. She had tied a little red fringed shawl over her wild red hair. Her face was red and her eyes were mad. I looked at her and felt that she could raise a rumpus.

I said, "You lead the army up to the Drip Mouth. Take that tin dishpan you have with you and your hammer, and when the scabs and the mules come up, begin to hammer and howl. Then all of you hammer and howl and be ready to chase the scabs with your mops and brooms. Don't be afraid of anyone."

Up the mountain side, yelling and hollering, she led the women, and when the mules came up with the scabs and the coal, she began beating on the dishpan and hollering and all the army joined in with her. The sheriff tapped her on the shoulder.

"My dear lady," said he, "remember the mules. Don't frighten them."

She took the old tin pan and she hit him with it and she hollered, "To hell with you and the mules!"

He fell over and dropped into the creek. Then the mules began to rebel against scabbing. They bucked and kicked the scab drivers and started off for the barn. The scabs started running down hill, followed by the army of women with their mops and pails and brooms.

A poll parrot in a near by shack screamed at the superintendent, "Got hell, did you? Got hell?"

There was a great big doctor in the crowd, a company lap dog. He had a little satchel in his hand and he said to me, "Mrs. Jones, I have a warrant for you."

"All right," said I. "Keep it in your pill bag until I come for it. I am going to hold a meeting now."

From that day on the women kept continual watch of the mines to see that the company did not bring in scabs. Every day women with brooms or mops in one hand and babies in the other arm, wrapped in little blankets, went to the mines and watched that no one went in. And all night long they kept watch.

The company was spending money among the farmers, urging them not to do anything for the miners. I went out with an old wagon and a union mule that had gone on strike, and a miner's little boy for a driver. I held meetings among the farmers and won them to the side of the strikers.

Sometimes it was twelve or one o'clock in the morning when I would get home, the little boy asleep on my arm and I driving the mule. Sometimes it was several degrees below zero. The winds whistled down the mountains and drove the snow and sleet in our faces. My hands and feet were often numb. We were living on dry bread and black coffee. I slept in a room that never had a fire in it, and I often woke in the morning to find snow covering the outside covers of the bed.

There was a place near Arnot called Sweedy Town, and the company's agents went there to get the Swedes to break the strike. I got the young farmers to get on their horses and go over to see that no Swede left town. They took clotheslines for lassos and any Swede seen moving in the direction of Arnot was brought back quick enough.

After months of terrible hardships the strike was about won. The president of the union, Mr. Wilson, when strikers were evicted, cleaned out his barn and took care of the evicted miners until homes could be provided. One by one he killed his chickens and his hogs. Everything that he had he shared. He ate dry bread and drank chicory. He knew every hardship that the rank and file of the organization knew. We do not have such leaders now.

The last of February the company put up a notice that all demands were conceded.

"Did you get the use of the hall for us to hold meetings?" said the women.

"No, we didn't ask for that."

"Then the strike is on again," said they.

They got the hall.

I was going to leave for the central fields, and before I left, the union held a victory meeting. The women came for miles in a raging snow storm, little children trailing on their skirts, and babies under their shawls. Many of the miners had walked miles. It was one night of real joy and a great celebration. The men opened a few of the freight cars out on a siding and helped themselves to boxes of beer. Old and young talked and sang all night long and to the credit of the company no one was interfered with.

Those were the days before the extensive use of gun men, of military, of jails, of police clubs. There had been no bloodshed. There had been no riots. And the victory was due to the army of women with their mops and brooms.

The March of the Mill Children

In the spring of 1903 I went to Kensington, Pennsylvania, where seventy-five thousand textile workers were on strike. Of this number at least ten thousand were little children. The workers were striking for more pay and shorter hours. Every day little children came into Union Headquarters, some with their hands off, some with the thumb missing, some with their fingers off at the knuckle. They were stooped little things, round shouldered and skinny. Many of them were not over ten years of age, although the state law prohibited their working before they were twelve.

The law was poorly enforced and the mothers of these children often swore falsely as to their children's age. In a single block in Kensington, fourteen women, mothers of twenty-two children all under twelve, explained it was a question of starvation or perjury. That the fathers had been killed or maimed at the mines.

I asked the newspaper men why they didn't publish the facts about child labor in Pennsylvania. They said they couldn't because the mill owners had stock in the papers.

"Well, I've got stock in these little children," said I, "and I'll arrange a little publicity."

We assembled a number of boys and girls one morning in

Independence Park and from there we arranged to parade with banners to the court house where we would hold a meeting.

A great crowd gathered in the public square in front of the city hall. I put the little boys with their fingers off and hands crushed and maimed on a platform. I held up their mutilated hands and showed them to the crowd and made the statement that Philadelphia's mansions were built on the broken bones, the quivering hearts and the drooping heads of these children.

The officials of the city hall were standing in the open windows. I held the little ones of the mills high up above the heads of the crowd and pointed to their puny arms and legs and hollow chests. They were light to lift.

I called upon the millionaire manufacturers to cease their moral murders, and I cried to the officials in the open windows opposite, "Some day the workers will take possession of your city hall, and when we do, no child will be sacrificed on the altar of profit."

The reporters quoted my statement that Philadelphia mansions were built on the broken bones and quivering hearts of children. The universities discussed it. Preachers began talking. That was what I wanted. Public attention on the subject of child labor.

The matter quieted down for a while and I concluded that people needed stirring up again.

The Liberty Bell that a century ago rang out for freedom against tyranny was touring the country and crowds were coming to see it everywhere. That gave me an idea. These little children were striking for some of the freedom that childhood ought to have, and I decided that the children and I would go on a tour.

I asked some of the parents if they would let me have their little boys and girls for a week or ten days, promising to bring them back safe and sound. They consented. A man named Sweeny was marshall for our "army." A few men and women went with me to help with the children. They were on strike and I thought they might as well have a little recreation.

The children carried knapsacks on their backs in which was a knife and fork, a tin cup and plate. We took along a wash boiler in which to cook the food on the road. One little fellow

13. Rev. and Dr. Anna Howard Shaw in her pulpit robes.

14. Susie King Taylor, ex-slave, teacher, and nurse.

15. "Mother" Mary Jones became a full-time union organizer at the age of 50.

16. Elizabeth Gertrude Stern grew up in a Jewish ghetto in a small Midwestern city and became a wife, mother, and career woman, who wrote under the pen name of Eleanor or Leah Morton.

17. Mountain Wolf Woman, a Winnebago Indian.

18. Mountain Wolf Woman and her husband, Bad Soldier, in 1908.

had a drum and another had a fife. That was our band. We carried banners that said, "We want more schools and less hospitals." "We want time to play." "Prosperity is here. Where is ours?"

We started from Philadelphia where we held a great mass meeting. I decided to go with the children to see President Roosevelt to ask him to have Congress pass a law prohibiting the exploitation of childhood. I thought that President Roosevelt might see these mill children and compare them with his own little ones who were spending the summer on the seashore at Oyster Bay. I thought, too, out of politeness, we might call on Morgan in Wall Street who owned the mines where many of these children's fathers worked.

On the Highway

The children were very happy, having plenty to eat, taking baths in the brooks and rivers every day. I thought when the strike is over and they go back to the mills, they will never have another holiday like this.

All along the line of march the farmers drove out to meet us with wagon loads of fruit and vegetables. Their wives brought the children clothes and money. The interurban trainmen would stop their trains and give us free rides.

Marshal Sweeny and I would go ahead to the towns and arrange sleeping quarters for the children, and secure meeting halls. As we marched on, it grew terribly hot. There was no rain and the roads were heavy with dust. From time to time we had to send some of the children back to their homes. They were too weak to stand the march.

We were on the outskirts of Trenton, New Jersey, cooking our lunch in the wash boiler, when the conductor on the interurban car stopped and told us the police were coming down to notify us that we could not enter the town. There were mills in the town and the mill owners didn't like our coming.

"All right," I said, "the police will be just in time for lunch."

Sure enough, the police came and we invited them to dine

with us. They looked at the little gathering of children with their tin plates and cups around the wash boiler. They just smiled and spoke kindly to the children, and said nothing at all about not going into the city.

We went in, held our meeting, and it was the wives of the police who took the little children and cared for them that night, sending them back in the morning with a nice lunch rolled up in paper napkins.

Everywhere we had meetings, showing up with living children, the horrors of child labor.

At one town the mayor said we could not hold a meeting because he did not have sufficient police protection. "These little children have never known any sort of protection, your honor," I said, "and they are used to going without it." He let us have our meeting.

One night in Princeton, New Jersey, we slept in the big cool barn on Grover Cleveland's great estate.

The heat became intense. The proprietor of the leading hotel sent for me. "Mother," he said, "order what you want and all you want for your army, and there's nothing to pay."

I called on the mayor of Princeton and asked for permission to speak opposite the campus of the University. I said I wanted to speak on higher education. The mayor gave me permission.

"Here's a text book on economics," I said, pointing to little James Ashworth, who was ten years old and who was stooped over like an old man from carrying bundles of yarn that weighed seventy-five pounds. "He gets three dollars a week and his sister who is fourteen gets six dollars. They work in a carpet factory ten hours a day while the children of the rich are getting their higher education."

That night we camped on the banks of Stony Brook where years and years before the ragged Revolutionary Army camped.

From Jersey City we marched to Hoboken. In New York we marched up Fourth Avenue to Madison Square and police officers, captains, sergeants, roundsmen and reserves from three precincts accompanied us. But the police would not let us hold a meeting in Madison Square. They insisted that the meeting be held in Twentieth Street.

There I told an immense crowd of the horrors of child labor and showed them Eddie Dunphy, a little fellow of twelve, whose job it was to sit all day on a high stool, handing in the right thread to another worker. Eleven hours a day he sat on the high stool with dangerous machinery all around him. All day long, winter and summer, spring and fall, for three dollars a week.

And then I showed them Gussie Rangnew, a little girl whose face was like an old woman's. Gussie packed stockings in a factory, eleven hours a day for a few cents a day.

We raised a lot of money for the strikers and hundreds offered their homes to the little ones while we were in the city.

The next day we went to Coney Island at the invitation of Mr. Bostick who owned the wild animal show. The children had a wonderful day. After the exhibition of the trained animals, Mr. Bostick let me speak to the audience. There was a back drop to the tiny stage of the Roman Colosseum with the audience painted in and two Roman emperors down in front with their thumbs down. Right in front of the emperors were the empty iron cages of the animals. I put my little children in the cages and they clung to the iron bars while I talked.

I told the crowd that the scene was typical of the aristocracy of the employers with their thumbs down to the little ones of the mills and factories, and people sitting dumbly by.

"I asked a man in prison once," I said, "how he happened to be there and he said he had stolen a pair of shoes. I told him if he had stolen a railroad he would be a United States Senator.

"We are told that every American boy has the chance of being president. I tell you that these little boys in the iron cages would sell their chances any day for good square meals and a chance to play. You see those monkeys in those cages over there," I pointed to a side cage. "The professors are trying to teach them to talk. The monkeys are too wise for they fear that the manufacturers would buy them for slaves in their factories."

We marched down to Oyster Bay but the president refused to see us and he would not answer my letters. But our march had done its work. We had drawn the attention of the nation to the crime of child labor. And while the strike of the textile workers in Kensington was lost and the children driven back to work, not long afterward the Pennsylvania legislature passed a child labor law that sent thousands of children home from the mills, and kept thousands of others from entering the factory until they were fourteen years of age.

How the Women Sang Themselves out of Jail

The miners in Greensburg, Pennsylvania, went on strike for more wages. One day a group of angry women were standing in front of the mine, hooting at the scabs that were taking the bread from their children's mouths. The sheriff came and arrested all the women "for disturbing the peace." Of course, he should have arrested the scabs, for they were the ones who really disturbed it.

I told them to take their babies and tiny children along with them when their case came up in court. They did this and while the judge was sentencing them to pay thirty dollars or serve thirty days in jail, the babies set up a terrible wail so that you could hardly hear the old judge. He scowled and asked the women if they had some one to leave the children with.

I whispered to the women to tell the judge that miners' wives didn't keep nurse girls; that God gave the children to their mothers and He held them responsible for their care.

Two mounted police were called to take the women to jail, some ten miles away. They were put on an interurban car with two policemen to keep them from running away. The car stopped and took on some scabs. As soon as the car started the women began cleaning up the scabs. The two policemen were too nervous to do anything.

The scabs, who were pretty much scratched up, begged the

motorman to stop and let them off but the motorman said it was against the law to stop except at the station. That gave the women a little more time to trim the fellows. When they got to the station, those scabs looked as if they had been sleeping in the tiger cat's cage at the zoo.

When they got to Greensburg, the women sang as the car went through the town. A great crowd followed the car, singing with them. As the women, carrying their babies, got off the car before the jail the crowd cheered and cheered them. The police officers handed the prisoners over to the sheriff and both of them looked relieved.

The sheriff said to me, "Mother, I would rather you brought me a hundred men than those women. Women are fierce!"

"I didn't bring them to you, sheriff," said I, "'twas the mining company's judge sent them to you for a present."

The sheriff took them upstairs, put them all in a room and let me stay with them for a long while. I told the women:

"You sing the whole night long. You can spell one another if you get tired and hoarse. Sleep all day and sing all night and don't stop for anyone. Say you're singing to the babies. I will bring the little ones milk and fruit. Just you all sing and sing."

The sheriff's wife was an irritable little cat. She used to go up and try to stop them because she couldn't sleep. Then the sheriff sent for me and asked me to stop them.

"I can't stop them," said I. "They are singing to their little ones. You telephone to the judge to order them loose."

Complaints came in by the dozens: from hotels and lodging houses and private homes.

"Those women howl like cats," said a hotel keeper to me.

"That's no way to speak of women who are singing patriotic songs and lullabies to their little ones," said I.

Finally after five days in which everyone in town had been kept awake, the judge ordered their release. He was a narrow-minded, irritable, savage-looking old animal and hated to do it, but no one could muzzle those women!

On Suffrage

Mother Jones, despite her own emancipated ways and her strong feelings for womanhood, was never a suffragette. One time, when five hundred women arranged a dinner at which she was invited to speak, they were rather shaken to hear her views, for, as Mother Jones put it, "most of those women were crazy about women's suffrage. They thought that Kingdom-come would follow the enfranchisement of women."

"You must stand for free speech in the streets," I told them.

"How can we," piped a woman, "when we haven't a vote?"

"I have never had a vote," said I, "and I have raised hell all over this country! You don't need a vote to raise hell! You need convictions and a voice!"

Someone meowed, "You're an anti!"

"I am not an anti to anything which will bring freedom to my class," said I. "But I am going to be honest with you sincere women who are working for votes for women. The women of Colorado have had the vote for two generations and the working men and women are in slavery. The state is in slavery, vassal to the Colorado Iron and Fuel Company and its subsidiary interests. A man who was present at a meeting of the mine owners told me that when the trouble started in the mines, one operator proposed that women be disenfranchised because here and there some woman had raised her voice in behalf of the miners. Another operator jumped to his feet and shouted, 'For God's sake! What are you talking about! If it had not been for the women's vote the miners would have beaten us long ago!'"

Some of the women gasped with horror. One or two left the room. I told the women I did not believe in women's rights nor in men's rights but in human rights. "No matter what your fight," I said, "don't be ladylike! God Almighty made women and the Rockefeller gang of thieves made the ladies. I have just fought through sixteen months of bitter warfare in Colorado. I have been up against armed mercenaries but this old woman, without a vote, and with nothing but a hatpin has scared them.

"Organized labor should organize its women along industrial lines. Politics is only the servant of industry. The plutocrats have organized their women. They keep them busy with suffrage and prohibition and charity."

Struggle and Lose; Struggle and Win

The steel strike was over. That is, the men were forced back to work. Only in Bible stories can David conquer the giant Goliath.

But the strike is not over. Injustice boils in men's hearts as does steel in its caldron, ready to pour, white hot, in the fullness of time.

In West Virginia, in 1923, the miners of Logan County were again on strike. I went among the women in the tent colonies on the hills. The story of coal is always the same. It is a dark story. For a second's more sunlight, men must fight like tigers. For the privilege of seeing the color of their children's eyes by the light of the sun, fathers must fight as beasts in the jungle. That life may have something of decency, something of beauty— a picture, a new dress, a bit of cheap lace fluttering in the window—for this, men who work down in the mines must struggle and lose, struggle and win.

There is never peace in West Virginia because there is never justice. Injunctions and guns, like morphia, produce a temporary quiet. Then the pain, agonizing and more severe, comes again. So it is with West Virginia. The strike was broken.

But the next year, the miners gathered their breath for another struggle. Sometimes they lost their battle through their own crooked leaders. And once it was my duty to go before the rank and file and expose their leaders who would betray them. And when my boys understood, West Virginia's climate wasn't healthy for them.

Medieval West Virginia! With its tent colonies on the bleak

hills! With its grim men and women; When I get to the other side, I shall tell God Almighty about West Virginia!

In spite of oppressors, in spite of false leaders, in spite of labor's own lack of understanding of its needs, the cause of the worker continues onward. Slowly his hours are shortened, giving him leisure to read and to think. Slowly his standard of living rises to include some of the good and beautiful things of the world. Slowly the cause of his children becomes the cause of all. His boy is taken from the breaker, his girl from the mill. Slowly those who create the wealth of the world are permitted to share it. The future is in labor's strong, rough hands.

Elizabeth Gertrude Stern

EXCERPTS FROM HER AUTOBIOGRAPHY
I AM A WOMAN—AND A JEW

ELIZABETH GERTRUDE STERN
1890–1954

Elizabeth Gertrude Stern, of Polish-Jewish ancestry, was born in a small Midwestern city in 1890 and grew up in its ghetto area.

Along with her two sisters and two brothers, she was raised in the Orthodox Jewish faith. In defiance of her father, who was an assistant rabbi, she married a non-Jew and their three children were raised without any religious instruction.

A strong advocate of women working outside the home, she was, at various times, a social worker, a saleswoman, a personnel director, a journalist and book writer, lecturer, and head of a leading settlement house.

"I was never," she declares in her autobiography, written when she was thirty-nine years old, "a leading feminist. I managed time to live, to be a wife, a mother and in charge of my home. I did my daily job, besides. Was it hard? Of course it was. Did it destroy my strength? Of course it did not. For it is nonsense, as any woman knows, to say that a woman's work—with her mind —outside her house, is harder than manual work in it."

She called her autobiography I Am a Woman—and a Jew and it was published in 1926 under the pseudonym of Leah Morton.

Going to the River

The first clear impression of my childhood is that of a warm day in summer. My mother, in her puffed sleeves and tight-fitting dress, walked near my father, in his long coat and high hat; for he was assistant to the rabbi in our city. We children—there were five of us—trudged behind our parents, looking neither to right nor left, but plodding steadily ahead. We dared not stop, for that would annoy father.

There was dimpled roly-poly Simeon; Etta, with her golden hair and Spanish skin—inherited from mother's own grandmother; Hannah, with her brown curls and sleepy hazel eyes exactly like our father's; Robert, the baby, all dark splendor like our father's father; and I, very tall for my age, very thin, with enormous brown eyes, an excessively high forehead that we all thought the acme of homeliness, and a funny nose that had neither the exquisite delicate curve of Hannah's, nor the round impudence of Simeon's.

Today I was so tired! I looked piteously at Mother, and she put her hand in her pocket, drew out a sweetmeat and, quietly, with her little dimpling smile, gave us each one. She put her finger on her lip, and went back to father.

It was a sin to eat the sweetmeats.

We were fasting that day and were not to eat, not even to wet our mouths with so much as a sip of water, until sundown.

I, who was thirteen, was particularly responsible for keeping the rule. I looked at my candy. My mother glanced back. Her face was mischievous and yet curiously sober under her "sheitel," the wig prescribed for pious Jewish women. It was as if she asked God to take lightly the sin we committed.

We came at last to the river's edge. Our father stood, waited a moment, and then prayed.

It was, surely, a strange sight. The river along which we stood was the Ohio. Great boats were steaming up its waters; giant loads of iron. Opposite our shore, far in the distance on the other side, burned furnaces of steel. The life of a new world was created here. And my father spoke in a tongue written more than five thousand years ago, prayed as his forefathers on an ancient river, the Jordan, had prayed, with the same simplicity and unaltered faith. He prayed that his sins should be washed away by the waters before us.

For it was for this reason that he had taken us all to the river, through the hot, long day. I looked into the muddy waters below us, and at my father. And I felt oddly numb. All my life I had so believed that, even when I resisted him, he was right. But today it seemed to me childish and perhaps even silly to be standing there, chanting that beautiful old tongue, the Hebrew, that I, too, had been taught, and asking that our sins be washed away.

Most of the people who lived near us were Catholics or Presbyterians, for ours was a small Scotch-Irish city. The Irish believed that if you told the priest what you had done, you would not be punished for your misdeeds.

The Presbyterians were so religious that, when they went to church on Sunday, they walked there and back, not using the street car.

These Presbyterians my father grudgingly approved; we Jews, also, did not ride on our Sabbath or our holy days; the Presbyterians had only copied us.

But when I told him one day of the Catholics, he looked down at me from his tall height, and said, "You can see how foolish and childish ignorant people are. A priest tells them that if they go to him and confess, he can forgive them. Can a sin be undone by a confession or even the wish to undo it?"

And yet here was my father, grave and pleading, sending our sins down the waters of the Ohio.

I looked at him, opened my mouth, but did not speak. I knew he would be angry.

From that day, however, I did not accept anything he told me about our faith until I analyzed it myself.

Friday Evenings

I used to tell myself that, when I was a big girl, sixteen perhaps, I would be free. I would do as I believed I ought then, and not as I was told.

I religiously observed all the rules of religious life, though they no longer meant anything to me. It was not necessary for me to observe them, for my father never supervised me. But it would have seemed to me I was untrue to the thing *he* believed if I failed to do as he believed.

I prayed three times a day—even taking my Hebrew book to high school, though I was terrified lest some fellow student should find what the book was through the words which my lips moved in study period.

I tied my handkerchief about my wrist on Saturday, rather than put it in my pocket; for the Law says one may not carry a handkerchief, even in a pocket, but clothing one may wear.

I did not eat meat on bread spread with butter, for milk and meat together are forbidden.

I did not speak to the Gentile boys at high school.

I thought of myself as very homely, as indeed I was. Hannah and Etta had grown to be lovely, in prescribed Semitic fashions, one plump and fair, the other like a languorous rose of Sharon. I looked like a studious boy who did not have enough to eat, and happened to be masquerading in pigtails.

In our biology class, our teacher, fair and plump and always slightly moist, spoke to us of animals, plants, amoeba, worms, and even the bony structure of a cat—and then closed the semester. But some of the girls told one another what they knew.

On Friday evenings others in the class went to a weekly party, but I was not permitted even to see them dance.

My mother did not permit the Gentile children in our little street to come into our home. It was not that their parents were working people—they were almost all mill workers—and our father a scholar. Mother did not wish Gentile children in the house because we could not afford to have them. Every time a Gentile child touched a dish, it was, in my father's eyes, defiled, and had to be thrown out.

It was simpler and wiser to forbid them the house, mother found.

She herself was conscientiously pious, and though she did not understand as much Hebrew as her daughters did, she religiously used it in daily prayer, and obeyed every one of the precepts a good housewife ought, as set down in the books.

We were poor, so poor that sometimes, to go to high school, I had to get up in the morning, wash my blouse and iron it; for I had no other.

After school I sewed for a neighbor, or taught Hebrew to a slow boy who was preparing to "enter the Covenant"—which I, as a mere female, had never been asked to do.

For lunch at high school I used to take bread and nothing else, and drink water. I used to pretend that I would not eat ice cream or candy as did the other girls, because they were not made by Hebraic laws regulating food; but I did not tell that I might have brought with me sweets so made by manufacturers of my own faith.

On Friday nights, however, I sat at the white tablecloth—the rest of the week it was checked—with my father sitting near the six glowing candles in the brilliantly polished brass candlesticks which my great-grandmother had lighted in her day, too. My mother wore the pretty close-fitting dress that was her "holiday dress," and a frilled apron over it, with handmade embroidery bordering its hem.

We all sat in spotless Sabbath cleanliness, and waited until the prayer over the homemade wine, and homemade bread, had been made by father and by each of the beggars he had collected after synagogue had closed.

Then we ate—gefullte fish, chicken soup, chicken boiled to the consistency of cheesecloth, sweets and nuts with raisins for dessert. Sometimes the beggars were very hungry. Once a wanderer from Rumania ate my portion, Etta's, and would have eaten Simeon's, too, but Simeon stopped him by a piteous wail. When the strangers ate my sisters' food and mine, mother would look at us, twinkle her dark eyes, and we would shrug resignedly, and eat white bread and wine, pretending we were not interested in food. But there was no need to pretend; the guests did not so much as notice us, who were only girls.

Learning to Dance

My father did not approve of my continuing high school. It was time for me to think of marrying a pious man. He and mother disagreed about it—their one quarrel.

It was perhaps due to my going to high school, mother said, gently and dubiously, that I wanted something new. I wanted to dance, to play, to have fun just like the other girls in my classes. I didn't mean to go to work at fourteen or fifteen, marry at sixteen, be a mother at eighteen and an old woman at thirty. I wanted a new thing—happiness. I was different from my sisters, who thought of marrying as soon as possible.

My mother drew her fine dark brows together. She took my face in her little hands, round and soft, in spite of her constant work. "You shall learn to dance," she said, "my daughter!"

And dance I did. I learned to dance in what, I suppose, was a dreadful public dance hall, for I paid a quarter a lesson there, once every Wednesday night, and I danced with the lady instructor when she thought of me; but I faithfully put my foot out— one, two, three, and turn—as the long line of men and women learned the steps of the waltz. I learned to two-step, and to schottische, and even—wild days, those—to do the barn dance. Mother took me to the hall, and came to take me back home at eleven.

Then I went to a dance. I went with Jack, a blue-eyed boy from my class, and wore a dress of mother's cut down and made to fit me. I did not tell her I was going with a Gentile. I simply told her I was going to a dance at school.

My swain met me after school, and we walked up together

to the chapel, there to talk until the pianist arrived, for we had no brass bands then. The room became crowded. He put out his arms, and said, "Shall we dance?"

Before me came my father's face, still and austere. I felt something chill me.

"Oh, Jack," I said. "I—I don't feel well. I'm going home." And home I went. I could not dance with a Gentile.

She went on to college, living with an aunt and uncle near the university buildings. At first she planned to become a doctor, then a writer, and then a social worker.

Leaving Home for All Time

I had heard that there was a school for social work, and that it was in New York. That was all I knew about it. During college I had saved a little money, barely enough to put me through one year of the school. I wrote, and was enrolled.

I broke every tie at home to do it.

My father insisted that it was time for me to marry. My aunts said the same. My sister Hannah and her husband were shocked that a girl of twenty-one planned to spend more time, wasting money, on just educating herself. My sister Etta, teaching school, felt that I might be doing the same. Only mother said nothing. She just listened. But I knew she did not disapprove.

My father called me into his study. "What is it you want?" he asked me. "You have a good home, and I think your mother and I have been kind to you in it. What are you seeking?"

I could not tell him that I wanted the same thing for which he had come to America. I wanted to live and act according to the faith I had, just as he wished it for himself. I wanted to be free to live as I believed, in every way. I wanted, first, the right to find out what I believed, what my faith was.

"If you go to New York," he said, "you will lose your Jewish spirit. What is this work for the poor? Is it work for their soul? Is it work for their religion? The synagogue will take care of its poor, and the rabbi. What sort of humanitarianism is it that does not see the need of each one's religion first of all?"

I waited, and then I answered, "I shall not lose my religion, father. I haven't had any for over two years."

He turned toward me, his face without color, his beard like gold brown flame. "You're a—you don't—you're not a Jewish woman?"

I answered, "I'm not anything you think, father. I've not been branded with a flaming iron. But I don't believe the way I used to any more."

"I warned your mother," he said quietly, "you would become lost to us if we let you have the education you wanted."

He left the room. He did not even bid me goodbye when I left for New York. All the time I was there, I received not a word from him, nor was his name mentioned in my mother's letters. I took summer courses, and worked in the winter between classes. The second year I did not return home before school.

Settlement Work and Anti-Semitism

When I had been going to high school, I had worked in the evening at a settlement, in charge of one of the clubs. My girls were nearly of age, and many of them lived in the streets near my home, for we did not move from the ghetto of our city to which my father had come when he first arrived as an immigrant. At social work school I specialized in settlement work because of my earlier experience in it. I wanted to get a position in some settlement house, at no matter how small a salary.

The school offered to help me find a job. It gave me a list of available openings, in the "Middle West and East." I asked why not in the West and South, and was told that it would not be advisable to try: "Jews are not usually wanted there."

The first opening was in a settlement in New York. The head worker, a harassed, middle-aged woman, met me herself, smiled affably, interviewed me, and then told me to come see her in a week.

In a week she interviewed me again, this time along with a board member who sat with her, a pretty young woman with dark, sweet eyes. "And you have had experience in club work?" the young woman asked, in a high, sweet voice.

"For more than two years," I told her.

"With girls? Or women, too? We may want you to have women, too."

"Just for a year with women, but a whole two years with girls," I said, "and with girls not easy to lead—Jewish immigrant girls."

"Jewish?" repeated the high, sweet voice, pausing on the word.

I explained that I had lived in the neighborhood, how well I knew the girls, and what I had been able to do.

"Oh, thank you very much for coming," said the sweet-faced board member. "We shall let you know in a week."

I waited a week, but did not hear from her and, when I called her up, was told that they were so sorry, but they had engaged a former candidate, one having experience with the sort of work they did—Protestant girls.

It was almost two months before I learned that I could not expect work in a settlement house as a Jewish worker. I gave up. I went to the school to ask what I could do. There was nothing to do but wait; perhaps a Jewish settlement house would want a Jewish worker. "But often," said the pleasant director of the "personnel department," "even Jewish settlements ask for non-Jewish workers, you see."

It was necessary to earn some money. I went to teach. I taught school in a foreign night school maintained by a labor organization— and my students were Jewish.

A New Job

Then, to my astonishment, I received a letter. I was offered a job. The head of one of the departments of a settlement house needed a "recreation and housing worker." The salary was tiny, but there was "maintenance" included. The name at the end was familiar; it was the name of a fellow-student at the school for social work, a graduate student who had done brilliant work in research.

He was in the office when I came in. I gave him my name, and then, before he could ask me further questions, I said, "I suppose you didn't see me in our big classes at the school. But we took the housing and children's lectures together. I want you to know I am a Jewess."

He nodded, absently. "And you are prepared to begin work at once?"

My work was not with Jewish people. It was to make a study of the homes of Polish people, to discover their various racial backgrounds, their reasons for coming to America, their social life here and so forth. I cannot, of course, speak Polish, and a young student whose native language that is was assigned to help me.

I liked my work. To gather the facts was like seeing a tapestry of history weave itself. My chief, Dr. Morton, was planning to write a book, and this was to be part of his material.

In the settlement I learned one thing—to be silent. There are few things that the social worker can do better than maintain discreet silence.

I found something else. In all my previous experience, the Gentile in contact with the Jew either resented him, patronized him or worshipped him as a super-being. These social workers, "non-Jews," when they worked with Jews, were genuinely fond of them, they found their characteristics, that were so often food for caricature or censure, lovable qualities that made them endearing. The emotional Jewess, too ready with affection and gratitude, was to them admirably appreciative. The studious little Jewish boys, mature when they should have been children at play, seemed to these social workers honorably eager for learning. Even the Jewish fear of poverty, that makes the Jew careful of his pennies, they found right and self-respecting.

Could it be, I wondered, that the Jew was disliked, feared, only when he was an equal?

Marrying the Chief

My chief, Dr. Morton, was the only male resident on the staff of the settlement house, and, although he was so young, and the others so ardently feministic, whatever he said was always greeted with a certain special respect. The elderly women who sat about the table at dinner would pause in their mutual enjoyment of gently clawing at one another as soon as he spoke.

His father had been a Frenchman, his mother an Englishwoman of good family. He was the only child, and though his youth was spent in America and he was, indeed, born in this country, many of his memories and some of his sympathies were with the two older countries from which his parents came, and to which, I found, they had often taken him as a child.

He liked my work and he enjoyed hearing me speak, too. To him it was not a question of the work I did being done by a Jewess or a Gentile. It was well done, if not brilliantly. Perhaps no one, therefore, made me so happy as did he.

For here, in his office, I was not a girl representing a race. I was not a Jewish maiden responsible to a race, as at home. I wasn't a strange young woman who took jests about her people with sensitive, chilling quiet. I was a worker, with an intelligent mind, doing the work of the community.

We completed our study, analyzed our findings. Dr. Morton wrote the thin pamphlet that gave the results of our work. In its preface he had a short sentence: "The research in housing was done by Miss Leah ———." It was the first time I had so much as thought of seeing my name in a book, a real book. I used to look at that page and that line, and find it as if it glowed in light out of all the surrounding text.

And then one day Dr. Morton turned to me and said, "Perhaps you have heard that I have been asked to go to another project and take charge of their housing and recreation work there?"

It did not seem strange to me when he asked me to go with him and to be his wife. I had known for months that I loved him. That was why I could speak to him of those things I felt most deeply, and why I felt the peace of my work.

I did not think, when he asked me to be his wife, that he was not a Jew. I only felt that, if he asked me at that moment to pour out my life for him, in our kiss, it would have been sweet to do so. I did not think then, that he was a man and I a woman. He was my love and I his.

It is needless to tell how bitter was the cry of my father. I felt, for a time, that I could not endure to hurt him so. I broke my engagement.

My lover came to me and asked me if I had not him, too, to consider. He asked me just two things: if I loved him and if I was certain of his love for me. I knew the answer to both. So we were married, and in my own city, with my mother giving us her blessing. Her eyes were swollen with crying, but she spoke her blessing to us and called my husband "my son." That is what he has always been to her.

Curiously enough, my husband's people did not even find our marriage incongruous. They were artists, writers, cosmopolites. They had no real religious or, perhaps, even national ties. They accepted me for his wife and a woman, and I entered our new life.

The settlement house was shocked, however. It was apparent that they felt a good man had gone astray. Our head worker gave us a set of silver butter-knives, and said she hoped we would be happy, but she spoke as if she hoped we would repent.

Not one of my cousins in New York would come to see us. I had married a Gentile. But my brother Simeon sent me a very lovely little jade god that he must have sought for weeks, and with it came a note: "New gods."

Honeymoon and Conflicts

My lover was a Doctor of Philosophy and twenty-seven, and I a staid social worker, a Bachelor of Arts and twenty-two, but the education of our time had not thought it necessary to teach two young people how to be man and wife.

For a little while we were just brother and sister, only clinging close to one another, seeking one another. It may seem curious, but this is just as it was with us.

Then we bought an old medical book and read about marriage, and made our marriage solemn and complete. It is strange that so much has been written about the love of men and women not married, and so little of the love of man and wife!

We were young, and we were well. We were mysterious and beautiful to one another. I had, all my life, thought of the womanhood in me as something rather to be deprecated; a man, I knew, of my faith, must absent himself from his wife, as from defilement, at certain holy times of his life. And always, she must humbly beg God to pardon her that she is a woman. Had I not read, in the prayer book, the words my brothers, my father, all my uncles, spoke daily—thanking God they were not women?

But my love found me God-worthy because I was a woman. He found me holy.

Of children we did not speak. At that time birth control was not a word spoken. There was a sin called preventing the conception of children, but Margaret Sanger had not yet appeared. Girls became pregnant and had abortions.

But married women had as many children as fate chose. If they were much advanced they might live only at certain times with their husbands, and have protection against pregnancy so. That was mentioned, in an awed whisper, by prurient-minded, but kindly, married women, to young brides.

I did not know whether I wanted to be a wife, living in my husband's love, or a woman building her career.

My husband was modern. He said I must do anything I wanted to do, just as he did what he chose. Only, he added, *he* must earn our living. Whatever *I* did I could do without thinking whether it was successful or not; only whether it made me happy.

I took his hands in mine, I recall, and put his palms against my cheek. But he did not feel how hot my cheeks were against his palms. I kissed him. But as I kissed him then, I know I wished he had said that my work was as *practically* a need to me, as his— that it was as essential to our life as his. If work was to be judged by him by its practical value to his life and mine, I would have wanted him to see that which I chose to do, too, as practical, and helpful as his own.

He thought I might do social work as a volunteer, without pay—

I was, however, determined not to do that, not to be an amateur. I wanted to work just as he did. I would not be happy otherwise, I told him.

He took me on his knee then, kissed me, and told me I was a violent feminist. But he liked it in me, I know. In fact, he was, himself, in his quiet way a feminist, too. I had been a member of a committee to arrange a meeting for Anna Howard Shaw, and when she came, he did the then striking thing of standing at the door of the little hall and greeting each person as she came in—for alas, only one other man came. I did not go with the suffrage party to Washington on any of its trips, but I saved money from lunches, and sent it to them anonymously.

"So you want a career," he smiled, "and a husband tacked on?"

It was a striking thing, but I said, seriously, "Haven't you one with me tacked on?"

He kissed me then, and laughed, very tenderly indeed.

Supporting the Family

In 1917, during the influenza epidemic, her husband came down with the sickness, and it took a long time for him to recover his strength. They already had two children.

I knew I must get work. Not now, work to fill the time, or to "express myself," but to earn the living of my family.

I could not teach in this state, for I had not passed the examinations here. What could I do?

In the columns of the newspapers I searched daily for the answer. One day it came. A big store wanted a "personnel director."

The store manager spoke to me, smiled to hear I was a college woman, was interested but not antagonistic when he heard I was married, saying, "The war's changing that. We need a lady in this job. Some one that will make a high-class appearance. Now, if you prove to be what we're looking for, there's a big job ahead of you! But first, you must know the work. First you must be a saleswoman."

I was sent to the linen department, then promoted to the dress department, from that to the hats and then to the books and to jewelry.

I knew merchandise, sales people, and most of all, the psychology of the customer.

They were not easy months. But I had a problem not different from those many of the other women were facing. A great many of the women had mothers or husbands dependent on them. Almost all the married women had children whom they supported.

From them I learned how to adjust things a bit.

I taught my young daughter how to feed her little brother and prepared breakfast the night before. I would set it out on the table, and let her feed her brother, only dressing him myself in the morning. With a woman near the school, I arranged for lunches for the children, and felt easier about them. I had an old German woman come in to help my husband at noon, and take him out on the porch. Sometimes I would run out to my home at noon, missing lunch, but having the peace of seeing that everything was well with my husband. He was tired and lonely, miserable as he grew well enough to understand our situation; but he said nothing. He would only sit, thin, and drawn, waiting until the children came home.

Presently he was able to hobble around. He used a cane and a crutch and managed to see the children at noon. He was able to help me with them in the morning. We did not speak of my working. But he suffered the more bitterly because of it, I knew well enough.

When we had a sale at the store, I could not come home on the usual hour, because of the need to put the things away, to add up sales slips, and to arrange the aisles neatly for the following morning.

Moving Up

After some months she was promoted to the post of personnel director of the store.

I was shown to my office, a pretty little office with a real desk, a typewriter, a telephone and a tray—for what? For letters. It looked like the wire tray in which I drained dishes.

Forty dollars a week. I had never earned so much before. My own desk. My own telephone. My own letter tray. I was a woman with a career for certain now.

I was thin. I pinned my skirt all around me because it would slip down. My coat fitted me like a loose sack. I wore high collars and ties, and so the boniness of my neck did not show, but the hollows in my cheeks were plain enough. But my thinness was "stylish." I was not cringing and thin; it was a proud thinness.

Oh, say what one wanted, it was a great thing!

I was successful. I was as successful as a man.

I held my little son and daughter close. I put my arms around my husband's thin shoulders, and when I leaned my cheek against his he did not see my eyes were happy. After all, these three people were my own—and I was their source not only of love, but of life. That, too, I could do for them.

I wanted to write. Sometimes it seemed to me my fingers burned with the need to write. I wanted to write the things I had seen and lived, that I had learned from women about men, from the men with me.

But I pressed all that back. Writing did not pay. And, first of all, I must prove that I was really able to take care of this family of mine, this little group, these three that I loved best. These—and my mother. I would send her a gift, something out of my new salary.

My husband lifted his head, grown gray these past months of illness. "I am getting well. It won't be long you'll have to do this."

My heart sank then. Didn't he know, didn't he see, that I wanted this to be—not something I did just because he had to drop the burden of our support, but because I was as capable as he of assuming that burden?

"Little woman," he whispered. "Forgive me."

I cried then. I cried because he asked me to forgive him because he was sick. But, yes, I cried too because he felt it necessary to ask that of me; because he did not feel that I was as hungry for the full measure of human responsibility as he was.

"I like to work," I said then, quietly. "I enjoy—being important," I said with a half laugh.

He laughed then, relieved. He was delighted that I spoke like a child about my work. He kissed me and held me close.

"No Jews in This Store"

In my marriage and in the social life which my husband and I shared, it had been for me to determine the values expressed in the fact that I was a Jewess. In business, however, I found now, abruptly, the values were set; they were old. I had thought from my experience it meant nothing that one were Jewish. "One makes one's own divisions when one is Jewish," I had once said.

Now the store manager called me in, beamed and said that the dance I had arranged for the employees the night before had been a success.

"I'm planning another," I said. "Have you any suggestions?"

He nodded. "Yep. One criticism. Nice dance. Nice crowd. But there were too many Jews from other stores. Cut that out."

I stared at him.

He said, briskly, "Lots of the girls said they saw sales girls from Oppenheimer's and Fields', too. Too many Jews. Spoil our class."

"But," I said, "you remember no one came here except by invitation. Those girls were invited by our men and our girls."

He smiled then. "Well, tell them they can't repeat."

I sat quietly, and then I heard my lips speak: "I couldn't do that. If I do that, I'll have to say I won't come either, for I am a Jewess myself."

He looked startled. "Really?"

I rose then. "I never thought it made any difference. But if it does, I'll leave today. Anyhow, I'll leave at the end of the month."

He protested, spoke rapidly of the respect he had for the Jewish business men in the city, took back what he said and explained that he was just expressing the feeling of their customers. Hadn't I noticed how few Jewish employees they had? It was just a matter of business, that was all. As for me, no one knew I was Jewish, and it didn't matter at all.

I nooded quietly and went up to my office.

I was determined to leave by the first.

If my people suffered a handicap, I could, of course, seek shelter under my husband's non-Jewishness. But I did not, of course. I went to look for another post. I'd work with Jews.

I went to Fields', one of the two Jewish stores in the city. They told me they could not take a married woman.

I went to Oppenheimer's, and was told they could not take a' Jewish woman. They had "mostly Jewish girls," it was true. But Jewish girls "respected a Christian woman better," they found.

I' came home, and my husband was at the door waiting for me. "Read this letter," he said, his voice husky. "Read it." It was a request for him to undertake new work in another city, a new work in a new field, where he would be not only a well-paid executive, but the pioneer to blaze a trail. He could begin in two or three months if he wished, when he was fully recovered. He would have a staff of five.

"Will you—take a job on my staff?" he said.

"As a paid employee?" I asked, my arm tightening in his.

He smiled down then: "As assistant, on my staff."

We went over his budget. My salary of $1000 would be half what I was receiving before. And I would be in a work utterly alien to my interests.

Side by Side?

How false it would be to say, though, I was not thrilled the day my husband and I walked to the office together. I was a "new woman"; I'd just read a paper at our club on the "right of the girl-child to her own personality"—and yet I was happy to lose mine in my husband's. My husband was well. He was well enough to go to work at once. The months that had stretched so long in prospect were over. He could command not only his body now, but his mind. He believed in himself again.

I was very modern. I believed in my equal rights as a woman. But I was happy that day because he was head again of our life and of our home. That was something I yielded to him as I gave my love to him. I knew that he was wiser than I, that he knew more than I. I had a certain knack that he had not, of knowing people, understanding them. He was impersonal. He was not interested in people, but in ideas that would help people. My gift would be brought to work side by side with his, as I lived side by side with him. That was how I would "express my personality."

Much of the work I could do at home, and our children were therefore under my direct care a great part of the day. Things were pleasant for us, for although living was high, our joint salary of $4500 a year was enough to meet our simple requirements. We paid our debts and we were able, for the first time in our lives, to go to the movies, even to a play, without feeling that we ought to ask protection from our selfishness. We bought, at last, the bookcase we had wanted and the books we had said we wished to buy. We sent money to my mother, gifts for her birthday—and on Jewish holidays.

My husband's work was recognized and it was respected. I cut clippings about him from the papers when they appeared and showed them to our children.

Women wrote to ask me to join clubs interested in "women's points of view"; sometimes I was asked to speak about my husband's work from the "woman's standpoint."

One day in late winter, a long important envelope came with the name of a well-known woman in the corner. The letter told me that they were planning to open a "health center" in the industrial neighborhood where the Hungarians lived. They would eventually open a camp also for children, and during the summer, clubs, classes and community activities would be developed. They wanted me to talk the matter over with them. The director's salary was stated. It was almost as much as that which my husband was receiving.

I thought over my teaching, my store work, my work with my husband. Curious. I had been an "executive"—why, for years. I had been doing these things that people thought valuable enough to train one for "a big job."

A New Stage

Although she did not take that "big job," six months later, when she was offered the position as head worker in a settlement house, she did so. After some years, her husband was offered a post in New York, and she resigned her position to go with him.

My children did not need me. I was thirty-eight. More than half my life had been lived. And I was doing nothing. I was fretting at the long days, bored with the long evenings. There was nothing for me to do now. My husband was earning an income big enough now for our needs.

I went to my desk, and there, like an old friend, stood an old typewriter. I had rented it for $5 for the first three months, and then for $12 a year. Finally, I had bought it, in installments, for $20.

I went to a magazine editor and asked to see him. We talked, and I found that all these years of my work were a mine on which I could draw, that I had been living through all these years, that I might build up a treasure from which I could draw my writing.

I received my first assignment, and another. I found other editors glad to have my work. At the end of the first year, I had earned almost three thousand dollars, as much as in the years I did social work. I earned it so easily! And it seemed criminal to have been so successful, for I was so happy in this work. I was happy in my work and in my home.

I am a Jewess, though I do not belong to any church, nor have my world enclosed among my people. The divisions are in my memories, in my heart.

Last winter I sat at the table of a famous governor, discussing with him a national crisis that I was sent to write about.

We touched, unexpectedly, an international angle of it and I said, "Do you think that will be hard on us Jews?"

He told me, startled, he had not thought me a Jewess.

I answered, *"I know I am."*

I am that before everything. Perhaps not in my work or in my daily life.

But in that inner self that cannot change. I belong to my people. My life is only a tiny atom of their long history.

Curiously, although she used the pseudonym of Leah Morton for her autobiography, she had already published under her own name of Elizabeth G. Stern the memoir My Mother and I, *which appeared in 1917 with a foreword by Theodore Roosevelt. Again using her own name, she collaborated with Leon Stern in* Friend at Court, *which was brought out in 1923. Then, under the by-line of Eleanor Morton, she published in 1937* Not All Laughter, *subtitling it "A Mirror to Our Times." Her last book, also under the name of Eleanor Morton, was* The Women in Ghandi's Life; *it appeared in 1953. She died the following year.*

Mountain Wolf Woman

EXCERPTS FROM HER AUTOBIOGRAPHY

MOUNTAIN WOLF WOMAN
1884–1960

Mountain Wolf Woman, a Winnebago Indian, was born in Wisconsin, the youngest of eight children in the family. She was seventy-three years old when she permitted her adopted kinswoman, anthropologist Nancy Lurie, to tape-record reminiscences of her life. Mountain Wolf Woman spoke first in Winnebago, and then immediately translated her own words into English.

Traditionally, the Winnebagos subsisted by male hunting and female gardening and wild food gathering. As the tribes were driven from their homelands by white settlers, they gradually became dependent on a cash economy and went to work harvesting crops for white employers or producing basketry and beadwork for the increasing tourist trade. Mountain Wolf Woman became a basket-maker, although this is not remarked upon in her autobiography. As Dr. Lurie notes in an appendix to the reminiscences, "Mountain Wolf Woman takes her productive activity so much for granted that she does not even mention that during most of her adult life and throughout her wide travels and changes of residence she has made baskets to obtain cash. She implies that men are the providers and speaks approvingly of her second husband as industrious. In plain fact, she has always contributed a large amount to the family income and furthermore exercised primary control over family finances."

Mountain Wolf Woman died in her sleep, at her home in Black River Falls, Wisconsin, after having caught pneumonia and pleurisy while sealing up windows and preparing her house for the winter months. Her life spanned traveling by pony to flying in an airplane, from baking bread in the embers of an open fire to purchasing a television set for her young granddaughters as an inducement for them to stay home evenings.

Earliest Recollections

Mother said she had me at our grandfather's home,—at East Fork River. We lived there in the spring, April, at the time they were making maple sugar. She said that after a while the weather became pleasant, everything was nice and green, and we moved from this place back to where we usually lived,—at Levis Creek, near Black River Falls. There father built a log house. I suppose it took a long time to build it because mother said the log house was newly finished when I walked there for the first time. There, where we regularly lived, mother and father planted their garden.

In the summer that followed the second spring,—after my first birthday, we went to Black River Falls. Mother, oldest sister White Thunder and I went to town. We were returning and mother carried me on her back. I was restless and she had taken me off the cradleboard. I remember being there on mother's back. We crossed a creek and I saw the water swirling swiftly. Mother said, "Ahead is your older sister." A woman was walking in front of us carrying an empty cradleboard. I saw that she held up her skirt just high enough to wade through the water. After that I forgot.

Once I asked mother if that ever happened. I told her what I had seen.

"Oh," mother said, "I remember, that was your oldest sister White Thunder who carried your empty cradle on her back.—Do you remember that?"

"Yes," I said.

"You were probably frightened," she said, "and perhaps that is why you remember."

White Thunder was the oldest child in our family and Crashing Thunder was second. Then followed second older sister Wihanga Bald Eagle. Next was Henaga, the second son; he was called Strikes Standing. Then came the third son, Hagaga, and he was called Big Winnebago. Haksigaga, the third daughter, died when she was quite small. They did not know how this death came about. However, there was an old lady who was related to my mother, and any time that my father brought home deer from hunting, summer, winter, any time my father killed deer, this old lady got some. Yet, the old lady was envious of my mother about her share of the meat. Mother used to say that she poisoned Haksigaga. She killed her because of jealousy about meat. Next was the fourth daughter Hinakega. She was called Distant Flashes Standing. And then I was the last child.—"Poor quality" they used to say of that one.

According to Winnebago tradition, children were given sex-birth order names along with more formal names aligned with their particular clan. After the fourth son, succeeding boys' names were diminutive forms of that given the fourth, while succeeding girls' names after the fourth daughter were diminutive forms of the third girl's name. Mountain Wolf Woman's sex-birth order name was Haksigaxunuga. She was usually called Haksigaxununinka—Little Fifth Daughter—because of her small size.

Once when I recalled that we camped at a place where the country was very beautiful, Mother said, "You were then about two years old." I remember there was a fish there. That beautiful country where we were camping was at Black River Falls at the old depot in back of what is now the general store. There was not a house around.

We lived there in the spring of the year and my father fished. I suppose all of the Indians fished. There my father speared a big fish, an enormous fish, a sturgeon. When my father brought it home, carrying it over his shoulder, the tail dragged on the ground.

He brought it back to where we were living. There I saw this big fish that looked like a man with a big fat belly, lying on his side with his belly protruding. I remembered that and then I forgot.

We must have been camped at the Black River where the bank is very steep. There they lost me and everybody helped my mother look for me.

They were afraid I fell in the water there, over on that high bank. There was an old lady and my mother brought her tobacco. Anything they asked of her, the old lady always knew the answer. They brought her tobacco because she was able to do this. Before she was able to say anything, somebody came back from town. They all said, "Sigaxunuga is lost! Sigaxunuga is lost!"

Then the person who returned from town said, "Oh, her father is in town with his daughter, leading her by the hand."

It seems that father was going toward town. On the way there was a cow which was probably tethered there and I was frightened by that cow. Father did not know that I was following along behind him. Evidently, in fear of that cow, I began to cry. Then father led me by the hand. He went to town, taking me with him. In time we returned, and so they brought me back alive.

We probably went back to our home again that spring as it must have been at that time that I was sick. I was very sick and my mother wanted me to live. She hoped that I would not die, but she did not know what to do. At that place there was an old lady whose name was Wolf Woman and mother had them bring her. Mother took me and let the old woman hold me.

"I want my little girl to live," mother said, "I give her to you. Whatever way you can make her live, she will be yours."

That is where they gave me away.

That old lady wept. "You have made me think of myself. You gave me this dear little child. You have indeed made me think of myself. Let it be thus. My life, let her use it. My grandchild, let her use my existence. I will give my name to my own child. The name that I am going to give her is a holy name. She will reach an old age."

There they named me with a Wolf Clan name; Xechaciwinga

they called me.—It means to make a home in a bluff or a mountain, as the wolf does, but in English I just say my name is Mountain Wolf Woman.

Family Work

In March we usually traveled to the Mississippi River close to La Crosse, sometimes even across the river, and then we returned again in the last part of May. We used to live at a place on the edge of the Mississippi called Caved In Breast's Grave.

My father, brother-in-law and brothers used to trap there for muskrats. When they killed the muskrats my mother used to save the bodies and hang them up there in great numbers. When there were a lot of muskrats then they used to roast them on a rack.

They prepared a lot of wood and built a big fire. They stuck four crotched posts into the ground around the fire and placed poles across the crotches. Then they removed the burning wood and left the embers. They put a lot of fine wood crisscross and very dense on the frame. On this the muskrats were roasted, placed all above the fireplace.

As the muskrats began roasting, the grease dripped off nice and brown and then the women used long pointed sticks to turn them over and over. The muskrat meat made a lot of noise as it cooked.

When these were cooked, the women put them aside and placed some more on the rack. They cooked a great amount of muskrats. —When they were cooled, the women packed them together and stored them for summer use.

In the spring when my father went trapping on the Mississippi and the weather became very pleasant my sister once said, "It is here that they dig yellow water lily roots."

So, we all went out, my mother and sisters and everybody. When we got to a slough where the water lilies were very dense, they took off their shoes, put on old dresses and went wading into the water.

They used their feet to hunt for the roots. They dug them out with their feet and then the roots floated up to the surface.

Eventually, my second oldest sister happened upon one. My sister took one of the floating roots, wrapped it about with the edge of her blouse and tucked it into her belt.

I thought she did this because it was the usual thing to do. I saw her doing this and when I happened upon a root I took it and did the same thing. I put it in my belt too.

And then everybody laughed at me! "Oh, Little Siga is doing something! She has a water lily root in her belt!"

Everybody laughed at me and yelled at me. My sister had done that because she was pregnant.

I suppose she did that to ward off something because she was pregnant. Thus she would not affect the baby and would have good luck finding the roots. Because I saw her do that, I did the same thing, and so they teased me.

When they dug up a lot of roots in this fashion they put them in a gunny sack, filling it half full and even more. Then we carried them back to camp and my mother and all my sisters scraped them.

The roots have an outside covering and they scraped that off and sliced them.—They look something like a banana. The women then strung the slices and hung them up to dry in order to store them. They dried a great amount, flour sacks full. During the summer they sometimes cooked them with meat and they were really delicious.

Feasting and Fasting

At the place where they hunted, father and older brother killed as many deer as they would need for a feast.

They set aside ten deer on a high, narrow rack made for storing meat. They cut down crotched poles and set them up in a rectangle with poles across the crotches and other poles forming a platform, similar to the open-sided square shelters used as sun shades, but narrower and higher. They put the deer on it and covered them with the hides.

Father used to hold big feasts, ten fireplaces they said. The row of fireplaces used to stretch off into the distance. Many Indians attended and father used to feed a wigwam full of people.

There we would dance all night. Sometimes children were named at feasts. This is what they used to do time and again. Sometimes, those who had been fasting would then eat at the feast.

My older brother Hagaga fasted in the woods.—Brother was allowed to return at the time of the feast since at that time one who fasts for a vision may eat.

My older sister Hinakega and I also used to fast.

In Dr. Lurie's notes to the reminiscences, she observes that girls fasted without the specific intention of the vision quest although occasionally they were so blessed. The basic idea was that such appeals to the spirits would reward girls in a general way with a long and useful life, a good husband, and a large family of helathy children.

They used to make us do this. We would blacken our cheeks and would not eat all day. That was at the time of the hunting I have told about, before we returned from hunting. We used to blacken our cheeks with charcoal at the time father left in the morning to go hunting. We used coals from the fire to blacken our cheeks and we did not eat all day.

I used to play outside but my older sister used to sit indoors and weave yarn belts. When my father returned from hunting in the evening he used to say to us, "Go cry to the Thunders." When father was ready to eat he would give us tobacco and say to us, "Here, go cry to the Thunders."

Just as it was getting dark my sister and I used to go off a certain distance and she would say to me, "Go stand by a tree and I am going to go farther on." We used to stand there and look at the stars and cry to the Thunders. This is what we used to sing:

> "Oh, Good Spirits
> Will they pity me? Here am I, pleading."

We used to sing and scatter tobacco, standing there and watching the stars and the moon.

Many American Indian tribes held tobacco to be a sacred plant. It was offered to the spirits to ward off evil and also used as a gift of thanks for benefits supposedly derived from the supernatural.

We used to cry because, after all, we were hungry. We used to think we were pitied by the spirits. We really wanted to mean what we were saying.

When we finished with our song we scattered tobacco at the foot of the tree and returned home. When we got back home father ate and we ate too. We did not eat all day, only at night, and when we had finished eating we put the dishes away.

Then father used to say, "All right, prepare your bedding and go to bed and I will tell you some stories."

I really enjoyed listening to my father tell stories. Everybody, the entire household, was very quiet and in this atmosphere my father used to tell stories. He used to tell myths, the sacred stories, and that is why I also know some myths. I do not know all of them any more, I just remember parts of stories.

Becoming a Woman

The family went on a short hunting trip. After that they went off to find cranberries and on our return we stopped at the home of grandfather Naqi-Johnga. There it was that mother told me how it is with little girls when they become women.

"Some time," she said, "that is going to happen to you. From about the age of thirteen years this happens to girls. When that happens to you, run to the woods and hide some place. You should not look at any one, not even a glance. If you look at a man you will contaminate his blood. Even a glance will cause you to be an evil person. When women are in that condition they are unclean."

Once, after our return to grandfather's house, I was in that condition when I awoke in the morning.

Because mother had told me to do so, I ran quite far into the woods where there were some bushes. The snow was still on the ground and the trees were just beginning to bud. In the woods there was a broken tree and I sat down under this fallen tree.

I bowed my head with my blanket wrapped over me and there I was, crying and crying. Since they had forbidden me to look around, I sat there with my blanket over my head. I cried.

Then, suddenly I heard the sound of voices. My sister Hinakega and my sister-in-law found me. Because I had not come back in the house, they had looked for me. They saw my tracks in the snow, and by my tracks they saw that I ran. They trailed me and found me.

"Stay here," they said. "We will go and make a shelter for you," and they went home again.

Near the water's edge of a big creek at the rapids of East Fork River, they built a little wigwam. They covered it with canvas. They built a fire and put straw there for me, and then they came to get me.

There I sat in the little wigwam. I was crying. It was far, about a quarter of a mile from home. I was crying and I was frightened. Four nights they made me sleep there. I never ate. There they made me fast. That is what they made me do. After the third time that I slept, I dreamed.

There was a big clearing in my dream. I came upon it, a big, wide open field, and I think there was a rise of land there. Somewhat below this rise was the big clearing. There, in the wide meadow, there were all kinds of horses, all colors. I must have been one who dreamed about horses.

Marriage

As a teen-age girl, Mountain Wolf Woman attended a Lutheran mission school.

I stopped attending school. They took me out of school. Alas, I was enjoying school so much, and they made me stop. They took me back home. They had let me go to school and now they made me quit. It was then that they told me I was going to be married.

I cried but it did not do any good. What would my crying avail me? They had already arranged it. As they were telling me about it my mother said, "My little daughter, I prize you highly. You alone are the youngest child. I prize you highly but nothing can be done about this matter. It is your brothers' doing. You must do whatever your brothers say. If you do not do so, you are going to embarrass them. They have been drinking again, but if you do not do this they will be disgraced. They might even experience something unfortunate." Thus mother spoke to me. She rather frightened me.

To go against the brothers' decision would be to break a taboo, and the men would suffer for it.

My father said, "My little daughter, you do not have very many things to wear, but you will go riding on your little pony. You do not have anything, but you will not walk there."

I had a little horse, a dapple gray kind of pony that was about three years old. Father brought it for me and there the pony stood.

They dressed me. I wore a ribbon embroidery skirt and I wore one as a shawl. I wore a heavily beaded binding for the braid of hair down my back, and I had on earrings. It looked as if I were going to a dance.

It was the custom among Winnebago women to wear as many as five or six pairs of long earrings.

That man was sitting nearby. He started out leading the pony and I followed after. When we reached a road that had high banks on the side he mounted the horse and I got on behind him.

That is the way he brought me home. We rode together. That is how I became a daughter-in-law.

As a daughter-in-law I arrived. When I arrived he had me

go in the wigwam and I went in and sat down. They told me to sit on the bed and I sat there.

I took off all the clothing that I was wearing when I got there. I took it all off. I laid down a shawl and whatever I had, all the finery, I put on it; beads, the necklaces, clothing, even the blouse that I was wearing.

Finally, the man's mother came in. Outside the wigwam there were canvas-covered wigwams standing here and there. The woman took the things and left.

There were women sitting all about outside. They were his female relatives. They divided the things among themselves. As they distributed the things around, everybody contributed something in return.

Two or three days from the time of my arrival they took me back with four horses and a double shawl so full of things they could barely tie the corners together. They took me home and later I received two more horses, so they gave me six horses in all.

Young married couples frequently remained with the wife's family for a while, the husband working for them, but when they began to have children of their own, they left—going back to the husband's family or setting up near them.

That is how they used to arrange things for young women in the past. They made the girls marry into whatever family they decided upon. They made the arrangements. That is the way they used to do.

At the time that my mother was combing my hair and I was weeping at the prospect of becoming a daughter-in-law she told me, "Daughter, I prize you very much, but this matter cannot be helped. When you are older and know better, you can marry whomever you yourself think that you want to marry." Mother said that to me and I did not forget it!

In the first place, before they made me get married, my older brother had been drinking and was asleep. I guess he slept there all day and when he awoke, that man they made me marry, who was not a drinker, was there.

He sat there using his hat to fan away the mosquitoes from my brother's face. That is why they made me marry that man. My brother awoke and he surmised, "He is doing this for me because I have sisters. That is what he is thinking to himself." So they made me marry that man. That is what the Indians used to do in the past.

Mountain Wolf Woman determined that her own children would not have arranged marriages, and all her children chose their own mates.

Leavetaking

That man was very easily aroused to jealousy of other men. He used to accuse me of being with other men. That made me angry. I hated him. He used to watch me too.

So, I said to him one time, "No matter how closely you watch me, if I am going to leave you, I am going to leave you! There are a lot of things right now that I do not like."

It was considered acceptable among the Winnebago for a wife to leave a jealous husband.

But that man was jealous. He used to accuse me of having affairs with other men, even my own male relatives. I hated him. Then when my second daughter was an infant I wanted to go to Black River Falls. They said there was going to be a powwow there.

We arrived there in a two-seated buggy I had which belonged to my mother and father. I owned a horse but we left my horse behind and used a horse that belonged to his family. We also used the new harness that his parents owned.

Soon after we arrived, father and mother left for Nebraska. Father was sick and they said he might get better if he went there. So they went to Nebraska.

When the powwow was over and the people were going home, he said, "Well, are we not going to return?"

"No," I said to him, "for my part, I am not going back."

"Well," he said, "we have to take back the things that we borrowed. We brought a horse of theirs. After all, it belongs to them."

"And you belong to them too," I said. "Take the horse and let him carry the harness on his back and ride him and go home," I told him. "Leave the wagon here for me, it belongs to my mother and father."

That man stayed around for a while but I would not go back so he finally left.

As for myself, I went to my grandmother. We had our own tent. "Grandmother," I said, "I am going to borrow some things."

"All right," she said, "I am caring for the baby."

I said to her, "When I come back, we are going to move."

My sister was also going to move. I went to the mission, to my niece, the wife of Bright Feather. I said to her, "Niece, I came to borrow something."

"All right," she said, "what did you come to borrow?"

"A one-horse harness and buggy hitch."

"All right, wherever they are take them. What am I using them for? They are yours," she said.

There was a wagon going back to the powwow ground and I asked the people to carry the harness and the hitch. I rode back with them too.

When we got back, the man with the wagon attached the single hitch to the buggy and took our double harness and hitch. He said, "I will take these back to your niece at the mission because I will be going that way. They can probably use them."

That is what he did. The only horse I had was a big one and I let him pull the buggy alone. I packed everything and headed for the home of my older sister. Thus I left that man.

I took grandmother with me in the one-horse buggy. We stayed for a while where one of my sisters was living at Black River Falls. She was there at a cranberry marsh where picking was in progress.

Then I moved again to a different marsh where another older sister lived. We used to pick cranberries there every day.

We stayed there and picked cranberries until the end of the season, and then we moved back to my other older sister's place. There my older brother asked for the use of a horse, and there Four Women, my brother's wife, gave me some things: a blouse decorated with little silver brooches, a very nice one, and necklaces and a hair ornament and earrings. They gave me much finery and again I became a woman to be envied.

I remained single and lived at my sister's place all winter long. Whenever there was a feast that winter my niece Queen of Thunder and I used to go to the feast, and we used to dance. There they accused me concerning a man. They gossiped at the winter feast. Alas, I was not even looking at any men.

The man that they linked me with began writing letters to me. Well, after all, they were accusing him of it.

Second Marriage

Then it became spring and in the spring we camped near Black River Falls where my sister was staying. I went to town to get some things and as I was coming back somebody behind me said, "Sister, sister."

I stopped. It was my oldest brother. "Sister," he said, "whoever is saying things to you, I would like it if you do as he says. Little sister, your first husband was not any good. You would never have had any place for yourself and at his home you would have always been doing all the work. But this lad who is now talking to you lives alone. He knows how to care for himself. If you make a home someplace, then I will have someplace to go to visit." That is what my older brother said to me.

I did not say anything. And just standing right there was that man, Bad Soldier.

The name Bad Soldier did not mean that he was cowardly, quite the reverse: "bad" in the sense of fierce.

I still did not say anything.

Then my brother went toward town and the man followed me

home. We arrived at the place where my sister was living temporarily near Black River Falls.

After we arrived, the man took the water pail and went after some water. He got the water and brought it back and then later he went into the woods and brought back a lot of firewood.

He began working for us, and sister was smiling broadly about it.

He said to me, "If you would like it, tomorrow we can go to the courthouse and get our marriage license. If she hears about it, she will give up." He was talking about his wife.

He had a wife and I did not want him, but he was persistent in courting me. "We will go to the courthouse and take out a marriage license so that woman cannot bother us," he said.

So that is what we did, we went to the courthouse and took out a marriage license. It was early spring when we did this.

Mountain Wolf Woman's sister Hinakega had no children of her own and she looked after the two daughters of Mountain Wolf Woman's first marriage. By her second husband, Mountain Wolf Woman had two sons who died, then a daughter was born and then another son, and eventually a large brood. They went west to where the Sioux lived in South Dakota. Bad Soldier rented a house for the family to live in, and he went to work for a white man who had a big general store. His job was to drive a truck out to the Sioux reservation and trade food for cowhides. After a few years Mountain Wolf Woman became homesick for her own people and they returned first to her parents in Nebraska and then to Black River Falls in Wisconsin. The children went to school there and the family all became Christians.

Widowhood

It was April 24, 1936, that my husband died. We told the undertaker, who took him and brought him back. They buried him in the mission cemetery. In the evenings I used to think as I sat there, "Maybe this is not happening to me. Maybe this is not happening to me. Maybe he did not die." Children of mine died. My relatives died, father and mother. My older sister died. But it was never as hard as when my man died.

"Maybe I am having a bad dream," I thought. I would pinch my arms to see if I were awake.

Then the doctor came. He used to come and see my husband when he was sick. He came there and said to me, "Have them dismantle this house and build it someplace else. Your husband had double pneumonia and tuberculosis set in. That is what he died of. Tear down your house and build it over. You have a lot of small children. Don't stay in this house."

So, one time I was sitting on the roof of the house with a hammer. The roof was covered with tarpaper and I was trying to get it off. A car came by and then it turned back. It was one of my nephews and another young man. "What are you doing, auntie?" he said.

"This house has to be taken apart to move some place else. I am supposed to get it rebuilt. I am trying to get the roof off."

"Oh, auntie, we will do that for you," he said, and they got out of the car and started to work. They took the whole house apart. They stacked the boards. They went home in the evening and they came back early in the morning. They took everything apart and piled the boards on top of each other. They said, "Auntie, where are you going to have them build the house?"

"Well, let it be on the mission grounds," I said. Then they told me that it was partly government land.

"Put it there," I said, and pointed out the spot to them and they hauled the boards over there. They certainly did me a great kindness.

The government agent and another man came. "How big a house do you want?" they said.

Across from the airport there was a little square house. I told them that I always liked that house. It was not too big and it was not too small. "I have a lot of little children and when my married children come back with their families I am crowded. Two of them with their children come home to visit. I used to be crowded. That square house is just about the right size. I like that one."

They went to look at it. They said I was right, that house was the right size. They made my little square house. There was no one around who could build houses, so the Indian boys got together and made the house. They finished it for me and I am living there today.

I am old, but though I am seventy-three years old my body is strong. I make my own clothing. There are women living here and there today who are younger than I am who are helplessly infirm. I am able to move about.

Where I live I care for myself. My children sometimes say they would take care of me. "Wait a while," I say, "until I am older. You can take care of me when I can no longer take care of myself."

I always say I am happy the way I am and that I hope to continue in that fashion. If I am good to people, after while, when my life ends, I expect to go to heaven. I say no more.

Attic

ATTIC

Here is a miscellany, an attic section for the reader to browse in. It consists of documents that did not fit into the framework proper yet were too valuable to omit altogether.

They range from the charming, prim little diary kept one summer by a Puritan girl in the 1700s to the stark testimony of a black woman in Reconstruction days testifying to the terror of the Ku Klux Klan. The speech of Elizabeth Cady Stanton was given to me by her granddaughter, Nora Stanton Barney, shortly before she died in 1971. Other materials—advertisements, records of speeches, letters, official historical statements—I have collected over the years and offer here as a sampling to which the reader may add independently.

As a last introductory note, I would be remiss if I did not warn the reader anew of Governor John Winthrop's observation in 1640:

"A godly young Woman of special parts, who was fallen into a sad infirmity, the loss of her understanding and reason, which had been growing upon her divers years by occasion of giving herself wholly to reading and writing and had written many books. Her husbande was loath to grieve hir; but he saw his error when it was too late. For if she had attended to her household affairs, and such things as belong to woman, and not gone out of hir way and calling to meddle in such things as are proper for men whose minds are stronger, she had kept hir Wits, and might have improved them usefully and honorably."

From The Private Journal kept by
MADAM KNIGHT
on a Journey
From Boston to New-York
in the year 1704

Sarah Kemble Knight grew up in Boston, married, and was widowed there. She took in boarders, used part of her house for a shop, taught children of the neighborhood to write, and also acted as a legal secretary and amateur lawyer—copying court records, drafting legal documents, writing letters for people. When she was thirty-eight, she made a trip on horseback that lasted five months; the journey was filled with mishaps and discomforts, but she was determined to get to New York to deal with the settlement of a cousin's estate. Every night, before going to sleep, she wrote down her account of that day's stage of the trip. The journal was first printed in 1825; the opening and closing journal entries follow here.

Monday, Octb'r. ye second, 1704.

About three o'clock afternoon, I begun my Journey from Boston to New-Haven, being about two Hundred Mile. My Kinsman, Capt. Robert Luist, waited on me as farr as Dedham, where I was to meet ye Western post. . . . We come to Billinges, where I was to Lodg.

My Guide dismounted and very Complasantly help't me down and shewd the door, signing to me with his hand to Go in; wch I Gladly did. But had not gone many steps into the Room, ere I was Interogated by a young Lady I understood afterwards was the Eldest daughter of the family, with these, or words to this purpose. (*viz.*) Law for mee—what in the world brings You here at this time a night!—I never see a woman on the Rode so Dreadfull late, in all the days of my versall life. Who are You? Where are you going! I'me scar'd out of my witts, with much now of the same Kind. . . .

I told her shee treated mee very Rudely, and I did not think it my duty to answer her unmannerly Questions. But to get ridd of them, I told her I come here to have the post's company with me tomorrow on my Journey, etc. Miss Star'd awhile, drew a chair, bid me sitt. And then run upstairs and putts on two or three Rings, (or else I had not seen them before), and returning, sett herself just before me, showing the way to Reding, that I might see her Ornaments, perhaps to gain the more respect. But her Granam's new Rung sow, had it appeared, would affected me as much. . . .

I pray'd Miss to shew me where I must Lodg. Shee conducted me to a parlour in a little back Lento, wch was almost fill'd with the bed that lay on it; on wch having Stretcht my tired Limbs, and lay'd my head on a Sad-Coloured pillow, I began to think on the transactions of ye past day.

Tuesday, October ye third.

About 8 in the morning, I with the Post proceeded forward without observing anything remarkable; And about two, afternoon, Arrived at the Post's second stage. . . .

Here, having called for something to eat, ye woman bro't in a Twisted thing like a cable, but something whiter; and laying it on the bord, tugg'd for life to bring it into a capacity to spread; wch having with great pains accomplished, she serv'd in a dish of Pork and Cabage, I suppose the remains of Dinner. The sause was of a deep Purple, wch I tho't was boil'd in her dye Kettle; the bread was Indian, and every thing on the Table service Agreeable to these. I, being hungry, gott a little down; but my stomach was soon cloy'd, and what cabbage I swallowed serv'd me for a Cudd the whole day after.

The final entry.

January 6th.

Being now well Recruited and fitt for business I discoursed the persons I was concerned with, that we might finnish in order to my return to Boston. They delayed as they had hitherto done hoping to tire my Patience. But I was reslute to stay and see an End of the matter let it be never so much to my disadvantage. So January 9th they come again and promise the Wednesday following to go through with the distribution of the Estate which they delayed till Thursday and then come with new amusements. But at length by the mediation of that holy good Gentleman, the Rev. Mr. James Pierpont, the minister of New Haven, and with the advice and assistance of other of our Good Friends we come to an accomodation and distribution, which having finished though not till February, the man that waited on me to York taking the charge of me I sit out for Boston. We went from New Haven upon the ice (the ferry being not passable thereby). We went forward without any thing Remarkable till we come to New London. I stayed a day here Longer than I intended by the Commands of the Honbble Govenor Winthrop to stay and take a supper with him whose wonderful civility I may not omitt. The next morning I crossed ye Ferry to Groton—And that night Lodgd at Stonington and had RostBeef and pumpkin sause for supper. The next night at Haven's and had Rost fowle, and the next day we come to a river which by Reason of ye Freshetts coming down was swelld so high wee feared it impassible and the rapid stream was very terryfying. However we must over and that in a small Cannoo . . .

Wee were now in the colony of the Massachusetts and taking Lodgings at the first Inn we come to had a pretty difficult passage the next day which was the second of March by reason of the sloughy ways then thawed by the Sunn. . . . And the next day being March 3d wee got safe home to Boston, where I found my aged and tender mother and my Dear and only Child in good health with open arms redy to receive me, and my Kind relations and friends flocking in to welcome mee and hear the story of my transactions and travails I having this day bin five months from home and now I cannot fully express my Joy and Satisfaction. But desire sincearly to adore my Great Benefactor for thus graciously carying forth and returning in safety his unworthy handmaid.

Mary Osgood Sumner, of Puritan descent, grew up in Georgia in the eighteenth century. Married at eighteen, she was widowed at twenty, and some time after was drowned at sea. Among her effects were sermon notes and a "Monitor," wherein she had kept an account of her misdeeds and duties performed during one summer period of her girlhood.

The misdeeds were listed on the "Black Leaf" as follows:

July 8. I left my staise on the bed.
"   9. Misplaced Sister's sash.
"   10. Spoke in haste to my little Sister, spilt the cream on the floor in the closet.
"   12. I left Sister Cynthia's frock on the bed.
"   16. I left the brush on the chair; was not diligent in learning at school.
"   17. I left my fan on the bed.
"   19. I got vexed because Sister was a-going to cut my frock.
"   22. Part of this day I did not improve my time well.
"   30. I was careless and lost my needle.
Aug. 5. I spilt some coffee on the table.

The entries of duties performed were carried on the "White Leaf":

July 8. I went and said my Catechism today. Came home and wrote down the questions and answers, then dressed and went to the dance, endeavored to behave myself decent.
"   11. I improved my time before breakfast; after breakfast made some biscuits and did all my work before the sun was down.
"   12. I went to meeting and paid good attention to the sermon, came home and wrote down as much of it as I could remember.
"   17. I did everything before breakfast; endeavored to improve in school; went to the funeral in the afternoon,

attended to what was said, came home and wrote down as much as I could remember.

" 25. A part of this day I parsed and endeavored to do well and a part of it I made some tarts and did some work and wrote a letter.

" 27. I did everything this morning same as usual, went to school and endeavored to be diligent; came home and washed the butter and assisted in getting coffee.

" 28. I endeavored to be diligent to-day in my learning, went from school to sit up with the sick, nursed her as well as I could.

" 30. I was pretty diligent at my work to-day and made a pudding for dinner.

Aug. 1. I got some peaches for to stew after I was done washing up the things and got my work and was midlin Diligent.

" 4. I did everything before breakfast and after breakfast got some peaches for Aunt Mell and then got my work and stuck pretty close to it and at night sat up with Sister and nursed her as good as I could.

" 8. I stuck pretty close to my work to-day and did all that Sister gave me and after I was done I swept out the house and put the things to rights.

" 9. I endeavored to improve my time to-day in reading and attending to what Brother read and most of the evening I was singing.

STORY

from an eighteenth-century book called
The Father's Gift, or How to be Wise and Happy

There were two little Boys and Girls, the Children of a fine Lady and Gentleman who loved them dearly. They were all so good and loved one another so well that every Body who saw them talked of them with Admiration far and near. They would part with any Thing to each other, loved the Poor, spoke kindly to Servants, did every Thing they were bid to do, were not proud, knew no Strife, but who should learn their Books best, and be the prettiest Scholar. The Servants loved them, and would do any Thing they desired. They were not proud of fine Clothes, their Heads never ran on their Playthings when they should mind their Books.

They said Grace before they ate, and Prayer before going to bed and as soon as they rose. They were always clean and neat, would not tell a Fib for the World, and were above doing any Thing that required one. God blessed them more and more, and their Papa, Mama, Uncles, Aunts and Cousins for their Sakes. They were a happy Family, no one idle; all prettily employed, the little Masters at their Books, the little Misses at their Needles. At their Play hours they were never noisy, mischievous or quarrelsome. No such word was ever heard from their Mouths as "Why mayn't I have this or that as well as Betty or Bobby." Or "Why should Sally have this or that any more than I;" but it was always "as Mama pleases, she knows best," with a Bow and a Smile, without Surliness to be seen on their Brow.

They grew up, the Masters became fine Scholars and fine Gentlemen and were honoured; the Misses fine Ladies and fine Housewives. This Gentleman sought to marry one of the Misses, and that Gentleman the other. Happy was he that could be admitted into their Company. They had nothing to do but pick and choose the best Matches in the Country, while the greatest Ladies for Birth and most remarkable for Virtue thought themselves honoured by the Addresses of the two Brothers. They all married and made good Papas and Mamas, and so the blessing goes round.

AN EIGHTEENTH-CENTURY SPINSTER IN BOSTON
from Weeden's *Economic and Social History of New England*

It is true, an *old* (or superannuated) maid in Boston is thought such a curse, as nothing can exceed it (and looked on as a *dismal spectacle*); yet she, by her good nature, gravity, and strict virtue, convinces all (so much as the fleering Beaus) that it is not her necessity, but her choice, that keeps her a Virgin. She is now about thirty years (the age which they call a *Thornback*), yet she never disguises herself, and talks as little as she thinks of Love. She never reads any Plays or Romances, goes to no Balls, or Dancing-match, as they do who go (to such Fairs) in order to meet with Chapmen. Her looks, her speech, her whole behavior, are so very chaste, that but one at Governor's Island, where we went to be merry at roasting a hog, going to kiss her, I thought she would have blushed to death.

Our *Damsel* knowing this, her conversation is generally amongst the Women . . . so that I found it no easy matter to enjoy her company, for some of her time (save what was taken up in Needle-work and learning French, etc.,) was spent in Religious Worship. She knew Time was a dressing-room for Eternity, and therefore reserves most of her hours for better uses than those of the Comb, the Toilet, and the Glass.

A YOUNG GIRL'S DAY'S WORK, 1775
from Sydney G. Fisher's *Men, Women and Manners in Colonial Days*

Fix'd gown for Prude,—Mend Mother's Riding-hood, Spun short thread,—Fix'd two gowns for Welsh's girls,—Carded tow,—Spun linen,—Worked on Cheese-basket,—Hatchel'd flax with Hannah, we did 51 lbs. apiece,—Pleated and ironed,—Read a Sermon of Dodridge's,—Spooled a piece,—Milked the Cows,—Spun linen, did 50 knots,—Made a Broom of Guinea wheat straw,—Spun thread to whiten,—Set a Red dye,—Had two Scholars from Mrs. Taylor's,—I carded two pounds of whole wool and felt,—Spun harness twine,—Scoured the pewter,—Ague in my face,—Ellen was spark'd last night,—spun thread to whiten—Went to Mr. Otis's and made them a swinging visit—Israel said I might ride his jade—Prude stayed at home and learned Eve's Dream by heart.

Advertisement in
The Pennsylvania Packet

September 23, 1780

Wanted at a Seat about half a day's journey from Philadelphia, on which are good improvements and domestics, a single Woman of unsullied Reputation, an affiable, cheerful, active and amiable Disposition; cleanly, industrious, perfectly qualified to direct and manage the female Concerns of country business, as raising small stock, dairying, marketing, combing, carding, spinning, knitting, sewing, pickling, preserving, etc., and occasionally to instruct two Young Ladies in those Branches of Oeconomy, who, with their father, compose the Family. Such a person will be treated with respect and esteem, and meet with every encouragement due to such a character.

A FEW RULES OF ETIQUETTE
from Alice Morse Earl's *Child Life in Colonial Days*

Never sit down at the table till asked, and after the blessing.
Ask for nothing; tarry till it be offered thee.
Speak not.
Bite not thy bread but break it.
Take salt only with a clean knife.
Dip not the meat in the same.
Hold not thy knife upright but sloping, and lay it down at the
  right hand of plate with blade on plate.
Look not earnestly at any other that is eating.
When moderately satisfied leave the table.
Sing not, hum not, wriggle not.
Smell not of thy Meat; make not a noise with thy Tongue, Mouth,
  Lips, or Breath in Thy Eating and Drinking.
When any speak to thee, stand up.
Say not I have heard it before.
Never endeavor to help him out if he tell it not right.
Snigger not; never question the Truth of it.

A BRIDE IN NEW YORK—1800

My head is almost turned, and yet I am very happy. I am enraptured with New York. You cannot imagine anything half so beautiful as Broadway, and I am sure you would say I was more romantic than ever, if I should attempt to describe the Battery,—the fine water prospect,—you can have no idea how refreshing in a warm evening. The gardens we have not yet visited; indeed, we have so many delightful things to see 'twill take me forever. My husband declares he takes as much pleasure in showing them to me as I do in seeing them; you would believe it if you saw him.

I went shopping yesterday, and 'tis a fact that the little white satin Quaker bonnets, cap-crowns, lined with pink or blue or white, are the most fashionable that are worn. But I'll not have one, for if any of my old acquaintance should meet me in the street, they would laugh: I would if I were they.

I have been to two of the Columbia gardens, near the Battery, a most romantic place, it is enclosed in a circular form and has little rooms and boxes all around, with chairs and tables, these full of company; the trees are all hung with lamps, twinkling through the branches; in the centre is a pretty little building with a fountain playing continually, and the rays of the lamps on the drops of water gave it a cool sparkling appearance that was delightful. This little building, which has a kind of canopy and pillars all around the garden, had festoons of colored lamps, that at a distance looked like large brilliant stars seen through the branches; and placed all around were marble busts, beautiful little figures of Diana, Cupid and Venus, which by the glimmering of the lamps, partly concealed by the foliage, give you an idea of enchantment.

As we strolled through the trees, we passed a box that Miss Watts was in. She called to us, and we went in, and had a charming refreshing glass of ice cream, which has chilled me ever since. They have a fine orchestra and have concerts here sometimes.

We went on toward the Battery. This is a large promenade by the shore of the North River: there are rows and clusters of trees in every part, and a large walk along the shore, almost over the water, gives you such a fresh delightful air, that every evening in summer it is crowded with company. Here, too, they have music playing in boats on the water of a moonlight night.

I am in raptures, as you may imagine, and if I had not grown sober before I came to this wonderful place, it would have turned my head.

Correspondence by Dolly Madison

Two letters from Dolly Madison show strikingly her mental coming of age. In the first, all frivol and frippery, there is, nevertheless, a sense of selective order. In the second, she is clearly aware of her role in historic events, not unlike Lady Bird Johnson taking shorthand notes for the future.

1. A Letter from Philadelphia, 1791

And now, my dear Anna, we will have done with judges and juries, courts, both martial and partial, and we will speak a little about Philadelphia and the fashions, the beaux, Congress, and the weather. Do I not make a fine jumble of them? What would Harper or beau Dawson say were they to know it, ha, ha,—mind you laugh here with me. Philadelphia never was known to be so lively at this season as at present; for an accurate account of the amusements, I refer you to my letter to your sister Mary.

I went yesterday to see a doll, which has come from England, dressed to show us the fashions, and I saw besides a great quantity of millinery. Very long trains are worn, and they are festooned up with loops of bobbin and small covered buttons, the same as the dress; you are not confined to any number of festoons, but put them according to your fancy, and you cannot imagine what a beautiful effect it has. There is also a robe which is plaited very far back, open and ruffled down the sides, without a train, even with the petticoat. The hats are quite a different shape from what they used to be: they have no slope in the crown, scarce any rim, and are turned up at each side, and worn very much on the side of the head. Several of them are made of chipped wood, commonly known as cane hats; they are all lined: one that has come for Mrs. Bingham is lined with white, and trimmed with broad purple ribbon, put round in large puffs, with a bow on the left side. The bonnets are all open on the top, through which the hair is passed, either up or down as you fancy, but latterly they wear it more up than down; it is quite out of fashion to frizz or curl the hair, as it is worn perfectly straight.

Earrings, too, are very fashionable. The waists are worn two inches longer than they used to be, and there is no such thing as long sleeves. They are worn half way above the elbow, either drawn or plaited in various ways, according to fancy; they do not wear ruffles at all, and as for elbows, Anna, ours would be alabaster, compared to some of the ladies who follow the fashion; black or a colored ribbon is pinned round the bare arm, between the elbow and the sleeve.

Some new-fashioned slippers for ladies have come made of various colored kid or morocco, with small silver clasps sewed on; they are very handsome, and make the feet look remarkably small and neat. Everybody thinks the millinery last received the most tasty seen for a long time.

All our beaux are well; the amiable Chevalier is perfectly recovered, and handsomer than ever. You can have no idea, my dear girl, what pleasant times I have; there is the charming Chevalier, the divine Santana, the jolly Vicar, the witty and agreeable Fatio, the black-eyed Lord Henry, the soft, lovemaking Count, the giggling, foolish Duke, and sometimes the modest, good Meclare, who are at our house every day. We have fine riding parties and musical frolics.

2. *From the Mistress of the White House*

Tuesday, August 23, 1814.

Dear Sister: My husband left me yesterday morning to join General Winter. He inquired anxiously whether I had courage or firmness to remain in the President's house until his return on the morrow, or succeeding day, and on my assurance that I had no fear but for him, and the success of our army, he left, beseeching me to take care of myself, and of the Cabinet papers, public and private. I have since received two despatches from him written with a pencil. The last is alarming, because he desires that I should be ready at a moment's notice to enter my carriage and leave the city; that the enemy seemed stronger than had at first been reported, and it might happen that they would reach the city with the intention of destroying it.

I am accordingly ready; I have pressed as many Cabinet papers into trunks as to fill one carriage; our private property must be sacrificed, as it is impossible to procure wagons for its transportation. I am determined not to go myself until I see Mr. Madison safe, so that he can accompany me, as I hear of much hostility to him. Disaffection stalks around us. My friends and acquaintances are all gone, even the Colonel with his hundred who were stationed as a guard in this enclosure. French John (a faithful servant), with his usual activity and resolution, offers to spike the cannon at the gate, and lay a train of powder, which would blow up the British, should they enter the house. To the last proposition I positively object, without being able to make him understand why all advantages in war may not be taken.

Wednesday morning, twelve o'clock—Since sunrise, I have been turning my spy-glass in every direction, and watching with unwearied anxiety, hoping to discover the approach of my dear husband and his friends; but alas! I can descry only groups of military, as if there was a lack of arms, or of spirit to fight for their own fireside.

Three o'clock—Will you believe it, my sister? we have had a battle or skirmish near Bladenburgh, and here I am still within sound of the cannon! Mr. Madison comes not. May God protect us! Two messengers, covered with dust, come to bid me fly; but here I mean to wait for him.

At this late hour a wagon has been procured, and I have had it filled with plate, and the most valuable portable articles, belonging to the house. Whether it will reach its destination, the "Bank of Maryland," or fall into the hands of British soldiery, events must determine. Our kind friend Mr. Carroll, has come to hasten my departure, and in a very bad humour with me, because I insist on waiting till the large picture of General Washington is secured, and it requires to be unscrewed from the wall. This process was found too tedious for these perilous moments; I have ordered the frame

19. A "morning negligee" worn in 1862.

20. The Working Women's Protective Union hearing a complaint against a sewing-machine dealer.

21. Ladies' and children's bathing and walking suits, 1874.

Young Girls

Mrs. Pinkham is a true friend to young girls, who naturally hesitate to communicate their private afflictions to the male physician.

Chlorosis, or Green Sickness, is a disorder noted in young girls about a year after the first menses. The symptoms are a heavy, tired condition, and a dislike of wholesome food. Dark greenish circles appear round the eyes, the patient seems bloodless, is apt to be dizzy, the heart palpitates, fainting spells occur, the menses are irregular, the head aches, there are pains in the back and hips, dyspepsia appears, and there is gas in the bowels.

Take Lydia E. Pinkham's Blood Purifier alternately with her Vegetable Compound and be cured.

to be broken, and the canvas taken out. It is done and the precious portrait placed in the hands of two gentlemen of New York for safe keeping. And now, dear sister, I must leave this house, or the retreating army will make me a prisoner in it by filling up the road I am directed to take. When I shall again write to you, or where I shall be tomorrow, I cannot tell!

Dolly

FASHIONABLE EDUCATION—1821
by Reverend Timothy Dwight

Miss, the darling of her father and the pride of her mother, is taught from the beginning to regard her dress as a momentous concern. She is instructed in embroidery merely that she may finish a piece of work, which from time to time is to be brought out, to be seen, admired, and praised by visitors; or framed, and hung up in the room, to be still more frequently seen, admired and praised. She is taught music, only that she may perform a few times, to excite the same admiration, and applause, for her skill on the forte piano. She is taught to draw, merely to finish a picture, which, when richly framed, and ornamented, is hung up, to become an altar for the same incense.

The reading of girls is regularly lighter than that of boys. When the standard of reading for boys is set too low, that for girls will be proportionately lowered. Where boys investigate books of sound philosophy, and labour in mathematical and logical pursuits; girls read history, the higher poetry, and judicious discourses in morality, and religion. When the utmost labour of boys is bounded by history, biography, and the pamphlets of the day: girls sink down to songs, novels, and plays.

Of this reading what, let me ask, are the consequences? By the first novel which she reads, she is introduced into a world, literally new. Instead of houses, inhabited by mere men, women and children, she is presented with a succession of splendid palaces, and gloomy castles inhabited by tenants, half human and half angelic, or haunted by downright fiends. Every thing in the character and circumstances, of these beings comes at the wish, or the call of the enchanter. Whatever can supply their wants, suit their wishes, or forward, or frustrate, their designs, is regularly at hand. The heroes are as handsome, as dignified, as brave, as generous, as affectionate, as faithful, and as accomplished, as he supposes will satisfy the demands of his readers. At the same time, they have always a *quantum sufficit* of money: or, if not, some relation, dies at the proper time, and leaves them an ample supply. Every heroine is, also a compound of all that is graceful and lovely. Her person is fashioned 'by the hand of harmony.' Her complexion outvies the snow, and shames the rose.

I know, that this education is expressly attempted with a view to superior refinement: but it is not a refinement of the taste, the understanding, or the heart. It is merely a refinement of the imagination; of an imagination, already soft, and sickly, of a sensibility, already excessive; of a relish, already fastidious. To a genuine perfection of taste it bears no more resemblance, than the delicate white of decay to the native fairness of complexion; or than the blush of a hectic to the bloom of health.

From *The New England Farrier*—1827

For Female Weakness or Weaknesses
Take two or two and a half pails full of double tansy closely
packed in a pot, put on a tin still, draw out two quarts of essence,
add a quarter of spirits or less, so as to keep it, cork it up. Take a
glass at a time, half an hour before eating, two or three times a day,
and thus continue till you take a quart or more. If you use single
tansy you must use twice the quantity above mentioned.

For Weakly Obstructions in the Female Sex
Take hearts ease herbs, spikenard roots, with the pith out, a small
part of blood root, turkey root, wild liquorice, a few roots of white
pond lilies, a good parcel of female flowers, so called. . . . This is
one of the finest of roots for the female use in the world. Take
double the quantity of this, and equal parts of the others, make a
syrup of them, boil them in fair water until all the substance is out,
strain it off, sweeten it with honey, add as much rum to it as will
keep it from souring. . . . Drink half a gill going to bed every
night.

To Cure Hard Drinking
Take Roman wormwood, gather it in the full of the moon when it
is in the blossom, and in the morning when the dew is on; dry it one
day in the sun, then under cover until it is dry, roll it up in paper,
then put it into a tight place, and make a bitter of this by putting
it into water—drink this frequently and when you are faint—so
continue one year, and it will deliver you from the desire of ardent
spirit. This is called Roman wormwood, because it cured the
Romans of a stinking breath.

To Kill Worms in Children

Take sage, boil it with milk to a good tea, turn it to whey with alum or vinegar, and give the whey to the child, if the worms are not knotted in the stomach, and it will be a sure cure. If the worms are knotted in the stomach, it will kill the child.

TURN-OUT—1836
by Harriet Hanson Robinson
From *Loom and Spindle* Published by Thomas Y. Crowell
in 1898

One of the first strikes of cotton-factory operatives that ever took place in this country was that in Lowell, in October 1836. When it was announced that wages were to be cut down, great indignation was felt, and it was decided to strike, en masse. This was done. The mills were shut down, and the girls went in procession from the several corporations to the grove on Chapel Hill, and listened to "incendiary speeches" from early labor reformers.

One of the girls stood on a pump, and gave vent to the feelings of her companions in a neat speech, declaring that it was their duty to resist all attempts at cutting down the wages. This was the first time a woman had spoken in public in Lowell, and the event caused surprise and consternation among her audience. It was estimated that as many as twelve or fifteen hundred girls turned out, and walked in procession through the streets. They had neither flags nor music, but sang songs.

My own recollection of this first strike (or "turn-out," as it was called) is very vivid. I worked in a lower room, where I had heard the proposed strike fully, if not vehemently, discussed. I had been an ardent listener and naturally I took sides with the strikers. When the day came on which the girls were to turn out, those in the upper rooms started first, and so many of them left that our mill was at once shut down. Then when the girls in my room stood irresolute, uncertain what to do, asking each other, "Would you?" or, "Shall we turn out?" and not one of them having the courage to lead off, I, who began to think they would not turn out, after all their talk, became impatient, and started on ahead, saying with childish bravado, "I don't care what you do, I am going to turn out, whether any one else does or not," and I marched out, and was followed by the others.

The agent of the corporation where I then worked took some small revenge on the supposed ring-leaders, on the principle of sending the weaker to the wall; my mother was turned away from the boarding-house, that functionary saying, "Mrs. Hanson, you could not prevent the older girls from turning out, but your daughter is child, and her you could control."

It is hardly necessary to say that so far as results were concerned this strike did no good. The dissatisfaction of the operatives subsided, or burned itself out, and though the authorities did not accede to their demands, the majority returned to their work, and the corporation went on cutting down wages.

THE FACTORY GIRL

No more shall I work in the factory
To greasy up my clothes,
No more shall I work in the factory
With splinters in my toes.

> CHORUS: It's pity me, my darling,
> It's pity me, I say.
> It's pity me, my darling,
> And carry me away.

No more shall I hear the bosses say,
"Boys, you'd better daulf,"
No more shall I hear those bosses say,
"Spinners, you had better clean off."

CHORUS

No more shall I hear the drummer wheels
A-rolling over my head;
When factory girls are hard at work,
I'll be in my bed.

CHORUS

No more shall I hear the whistle blow
To call me up so soon;
No more shall I hear the whistle blow
To call me from my home.

CHORUS

No more shall I see the super come,
All dressed up so fine;
For I know I'll marry a country boy
Before the year is round.

CHORUS

No more shall I wear the old black dress,
Greasy all around;
No more shall I wear the old black bonnet,
With holes all in the crown.

CHORUS

From *Catalogue of the Alabama Female Institute Tuscaloosa, Alabama—1837*

Junior Class—First Year

History of the United States; Mental Arithmetic; English Grammar and Parsing; French History; Written Arithmetic; Grecian History; Sacred and Ancient Geography; Roman History.

Middle Class—Second Year

Natural Philosophy; Geometry; English History; Modern Geography, physical and political, with the use and drawing of Maps; Botany; Natural Theology; Philosophy of Natural History.

Senior Class—Third Year

Intellectual Philosophy; Ecclesiastical History; Rhetoric; Algebra; Evidences of Christianity; Astronomy and the use of the Globes; Chemistry; Moral Philosophy; Critical Reading, and Analysis of English Poets.

Calisthenics, Vocal Music, Composition, Letter Writing, and other general exercises, together with the daily study of the Bible or Sacred History, will be continued during the whole course, as parts of the regular system of education. Familiar instruction will also be given upon Female Manners and Deportment; Female Biography and Mythology; Logic; Political Economy; Geology; Mineralogy and other departments of useful female knowledge.

Every young lady on entering the Institute will be familiarly examined and her department and studies assigned according to attainments previously made.

At the close of each session, according to the established plan of the Institute, each pupil is examined privately, with a view to ascertain the amount of useful, communicable knowledge actually acquired.

MEN AND WOMEN
From *Woman in the Nineteenth Century*—1845
by Sarah Margaret Fuller Ossoli
Born in Cambridgeport, Mass., 1810
Perished by Shipwreck, Fire Island Beach, N. Y., 1850

If men look straitly to it, they will find that, unless their lives are domestic, those of the women will not be. A house is no home unless it contain food and fire for the mind as well as for the body. The female Greek, of our day, is as much in the street as the male to cry, "What news?" We doubt not it was the same in Athens of old. The women, shut out from the market-place, made up for it at the religious festivals. For human beings are not so constituted that they can live without expansion. If they do not get it in one way, they must in another, or perish.

As to men's representing women fairly at present, while we hear from men who owe to their wives not only all that is comfortable or graceful, but all that is wise, in the arrangement of their lives, the frequent remark, "You cannot reason with a woman,"—when from those of delicacy, nobleness, and poetic culture, falls the contemptuous phrase "women and children," and that in no light sally of the hour, but in works intended to give a permanent statement of the best experiences,—when not one man, in the million, shall I say? no, not in the hundred million, can rise above the belief that Woman was made *for Man*,—when such traits as these are daily forced upon the attention, can we feel that Man will always do justice to the interests of Woman? Can we think that he takes a sufficiently discerning and religious view of her office and destiny *ever* to do her justice, except when prompted by sentiment,—accidentally or transiently, that is, for the sentiment will vary according to the relations in which he is placed? The lover, the poet, the artist, are likely to view her nobly. The father and the philosopher have some chance of liberality; the man of the world, the legislator for expediency, none.

Under these circumstances, without attaching importance, in themselves, to the changes demanded by the champions of Woman, we hail them as signs of the times. We would have every arbitrary barrier thrown down. We would have every path laid open to Woman as freely as to Man. Were this done, and a slight temporary fermentation allowed to subside, we should see crystallizations more pure and of more various beauty. We believe the divine energy would pervade nature to a degree unknown in the history of former ages, and that no discordant collision, but a ravishing harmony of the spheres, would ensue.

Yet, then and only then will mankind be ripe for this, when inward and outward freedom for Woman as much as for Man shall be acknowledged as a *right,* not yielded as a concession. As the friend of the Negro assumes that one man cannot by right hold another in bondage, so should the friend of Woman assume that Man cannot by right lay even well-meant restrictions on Woman. If the Negro be a soul, if the woman be a soul, apparelled in flesh, to one Master only are they accountable. There is but one law for souls, and, if there is to be an interpreter of it, he must come not as man, or son of man, but as son of God. Were thought and feeling once so far elevated that Man should esteem himself the brother and friend, but nowise the lord and tutor, of Woman,— were he really bound with her in equal worship,—arrangements as to function and employment would be of no consequence. What Woman needs is not as a woman to act or rule, but as a nature to grow, as an intellect to discern, as a soul to live freely and unimpeded, to unfold such powers as were given her when we left our common home. If fewer talents were given her, yet if allowed the free and full employment of these, so that she may render back to the giver his own with usury, she will not complain; nay, I dare to say she will bless and rejoice in her earthly birthplace, her earthly lot. Let us consider what obstructions impede this good era, and what signs give reasons to hope that it draws near.

I was talking on this subject with Miranda, a woman who, if any in the world could, might speak without heat and bitterness of the position of her sex. Her father was a man who cherished no sentimental reverence for Woman, but a firm belief in the equality of the sexes. She was his eldest child, and came to him at an age when he needed a companion. From the time she could speak and go alone, he addressed her not as a plaything, but as a living mind. Among the few verses he ever wrote was a copy addressed to this child, when the first locks were cut from her head; and the reverence expressed on this occasion for that cherished head, he never belied. It was to him the temple of immortal intellect. He respected his child, however, too much to be an indulgent parent. He called on her for clear judgment, for courage, for honor and fidelity; in short, for such virtues as he knew. In so far as he possessed the keys to the wonders of this universe, he allowed free use of them to her, and, by the incentive of a high expectation, he forbade, so far as possible, that she should let the privilege lie idle.

Thus this child was early led to feel herself a child of the spirit. She took her place easily, not only in the world of organized being, but in the world of mind. A dignified sense of self-dependence was given as all her portion, and she found it a sure anchor. Herself securely anchored, her relations with others were established with equal security. She was fortunate in a total absence of those charms which might have drawn to her bewildering flatteries, and in a strong electric nature, which repelled those who did not belong to her, and attracted those who did. With men and women her relations were noble,—affectionate without passion, intellectual without coldness. The world was free to her, and she lived freely in it. Outward adversity came, and inward conflict; but that faith and self-respect had early been awakened which must always lead, at last, to an outward serenity and an inward peace.

Of Miranda I had always thought as an example, that the restraints upon the sex were insuperable only to those who think them so, or who noisily strive to break them. She had taken a course of her own, and no man stood in her way. Many of her acts had been unusual, but excited no uproar. Few helped, but none checked her; and the many men who knew her mind and her life, showed to her confidence as to a brother, gentleness as to a sister. And not only refined, but very coarse men approved and aided one in whom they saw resolution and clearness of design. Her mind was often the leading one, always effective.

When I talked with her upon these matters, and had said very much what I have written, she smilingly replied: "And yet we must admit that I have been fortunate, and this should not be. My good father's early trust gave the first bias, and the rest followed, of course. It is true that I have had less outward aid, in after years, than most women; but that is of little consequence. Religion was early awakened in my soul,—a sense that what the soul is capable to ask it must attain, and that, though I might be aided and instructed by others, I must depend on myself as the only constant friend. This self-dependence, which was honored in me, is deprecated as a fault in most women. They are taught to learn their rule from without, not to unfold it from within.

"This is the fault of Man, who is still vain, and wishes to be more important to Woman than, by right, he should be."

"Men have not shown this disposition toward you," I said.

"No; because the position I early was enabled to take was one of self-reliance. And were all women as sure of their wants as I was, the result would be the same. But they are so overloaded with precepts by guardians, who think that nothing is so much to be dreaded for a woman as originality of thought or character, that their minds are impeded by doubts till they lose their chance of fair, free proportions. The difficulty is to get them to the point from which they shall naturally develop self-respect, and learn self-help.

"Once I thought that men would help to forward this state of things more than I do now. I saw so many of them wretched in the connections they had formed in weakness and vanity. They seemed so glad to esteem women whenever they could.

"'The soft arms of affection,' said one of the most discerning spirits, 'will not suffice for me, unless on them I see the steel bracelets of strength.'

"But early I perceived that men never, in any extreme of despair, wished to be women. On the contrary, they were ever ready to taunt one another, at any sign of weakness, with

"'Art thou not like the women, who,'—

The passage ends various ways, according to the occasion and rhetoric of the speaker. When they admired any woman, they were inclined to speak of her as 'above her sex.' Silently I observed this, and feared it argued a rooted scepticism, which for ages had been fastening on the heart, and which only an age of miracles could eradicate. Ever I have been treated with great sincerity; and I look upon it as a signal instance of this, that an intimate friend of the other sex said, in a fervent moment, that I 'deserved in some star to be a man.' He was much surprised when I disclosed my view of my position and hopes, when I declared my faith that the feminine side, the side of love, of beauty, of holiness, was now to have its full chance, and that, if either were better, it was better now to be a woman; for even the slightest achievement of good was furthering an especial work of our time. He smiled incredulously. 'She makes the best she can of it,' thought he. 'Let Jews believe the pride of Jewry, but I am of the better sort, and know better.'

"Another used as highest praise, in speaking of a character in literature, the words 'a manly woman.'

"So in the noble passage of Ben Jonson:

"'I meant the day-star should not brighter rise,
     Nor lend like influence from its lucent seat;
     I meant she should be courteous, facile, sweet,
Hating that solemn vice of greatness, pride;
     I meant each softest virtue there should meet,
Fit in that softer bosom to reside.
Only a learned and a *manly soul*
     I purposed her, that should with even powers
The rock, the spindle, and the shears control
     Of Destiny, and spin her own free hours."

"Methinks," said I, "you are too fastidious in objecting to this. Jonson, in using the word 'manly' only meant to heighten the picture of this, the true, the intelligent fate, with one of the deeper colors."

"And yet," said she, "so invariable is the use of this word where a heroic quality is to be described, and I feel so sure that persistence and courage are the most womanly no less than the most manly qualities, that I would exchange these words for others of a larger sense, at the risk of marring the fine tissue of the verse. Read, 'A heavenward and instructed soul,' and I should be satisfied. Let it not be said, wherever there is energy or creative genius, 'She has a masculine mind.'"

From *The Operative's Friend, and Defence:*
or,
Hints to Young Ladies
who are
Dependent on Their Own Exertions

by Rev. James Porter, A.M.
Published in Boston, 1850

Health

Always have an umbrella by you. You will more than save the expense of one in preserving your clothes, and it will screen you from a fruitful source of disease. Getting wet seldom fails to produce a cold. To lose your dinner is not half as dangerous. Wet feet and wet clothes have sent thousands to eternity before their time. Be well supplied with umbrella and overshoes, and you will go safely where others will sicken and die.

Avoid unnecessary exposure to the evening air. In some localities, this is more injurious than in others. The practice of sitting at the door or window, with little or nothing over the head, is very imprudent. You had far better put on your bonnet and shawl, and take a walk. This in good weather may be a useful exercise.

It is always dangerous to set in a *current* of air, however warm the weather, particularly in the evening, after a day of heat and toil. It is scarcely possible to avoid a severe cold.

Dress

Permit me to caution you a little upon that delicate subject—*dress*. It is admitted, that none have a better right to good clothes, than those who *earn* them. And I am not about to say a word against their having them. It is pleasing to me, to see young ladies well dressed, especially when they are *deserving*.

But it cannot be denied, that many in trying to dress well, dress very *ill*; and others who wear expensive clothes, wear very poor ones.

Dr. Alcott has properly said, 'The threefold object of dress is to cover, warm, and defend us.' Perhaps you think this enumeration a little meagre. I admit, then, that *beauty* may be consulted. Many of the works of God are not only useful, but exceedingly *beautiful*. He has dressed the birds, the beasts, and flowers, the heavens, and the earth, and many other objects in great splendor. But I do not think of an instance in all his works, where he has sacrificed utility for this object. No, not one. While, therefore, we imitate the Creator in the beautiful, it must be in subordination to usefulness and virtue.

Economy

The habit of eating nuts, candies, seeds, apples, etc., is like any other habit, it gathers strength by indulgence. Hence some find it as difficult to resist their appetite for them, as the toper does to forsake his cups. It seems as though they *must* have them. They cannot be *easy* if denied. And often the tone of the stomach becomes so deranged by their use, they really seem necessary to health and comfort, as does alcohol to tipplers.

This explains why so many girls are forever *"nibbling"* at one thing or another, and cannot work, or go into company, or walk the street without a quid of some luxury in their mouths. They would seem as much lost, as a snuff-taker without her box, who would rather lose her dinner than her snuff. And yet, they have no conception of their *slavery*, or the *cost* of it.

But once settle it, that you will not purchase or use these articles, and all *hankering* for them will soon cease. Indeed, many of them will appear disgusting, and you can pass a world of others, without the slightest desire for, or thought concerning them. It will then be no sacrifice not to buy, and you will retain your money for useful purposes, preserve your health, and what is better than all, maintain a good conscience.

From the Worcester Spy—1855

It was my privilege to celebrate May day by officiating at a wedding in a farm-house among the hills of West Brookfield. The bridegroom was a man of tried worth, a leader in the Western Anti-Slavery Movement; and the bride was one whose fair name is known throughout the nation; one whose rare intellectual qualities are excelled by the private beauty of her heart and life.

I never perform the marriage ceremony without a renewed sense of the iniquity of our present system of laws in respect to marriage; a system by which "man and wife are one, and that one is the husband."

It was with my hearty concurrence, therefore, that the following protest was read and signed, as a part of the nuptial ceremony; and I send it to you, that others may be induced to do likewise.

REV. THOMAS WENTWORTH HIGGINSON

Protest

While acknowledging our mutual affection by publicly assuming the relationship of husband and wife, yet in justice to ourselves and a great principle, we deem it a duty to declare that this act on our part implies no sanction of, nor promise of voluntary obedience to such of the present laws of marriage, as refuse to recognize the wife as an independent, rational being, while they confer upon the husband an injurious and unnatural superiority, investing him with legal powers which no honorable man would exercise, and which no man should possess. We protest especially against the laws which give to the husband:

1. The custody of the wife's person.
2. The exclusive control and guardianship of their children.
3. The sole ownership of her personal, and use of her real estate, unless previously settled upon her or placed in the hands of trustees, as in the case of minors, lunatics, and idiots.

4. The absolute right to the product of her industry.

5. Also against laws which give to the widower so much larger and more permanent an interest in the property of his deceased wife, than they give to the widow in that of the deceased husband.

6. Finally, against the whole system by which "the legal existence of the wife is suspended during marriage," so that in most States, she neither has a legal part in the choice of her residence, nor can she make a will, nor sue or be sued in her own name, nor inherit property.

We believe that personal independence and equal human rights can never be forfeited, except for crime; that marriage should be an equal and permanent partnership, and so recognized by law; that until it is so recognized, married partners should provide against the radical injustice of present laws by every means in their power.

We believe that where domestic difficulties arise, no appeal should be made to legal tribunes under existing laws, but that all difficulties should be submitted to the equitable adjustment of arbitrators mutually chosen.

Thus reverencing law, we enter our protest against rules and customs which are unworthy of the name, since they violate justice, the essence of the law.

(*Signed*)   HENRY B. BLACKWELL,
                   LUCY STONE

WOMAN SUFFRAGE SONG—1867
(performed by the Singing Hutchinson Family who
had formerly been active in the anti-slavery campaign)

Who votes for woman suffrage now
Will add new laurels to his brow;
His children's children, with holy fire,
Will chant in praise their patriot sire.
No warrior's wreath of glory shed
A brighter lustre o'er the head
Than he who battles selfish pride,
And votes with woman side by side.

INVESTIGATION OF THE KU KLUX KLAN—
1871
Testimony Taken by the Joint Select Committee to
Inquire into the Condition of Affairs in the Late
Insurrectionary States

Jacksonville, Florida, November 10, 1871

Hannah Tutson (colored) sworn and examined.

State your age, where you were born, and where you now live?

As near as I can tell I am about forty-two or forty-three years old.
I was born in Gadsden, Florida, and I now live in Clay County,
near Waldo, on old Number Eleven Pond.

Are you the wife of Samuel Tutson?

Yes, sir.

Were you at home when he was whipped last spring?

Yes, sir; I was at home.

Tell us what took place then, what was done, and how it was
done.

When they came to my house that night the dog barked twice,
and the old man got up and went out of doors and then came back
and lay down; she flew out again, and I got up and went out of
doors; I knew the slut barked more than usual, but I could see
nothing; I went back into the house, and just as I got into bed
five men bulged right against the door, and it fell right in the
middle of the floor, and they fell down. George McRae was the
first to get up. I had no chimney in the house, but a board floor,
and he went where I had left all the children; went circling
around toward the children's bed, and I said "Who's that?" The old
man had not spoke. George McRae ran right to me and gathered
me by the arm. As I saw him coming I took up the child—the
baby—and held to him. The old man threw his arms around
my neck and held on to me. Cabell Winn catched hold of my
foot, and then there were so many hold of me I cannot tell who

they were. George McRae and Cabell Winn were the first to take hold of me. He said, "Come in, True-Klux." I started to scream, and George McRae catched me right by the throat and choked me. I worried around and around, and he catched the little child by the foot and slinged it out of my arms. I screamed again, and he gathered me again. Then there were so many hold of me that they got me out of doors. After they got me out, I looked up and I saw Jim Phillips, George McRae and Henry Baxter. I looked ahead of me and they had the old man; and they tore down the fence the same as if you saw people dragging hogs from the butcher-pen. And they went to another corner of the fence and jerked me over, just as if they were jerking a dumb beast. The old man was ahead of me, and I saw Dave Donley stamp on him. I said, "Sam, give up; it is not worth while to try to do anything; they will try to kill us here." They said, "O, God damn you, we will kill you." I said, "I will go with you." George McRae said, "Come right along." I said, "Yes, I am coming; I will come right along." After they carried me about a quarter of a mile from the house— maybe a little more; I cannot tell exactly how far it was; it was a good distance from the house—they took me through a path to a field, and down to the lower end of the field. When they got there he said, "Come here, True-Klux." The True-Klux came there and stopped and whispered about as far from here to this gentle- man [pointing to a member of the committee sitting at the table]. Then he said, "Now, old lady, you pretend to be a good Christian, you had better pray right off." I cast my eye up to the elements and begged God to help me. George McRae struck me over the head with a pistol, and said, "God damn you, what are you making this fuss for?" I said, "No." He said, "Where is the ropes?" They said they had lost the ropes. Now I never saw any horses; I did not see any that night. They went off next to a field and came back with a handful of saddle-girths, with the buckles on them. They took and carried me to a pine, just as large as I could get my arms around, and then they tied my hands there. They pulled off all my linen, tore it up so that I did not have a piece of rag on me as big as my hand. They tied me, and I said, "Men, what are you going to do with me?" They said, "God damn you, we will show you; you are living on another man's premises." I said, "No; I am living on my own premises; I gave $150 for it and Captain Buddington and Mr. Mundy told me to stay here." He said, "God damn you, we will give them the same as we are going to give you." I quit talking to them, only as they asked me anything. They tied me to a tree and whipped me for awhile. Then George McRae would say, "Come here, True-Klux." Then the True-Klux would come, and they would step off about as far as that gentleman and whisper; and then they would say that they would go off to where the saddles were. They would go, and then when they came back they would whip me again. Every time they would go off, George McRae would act scandalously and ridiculously toward me and treat me shamefully. When he saw them coming again he would make me get up. He would make me squat down by the pine, and say, "What are you trembling for?" I would say that I was cold, and was afraid that I would freeze. He would get his knees between my legs and say, "God damn you, open your legs." I tell you, men, that he did act ridiculously and shamefully, that same George McRae. He sat down there and said, "Old lady, if you don't let me have to do with you, I will kill you." I said, "No; do just what you are going to do." He said, "God damn you, I am going to kill you." They whipped me, and went off again to the horses, and got liquor of some kind and poured it on my head, and I smelled it for three weeks, so that it made me sick. They went off and whispered, and then he told them to go to my house and tear it down. He asked me where was my ox. It was in the field, but I would not tell him; I said that my son-in-law had got my cart. He said, "Where is your son-in-law?" I said, "He has gone to Palatka." He said, "Where is your ox?" I would not tell him. He would whisper to them, and tell them to go and get the ox, and to get my things and to start them off to-night. He said, "Let's start them right off to-night." They would go and hunt, and then come back. He would make me sit down while they were gone. Understand me, men, while they were going to hunt for that ox, George McRae would make me sit down there, and try to have me do with him right there. They came back and whipped me. I said, "Yes, men, if you will stop whipping me, I will give way to you." Gentlemen, you do not know what expressions Cabell Winn made out of his mouth. It was all smutty on their faces, only right from the ear down, and their hands were smutty. Some were in their shirtsleeves and some had their coats on. I had been working with them very nearly three years. You know that when any person gets half drunk, he cannot alter his voice but what you can tell him. I have been working and washing for them; I had not been two weeks from his mother's house, where I had been washing; I washed there every week. That is the way they did me; they came back and whipped me. George McRae said, "I came to dispossess you of this place once before." There were four men whipping me at once.

With what?

With saddle-girths, as I told you; with surcingles off the saddles. George McRae said, "We came to dispossess you once before, and you said you did not care if we did whip you." I said, "Stop, men, and let me see." One of them said, "Stop, and let her get her breath." Mr. Winn talked all kind of nasty talk to me. I got so I did not count Mr. Winn more than he counted me. I told Mr. Winn just exactly three weeks before they whipped me that I did not care what they did for me just so I saved my land. Said I, "In the red times, [slavery], how many times have they took me and turned my clothes over my head and whipped me? I do not care what they do to me now if I can only save my land." He again asked me if I said that, and I said, "Stop; I will see." After a minute I said, "Yes, I did say so." Cabell Winn says, "Yes, you damned bitch, you did say so." I did not tell anybody but Cabell Winn and his daddy, for my husband was gone. The night they came to whip me they did not expect to find the old man there, and when they found he had hold of me as they were carrying me to the door, he says, "O, God damn you, are you here?" And the time they were whipping me they said, "Now, listen, God damn you, at that poor old man; you were a God damned old bitch to get the poor old man in this fix; listen at him, you damned old bitch." I would have this just the way you hear me tell it now before the others, but they stopped me.

How many lashes did they give you in all?

I cannot tell you, for they whipped me from the crown of my head to the soles of my feet. I was just raw. The blood oozed out through my frock and around my waist, clean through, when I got to Captain Buddington's. After I got away from them that night I ran to my house. My house was torn down. I went in and felt where my bed was. It was along in the middle of the floor. I went to the other corner of the house and felt for my little children. I could not see one, and the bed was hoisted up in the corner of the house and hitched there, and is there now. I could not feel my little children and I could not see them. I said, "Lord, my little children are dead." I went to the box for my things and I picked up a dress I had there, but I went five miles before I put it on my back. When I got near one of my neighbor's house I hollered "murder," and they heard me, and they said they heard horses' feet go by. I did hear horses myself, and I hollered, for I was afraid. I cannot read, and I have got no clock, but as near as I can get to it, I got away from them an hour to day, and I went twelves miles by sunrise after I got away from them. I went through to Mr. Montgomery's house. I could not bear my clothes fastened on me. I told them to give me a light as quick as they could so that I might go back and hunt up my children. I have two grown sons and a daughter, who are married and gone off. I said, "Give me a light; I expect my husband is dead, and I want to go back and find my children." I went back again, and I heard him holler, but I could hear nothing of my children. They said, "Go by Mr. Ashley's and get him to ride up there." I went by Mr. Ashley's, and went in there. I turned up my clothes and let Mr. Ashley see how I was whipped. I had on nothing but a frock, and I could not fasten it. He said, "Woman, go back home and hunt for your husband and children. If he is dead, don't stand to bury him, but go right on to Whitesville." I told him I did not know how to go there. He said, "If you have not been it is right enough to hunt up your boys, and let them go with you; if your husband is dead don't stand to bury him."

Did you find your children?

I did next day at 12 o'clock.

Where were they?

They were there at my house, where the True-Klux had whipped me. Their father lay out to the middle of the night, and my children lay out there too. They said that when they got away from me they went out into the field, and my little daughter said that as the baby cried she would reach out and pick some gooseberries and put them into its little mouth. When she could hear none of them any more she went up into the field to a log heap and stayed there with her brother and the baby. At daylight the old man came by a little house I had been living in, and which I used to keep some corn and things in, and they had torn it down, and the hogs had been in there eating up what corn and little stuff I had there.

How old were your children?

One was about five years old, another betwixt nine and ten, and the other was not quite a year old, lacking two months.

That was the one you had in your arms when they jerked it away?

Yes, sir.

Did the baby get hurt?

Yes, sir; in one of its hips. When it began to walk one of its hips was very bad, and every time you would stand it up it would scream. But I rubbed it and rubbed it, and it looks like it was outgrowing it now.

How soon did you see your husband?

Only when I saw my children. He was whipped so bad he could not travel as I did; he stayed at home. When I got back there Mr. Chesnut, a white gentleman, had him there, and he and Mr. Chesnut were sitting there talking.

Did you see where he had been whipped?

Yes, sir; he could not sit up.

Where had he been whipped, on what part of his body?

All over it; his legs were whipped more than anywhere else. They did not begin to whip me as they did him. When I came Mr. Chesnut was there, and unfastening my frock, my daughter gave me some linen to put on, and Mr. Chesnut looked at me where I was whipped. I went by Mr. Rohan Wall's and let them look at me once. But they stand to it to-day, until yet, that that land is not mine; they say it is Tire's. Mr. Winn coaxed me and begged me to give it up before they whipped me.

He wanted to make you give up the land?

Yes, sir; they came there about three weeks before they whipped me to dispossess me of the place.

Who came there before?

George McRae, and old Mr. Sullivan, and Dave Donley, and Mr. Hagan and Jake Winn. Mr. Byrd Sullivan came on Saturday. I spoke to them very rash, and I was sort of sorry I spoke to them in that way. Mr. Hagan came back and wanted to give me some advice. He told me it was Judge Buddington and Barney Crocker. I said I did not believe it, because they told me that this was my land, and not Tire's land. Tire was the first one who made out that he entered my land. I said, "I am going to die on this land." Hagan said, "You better give it up." Mrs. Lane sent for me to come and wash for her one day in a week, to scour and wash, any day in the week I felt like it. They made me mad Saturday about driving me from my place, and I would not go to Mrs. Lane's the first of the week. I had to go through Jake Winn's yard to go to her house. My son was working there, and I went in and saw Mrs. Winn and told her good morning. She says, "Hannah, I thought you were gone." I said, "Gone where?" She said, "Off the place." I said, "No, I am not going off the place; didn't Captain Buddington tell me to stay here? I am not going; no law is going to move me from here except Tallahassee law. I said, "What are they going to do to me, Mrs. Hagan?" She said, "They are going to whip you." I said, "I wish they would whip me," and then I went off. I told Mrs. Lane about it, and she said, "I have nothing to do with it; it is your land; you ought to have your land." She went and told Mr. Byrd Sullivan. He pretended to be courting of her then; she told him what I had to say. That was on Wednesday. On Friday while I was eating my breakfast with nobody there but me and my little children,

Byrd Sullivan came to my house with Jake Winn and Dave Donley and George McRae. They went into the field and let down the fence; the old man was gone to the hammock. Old Byrd Sullivan came up to the house and said: "Aunty, these people are devilish people; they are determined to put you off this land. Now, pay good attention to what I say. When you get your hand into a lion's mouth you pull it out just as easy as you can. Pay good attention to me. I would like to see your old man this morning, but he is not at home. You can tell your old man to give it up, or in a month's time, or such matter, they will come here, and the lot will push him out of doors and let you eat this green grass." I began to cry, and he said, "You will stop this grieving and crying; tell your old man to keep on writing; I know what you paid for this land; you gave cotton for it." I said, "Yes; I gave cotton enough to come to $150." He said, "Tell your old man to keep on writing, and when he gets the papers for his land let him come to me and he will have his land back." I said, "Mr. Ashley, Mr. Rohan and Mr. Swindell told me not to give it up; that if I let anybody else come on the land I could not get it back."

How long had you been living there?

Nearly three years.

How many crops had you made?

Two crops.

And this crop would have been the last?

Yes, sir.

You spoke about some of them "wanting to do with you," as you expressed it.

Yes, sir.

What one was that?

George McRae.

Did you give way to him?

No, sir; George McRae acted so bad, and I was stark naked. I tell you, men, he pulled my womb down so that sometimes now I can hardly walk.

From *The Lady's Almanac for 1875*
(distributed by the New England News Company, American News Company, Western News Company, Central News Company, Baltimore News Company, and St. Louis Book and News Company.)

Daily Habits

The education of the girl, as a housekeeper, should be begun by the mother early, continued until the marriage of the daughter, and no other duty of the mother and no other study of the daughter, should interfere with it. This and the school education should go on simultaneously. If anything is to be postponed let it be music and drawing and philosophy, which, as experience shows, are usually unattended to and unpracticed after "the happy event." The more and higher the education, the better. But let us have a real and practical instead of a sham education.

To Clean Gold Chains

Put the chain in a small glass bottle with warm water, a little toothpowder and some soap. Cork the bottle and shake it for a minute violently. The friction against the glass polishes the gold, and the soap and chalk extract every particle of grease and dirt from the interstices of a chain of the most intricate pattern; rinse it in clear cold water, wipe with a towel, and the polish will surprise you.

THE WRONGS OF SEWING-WOMEN
from *Harper's Weekly*, February 21, 1874

The wrongs to which sewing-women are subjected in the metropolis have long been a familiar story to the public. Toiling wearily day and night for a mere pittance, they have found it hard, even with honest employers, to earn enough to keep soul and body together; but in thousands of instances they have been cheated out of even the small sums they have well earned by villainous shop-keepers, who increase their own profits by defrauding the poor women employed by them. Nor have these swindling operations been confined to the manufacturing branches. The latest scheme of the kind is that of letting sewing-machines on apparently fair but really disadvantageous terms to the hirer. A contract is drawn up by the unscrupulous agent in such terms as to be incomprehensible by the party hiring it, and then, after several payments have been made, the poor woman finds that the machine has been forfeited by some pretended failure of hers to meet the engagements. Of course nothing of this kind is ever done by the great companies or their accredited agents, but by irresponsible outsiders, who make a business of cheating poor people. Fortunately for the sewing-women, "The Women's Protective Union"—a worthy institution well known in this city—takes up such cases, and through their indefatigable lawyer prosecutes the villains, and compels them to deal fairly by their victims. An instance of the kind is [Illustration 19]. One of these agents, who has cheated a young woman, is summoned to appear before the attorney, who is engaged in investigating the circumstances. She protests tearfully that she has complied with all the terms of her agreement. There can be no doubt of the result. The trickster will be given his choice of refunding the ill-gotten money or else going to prison, and he will undoubtedly prefer the former.

The Housewife's Lament

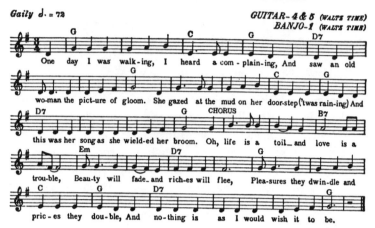

1. One day I was walking, I heard a complaining,
   And saw an old woman the picture of gloom.
   She gazed at the mud on her doorstep ('twas raining)
   And this was her song as she wielded her broom.
   CHORUS:
   Oh, life is a toil and love is a trouble,
   Beauty will fade and riches will flee,
   Pleasures they dwindle and prices they double,
   And nothing is as I would wish it to be.

2. There's too much of worriment goes to a bonnet,
   There's too much of ironing goes to a shirt,
   There's nothing that pays for the time you waste on it,
   There's nothing that lasts us but trouble and dirt. (CHO.)

3. In March it is mud, it is slush in December,
   The midsummer breezes are loaded with dust,
   In fall the leaves litter, in muddy September
   The wallpaper rots and the candlesticks rust. (CHO.)

4. There are worms on the cherries and slugs on the roses,
   And ants in the sugar and mice in the pies,
   The rubbish of spiders no mortal supposes
   And ravaging roaches and damaging flies. (CHO.)

5. With grease and with grime from corner to centre,
   Forever at war and forever alert,
   No rest for a day lest the enemy enter,
   I spend my whole life in a struggle with dirt. (CHO.)

The Housewife's Lament by Eliza S. Turner, courtesy of *Sing Out!*

From *A New England Girlhood*
by Lucy Larcom
Published by Houghton Mifflin Company
in 1889

The printed regulations forbade us to bring books into the mill, so I made my window-seat into a small library of poetry, pasting its sides all over with newspaper clippings. Some of the girls could not believe that the Bible was meant to be counted among forbidden books. We all thought that the Scriptures had a right to go where ever we went, and that if we needed them anywhere, it was at our work. I evaded the law by carrying some leaves from a torn Testament in my pocket.

SOLITUDE OF SELF

An Address by Elizabeth Cady Stanton Before the
Committee of the Judiciary of the United States
Congress
Monday, January 18, 1892

Mr. Chairman and gentlemen of the committee: We have been
speaking before Committees of the Judiciary for the last twenty
years, and we have gone over all the arguments in favor of the
sixteenth amendment which are familiar to all you gentlemen;
therefore, it will not be necessary that I should repeat them again.

The point I wish plainly to bring before you on this occasion
is the individuality of each human soul; our Protestant idea, the
right of individual conscience and judgment—our republican idea,
individual citizenship. In discussing the rights of woman, we are
to consider, first, what belongs to her as an individual, in a world
of her own, the arbiter of her own destiny, an imaginary Robinson
Crusoe with her woman Friday on a solitary island. Her rights under
such circumstances are to use all her faculties for her own safety
and happiness.

Secondly, if we consider her as a citizen, as a member of a great
nation, she must have the same rights as all other members, according to the fundamental principles of our government.

Thirdly, viewed as a woman, an equal factor in civilization, her
rights and duties are still the same—individual happiness and development.

Fourthly, it is only the incidental relations of life, such as
mother, wife, sister, daughter, that may involve some special duties
and training. In the usual discussion in regard to woman's sphere,
such men as Herbert Spencer, Frederic Harrison, and Grant Allen
uniformly subordinate her rights and duties as an individual, as
a citizen, as a woman, to the necessities of these incidental relations,
some of which a large class of women may never assume. In

discussing the sphere of man we do not decide his rights as an individual, as a citizen, as a man by his duties as a father, a husband, a brother, or a son, relations some of which he may never fill. Moreover he would be better fitted for these very relations and whatever special work he might choose to do to earn his bread by the complete development of all his faculties as an individual.

Just so with woman. The education that will fit her to discharge the duties in the largest sphere of human usefulness will best fit her for whatever special work she may be compelled to do.

The insolation of every human soul and the necessity of self-dependence must give each individual the right to choose his own surroundings.

The strongest reason for giving woman all the opportunities for higher education, for the full development of her faculties, forces of mind and body for giving her the most enlarged freedom of thought and action; a complete emancipation from all forms of bondage, of custom, dependence, superstition; from all the crippling influences of fear, is the solitude and personal responsibility of her own individual life. The strongest reason why we ask for woman a voice in the government under which she lives; in religion she is asked to believe; equality in social life, where she is the chief factor; a place in the trades and professions, where she may earn her bread, is because of her birthright to self-sovereignty; because, as an individual, she must rely on herself. No matter how much women prefer to lean, to be protected and supported, nor how much men desire to have them do so, they must make the voyage of life alone, and for safety in an emergency they must know something of the laws of navigation. To guide our own craft, we must be captain, pilot, engineer; with chart and compass to stand at the wheel; to watch the wind and waves and know when to take in the sail, and to read the signs in the firmament over all. It matters not whether the solitary voyager is man or woman.

Nature having endowed them equally, leaves them to their own skill and judgment in the hour of danger, and, if not equal to the occasion, alike they perish.

To appreciate the importance of fitting every human soul for independent action, think for a moment of the immeasurable solitude of self. We come into the world alone, unlike all who have gone before us; we leave it alone under circumstances peculiar to ourselves. No mortal ever has been, no mortal ever will be like the soul just launched on the sea of life. There can never again be just such environments as make up the infancy, youth and manhood of this one. Nature never repeats herself, and the possibilities of one human soul will never be found in another. No one has ever found two blades of ribbon grass alike, and no one will never find two human beings alike. Seeing, then, what must be the infinite diversity in human character, we can in a measure appreciate the loss to a nation when any large class of the people is uneducated and unrepresented in the government. We ask for the complete development of every individual, first, for his own benefit and happiness. In fitting out an army we give each soldier his own knapsack, arms, powder, his blanket, cup, knife, fork and spoon. We provide alike for all their individual necessities, then each man bears his own burden.

Again we ask complete individual development for the general good; for the consensus of the competent on the whole round of human interest; on all questions of national life, and here each man must bear his share of the general burden. It is sad to see how soon friendless children are left to bear their own burdens before they can analize their feelings; before they can even tell their joys and sorrows, they are thrown on their own resources. The great lesson that nature seems to teach us at all ages is self-dependence, self-protection, self-support. What a touching instance of a child's solitude; of that hunger of heart for love and recognition, in the case of a little girl who helped to dress a Christmas tree for the children of the family in which she served. On finding there was no present for herself she slipped away in the darkness and spent the night in an open field sitting on a stone, and when found in the morning was weeping as if her heart would break. No mortal will ever know the thoughts that passed through the mind of that friendless child in the long hours of that cold night, with only the silent stars to keep her company. The mention of her case in the daily papers moved many generous hearts to send her presents, but in the hours of her keenest sufferings she was thrown wholly on herself for consolation.

In youth our most bitter disappointments, our brightest hopes and ambitions are known only to ourselves; even our friendship and love we never fully share with another; there is something of every passion in every situation we conceal. Even so in our triumphs and our defeats.

The successful candidate for Presidency and his opponent each have a solitude peculiarly his own, and good form forbids either to speak of his pleasure or regret. The solitude of the king on his throne and the prisoner in his cell differs in characters and degree, but it is solitude nevertheless.

We ask no sympathy from others in the anxiety and agony of a broken friendship or shattered love. When death sunders our nearest ties, alone we sit in the shadows of our affliction. Alike mid the greatest triumphs and darkest tragedies of life we walk alone. On the divine heights of human attainments, eulogized and worshipped as a hero or saint, we stand alone. In ignorance, poverty, and vice, as a pauper or criminal, alone we starve or steal; alone we suffer the sneers and rebuffs of our fellows; alone we are hunted and hounded thro dark courts and alleys, in by-ways and highways; alone we stand in the judgment seat; alone in the prison cell we lament our crimes and misfortunes; alone we expiate them on the gallows. In hours like these we realize the awful solitude of individual life, its pains, its penalties, its responsibilities; hours in which the youngest and most helpless are thrown on their own resources for guidance and consolation. Seeing then that life must ever be a march and a battle, that each soldier must be equipped for his own protection, it is the height of cruelty to rob the individual of a single natural right.

To throw obstacles in the way of a complete education is like putting out the eyes; to deny the rights of property, like cutting off the hands. To deny political equality is to rob the ostracised of all self-respect; of credit in the market place; of recompense in the world of work; of a voice among those who make and administer the law; a choice in the jury before whom they are tried, and in the judge who decides their punishment. Shakespeare's play of Titus and Andronicus contains a terrible satire on woman's position in the nineteenth century—"Rude men" (the play tells us) "seized the king's daughter, cut out her tongue, cut off her hands, and then bade her go call for water and wash her hands." What a picture of woman's position. Robbed of her natural rights, handicapped by law and custom at every turn, yet compelled to fight her own battles, and in the emergencies of life to fall back on herself for protection.

The girl of sixteen, thrown on the world to support herself, to make her own place in society, to resist the temptations that surround her and maintain a spotless integrity, must do all this by native force or superior education. She does not acquire this power by being trained to trust others and distrust herself. If she wearies of the struggle, finding it hard work to swim upstream, and allows herself to drift with the current, she will find plenty of company, but not one to share her misery in the hour of her deepest humiliation. If she tries to retrieve her position, to conceal the past, her life is hedged about with fears lest willing hands should tear the veil from what she fain would hide. Young and friendless, she knows the bitter solitude of self.

How the little courtesies of life on the surface of society, deemed so important from man towards woman, fade into utter insignificance in view of the deeper tragedies in which she must play her part alone, where no human aid is possible.

The young wife and mother, at the head of some establishment with a kind husband to shield her from the adverse winds of life, with wealth, fortune and position, has a certain harbor of safety, secure against the ordinary ills of life. But to manage a household, have a desirable influence in society, keep her friends and the affections of her husband, train her children and servants well, she must have rare common sense, wisdom, diplomacy, and a knowledge of human nature. To do all this she needs the cardinal virtues and the strong points of character that the most successful statesman possesses.

An uneducated woman, trained to dependence, with no resources in herself must make a failure of any position in life. But society says women do not need a knowledge of the world; the liberal training that experience in public life must give, all the advantages of collegiate education; but when for the lack of all this, the woman's happiness is wrecked, alone she bears her humiliation; and the solitude of the weak and the ignorant is indeed pitiful. In the wild chase for the prizes of life they are ground to powder.

In age, when the pleasures of youth are passed, children grown up, married and gone, the hurry and bustle of life in a measure over, when the hands are weary of active service, when the old armchair and the fireside are the chosen resorts, then men and women alike must fall back on their own resources. If they cannot find companionship in books, if they have no interest in the vital questions of the hour, no interest in watching the consummation of reforms, with which they might have been identified, they soon pass into their dotage. The more fully the faculties of the mind are developed and kept in use, the longer the period of vigor and active interest in all around us continues. If from a lifelong participation in public affairs a woman feels responsible for the laws regulating our system of education, the discipline of our jails and prisons, the sanitary conditions of our private homes, public buildings, and thoroughfares, an interest in commerce, finance, our foreign relations, in any or all of these questions, her solitude will at least be respectable, and she will not be driven to gossip or scandal for entertainment.

The chief reason for opening to every soul the doors to the whole round of human duties and pleasures is the individual development thus attained, the resources thus provided under all circumstances to mitigate the solitude that at times must come to everyone. I once asked Prince Kropotkin, the Russian nihilist, how he endured his long years in prison, deprived of books, pen, ink, and paper. "Ah," he said, "I thought out many questions in which I had a deep interest. In the pursuit of an idea I took no note of time. When tired of solving knotty problems I recited all the beautiful passages in prose or verse I had ever learned. I became acquainted with myself and my own resources. I had a world of my own, a vast empire, that no Russian jailor or Czar could invade." Such is the value of liberal thought and broad culture when shut from all human companionship, bringing comfort and sunshine within even the four walls of a prison cell.

As women ofttimes share a similar fate, should they not have all the consolation that the most liberal education can give? Their suffering in the prisons of St. Petersburg; in the long, weary marches to Siberia, and in the mines, working side by side with men, surely call for all the self-support that the most exalted sentiments of heroism can give. When suddenly roused at midnight, with the startling cry of "fire! fire!" to find the house over their heads in flames, do women wait for men to point the way to safety? And are the men, equally bewildered and half suffocated with smoke, in a position to more than save themselves?

At such times the most timid women have shown a courage and heroism in saving their husbands and children that has surprised everybody. Inasmuch, then, as woman shares equally the joys and sorrows of time and eternity, is it not the height of presumption in man to propose to represent her at the ballot box and the throne of grace, do her voting in the state, her praying in the church, and to assume the position of priest at the family altar.

Nothing strengthens the judgment and quickens the conscience like individual responsibility. Nothing adds such dignity to character as the recognition of one's self-sovereignty; the right to an equal place, every where conceded; a place earned by personal merit, not an artificial attainment, by inheritance, wealth, family, and position. Seeing, then, that the responsibilities of life rest equally on man and woman, that their destiny is the same, they need the same preparation for time and eternity. Talk of sheltering woman from the fierce storms of life is the sheerest mockery, for they beat on her from every point of the compass, just as they do on man, and with more fatal results, for he has been trained to protect himself, to resist, to conquer. Such are the facts in human experience, the responsibilities of individual sovereignty. Rich and poor, intelligent and ignorant, wise and foolish, virtuous and vicious, man and woman, it is ever the same, each soul must depend wholly on itself.

Whatever the theories may be of woman's dependence on man, in the supreme moments of her life he cannot bear her burdens. Alone she goes to the gates of death to give life to every man that is born into the world. No one can share her fears, no one can mitigate her pangs; and if her sorrow is greater than she can bear, alone she passes beyond the gates into the vast unknown.

From the mountain tops of Judea, long ago, a heavenly voice bade His disciples, "Bear ye one another's burdens," but humanity has not yet risen to that point of self-sacrifice, and if ever so willing, how few the burdens are that one soul can bear for another. In the highways of Palestine; in prayer and fasting on the solitary mountain top; in the Garden of Gethsemane; before the judgment seat of Pilate; betrayed by one of His trusted disciples at His last supper; in His agonies on the cross, even Jesus of Nazareth, in these last sad days on earth, felt the awful solitude of self. Deserted by man, in agony he cries, "My God! My God! why hast Thou forsaken me?" And so it ever must be in the conflicting scenes of life, in the long weary march, each one walks alone. We may have many friends, love, kindness, sympathy and charity to smooth our pathway in everyday life, but in the tragedies and triumphs of human experience each mortal stands alone.

But when all artificial trammels are removed, and women are recognized as individuals, responsible for their own environments, thoroughly educated for all the positions in life they may be called to fill; with all the resources in themselves that liberal thought and broad culture can give; guided by their own conscience and judgment; trained to self-protection by a healthy development of the muscular system and skill in the use of weapons of defense, and stimulated to self-support by the knowledge of the business world and the pleasure that pecuniary independence must ever give; when women are trained in this way they will, in a measure, be fitted for those hours of solitude that come alike to all, whether prepared or otherwise. As in our extremity we must depend on ourselves, the dictates of wisdom point to complete individual development.

In talking of education how shallow the argument that each class must be educated for the special work it proposes to do, and all those faculties not needed in this special walk must lie dormant and utterly wither for want of use, when, perhaps, these will be the very faculties needed in life's greatest emergencies. Some say, "Where is the use of drilling girls in the languages, the sciences, in law, medicine, theology?" As wives, mothers, housekeepers, cooks, they need a different curriculum from boys who are to fill all positions. The chief cooks in our great hotels and ocean steamers are men. In large cities men run the bakeries; they make our bread, cake and pies. They manage the laundries; they are now considered our best milliners and dressmakers. Because some men fill these departments of usefulness, shall we regulate the curriculum in Harvard and Yale to their present necessities? If not, why this talk in our best colleges of a curriculum for girls who are crowding into the trades and professions; teachers in all our public schools rapidly filling many lucrative and honorable positions in life? They are showing, too, their calmness and courage in the most trying hours of human experience.

You have probably all read in the daily papers of the terrible storm in the Bay of Biscay when a tidal wave made such havoc on the shore, wrecking vessels, unroofing houses and carrying destruction everywhere. Among other buildings the woman's prison was demolished. Those who escaped saw men struggling to reach the shore. They promptly by clasping hands made a chain of themselves and pushed out into the sea, again and again, at the risk of their lives until they had brought six men to shore, carried them to a shelter, and did all in their power for their comfort and protection.

What special school of training could have prepared these women for this sublime moment of their lives. In times like this humanity rises above all college curriculum and recognizes Nature as the greatest of all teachers in the hour of danger and death. Women are already the equals of men in the whole realm of thought, in art, science, literature, and government. With telescopic vision they explore the starry firmament, and bring back the history of the planetary world. With chart and compass they pilot ships across the mighty deep, and with skillful finger send electric messages around the globe. In galleries of art the beauties of nature and the virtues of humanity are immortalized by them on their canvas and by their inspired touch dull blocks of marble are transformed into angles of light.

In music they speak again the language of Mendelssohn, Beethoven, Chopin, Schumann, and are worthy interpreters of their great thoughts. The poetry and novels of the century are theirs, and they have touched the keynote of reform in religion, politics, and social life. They fill the editor's and professor's chair, and plead at the bar of justice, walk the wards of the hospital, and speak from the pulpit and the platform; such is the type of womanhood that an enlightened public sentiment welcomes today, and such the triumph of the facts of life over the false theories of the past.

Is it, then, consistent to hold the developed woman of this day within the narrow political limits as the dame with the spinning wheel and knitting needle occupied in the past? No! no! Machinery has taken the labors of woman as well as man on its tireless shoulders; the loom and the spinning wheel are but dreams of the past; the pen, the brush, the easel, the chisel, have taken their places, while the hopes and ambitions of women are essentially changed.

We see reason sufficient in the outer conditions of human beings for individual liberty and development, but when we consider the self-dependence of every human soul we see the need of courage, judgment, and the exercise of every faculty of mind and body, strengthened and developed by use, in woman as well as man.

Whatever may be said of man's protecting power in ordinary conditions, mid all the terrible disasters by land and sea, in the supreme moments of danger, alone, woman must ever meet the horrors of the situation; the Angel of Death even makes no royal pathway for her. Man's love and sympathy enter only into the sunshine of our lives. In that solemn solitude of self, that links us with the immeasurable and the eternal, each soul lives alone forever. A recent writer says:

"I remember once, in crossing the Atlantic, to have gone upon the deck of the ship in midnight, when a dense black cloud enveloped the sky, and the great deep was roaring madly under the lashes of demoniac winds. My feelings was not of danger or fear (which is a base surrender of the immortal soul), but of utter desolation and loneliness; a little speck of life shut in by a tremendous darkness. Again I remember to have climbed the slopes of the Swiss Alps, up beyond the point where vegetation ceases, and the stunted conifers no longer struggle against the unfeeling blasts. Around me lay a huge confusion of rocks, out of which the gigantic ice peaks shot into the measureless blue of the heavens, and again my only feeling was the awful solitude.

"And yet, there is a solitude, which each and every one of us has always carried with him, more inaccessible than the ice-cold mountains, more profound than the midnight sea; the solitude of self. Our inner being, which we call ourself, no eye nor touch of man or angel has ever pierced. It is more hidden than the caves of the gnome; the sacred adytum of the oracle; the hidden chamber of eleusinian mystery, for to it only omniscience is permitted to enter."

Such is individual life. Who, I ask you, can take, dare take, on himself the rights, the duties, the responsibilities of another human soul?

Photo Credits

Culver Pictures—#4, 5, 12.
The Bettman Archive—#8, 15.
Moorland-Spingarn Collection, Howard University—#14.
From *The Century Magazine,* November 1909, engraved by H. E. Merrill; reproduced by courtesy of Appleton-Century-Crofts, Educational Division, Meredith Corporation—#11.
Courtesy of Leon T. Stern—#16.
The University of Michigan Press—#17.
American Ethnology Collection, Smithsonian Institution—#18.